"This is a remarkable encourage people fro cover to cover. The first few chapters feel chaotic and pressured... keep reading, persevere. That was life for the author. The genius of the book is partly how it moves from tragedy and disorder to triumph and serenity. I was moved to tears in parts, and then finished reading feeling like I shared the victory of a life gone sane. This is the story of a remarkable woman overcoming seemingly overwhelming challenges and beating the odds. Brava!"

—Portland City Commissioner Amanda Fritz, retired registered nurse who worked for twenty-six years in inpatient psychiatry at Oregon Health Sciences University and Strong Memorial Hospital in Rochester, NY.

"This vivid narrative delivers a powerful first-person impression of the author's lifelong struggle to grasp reality, hold on to it, and thrive as a fully functioning person. Her struggle has been doubly difficult, because the reality she sought has so often been abusive, heartbreaking, or tragic. But with love and determination, she is winning her ongoing battle, and her gentle, positive spirit strides brightly through."

—Jim Stinson

"Just as Sherry alluded in chapter 5 to her meeting me and my husband when she was a high-school sophomore, we had interaction with her for many years and especially after 1971, when she visited us on many occasions and stayed in our Coos Bay home many times. On some occasions she seemed perfectly normal, and at other times we could tell she was definitely unbalanced. To this day, she and Joe and I get together several times each year to catch up on one another's lives."

"I have followed her remarkable journey to sanity with amazement and admiration, as she continues her art and her work to help others in so many ways to find their true selves and ways to relate to the world around them."

"Her antiwar views on Vietnam connect to the rest of her life's story as a peace-loving, politically liberal-minded person. This continues to create a strong bond throughout her life, and today she is an active, outspoken voice in Portland political circles as well as in her most important work for NAMI."

—Mitzi Asai Loftus, author of From Here to Everywhere

"Sherry Goes Sane takes you on a captivating journey that dives into the intricate patterns and thoughts of a mind unraveling, while at the same time witnessing the blossoming of one of the most beautiful and loving recovery stories to date. A spectacular life filled with struggle, hope, love, inspiration, and determination must be shared."
—Jeana L. Wheeler, PSS.

"Sherry Goes Sane is an honest, raw, and intimate account of one woman's brave journey to find her sanity. I commend Sherry for exposing the details of her illness, compounded by physical abuse, and how she overcame these obstacles to be the vibrant person she is today. By sharing her story in her own words, Sherry inspires hope that someone living with schizo-affective disorder can reach a place of happiness and stability."

—Amy Myers, marketing consultant and former education programs coordinator of NAMI Multnomah

Sherry Goes Sane

LIVING A LIFE WITH SCHIZO-AFFECTIVE DISORDER

By

SHERRY M. JOINER

Copyright © 2013 Sherry M. Joiner
All rights reserved.

ISBN: 1490315136
ISBN 13: 9781490315133

Library of Congress Control Number: 2013910286
CreateSpace Independent Publishing Platform
North Charleston, South Carolina

Special Thanks

A special thanks to my loving sister, Diana, her husband, Bob, and my sweet, caring, husband, Joe, who have believed in me and supported me in my decision to write this book.

In Appreciation

Thank you to Ward T. Smith, MD, psychiatrist, and Todd Ransford, PhD, psychologist, for helping me through the rough times. Because you inspire, my world has been a better place.

My gratitude is extended to Jeana Wheeler for helping to set up www.ArtsAndWritingbySherry.com.

With love to Alice Savage, Amy Myers, Nancy Cook, Nancy Earwood, Mitzi Loftus, Nancy Gail Smith, and Justin and Heidi Loftus for standing by me. The experiences we have shared in the past have made coping possible. It is from you that I have gained new insight into my disease.

In Loving Memory of
My mother, Maria, and My Brother, Doug

CHAPTER 1

SALEM

Salem! I'm in Salem. Not the rainy capital of Oregon, but the Salem that kids taunted you with when they wanted to imply that you were insane. Salem, the state mental hospital, which was the site used for the filming of much of *One Flew Over the Cuckoo's Nest*. But I shouldn't be here. I'm not crazy. I'm pissed off, but not crazy. That damn Connie Funkle with her insane desire to belittle me and challenge every good thing I try to do, throwing all the stuff from my hall locker onto the floor then loudly telling me to pick up my mess.

I'll show them how not crazy I am!

I am so sedated that I am a zombie. I'm imitating a duck: squatting down, grabbing my heels, walking on my tiptoes. The only way that I can keep my balance is to do deep knee bends. Later in my room, I am more agile. I take a white blouse that my brother, Doug, packed for me, tie it around my waist and, in my bra, stand on the frame of my bed by my window. With my feet pressed together, one knee bent, arms to the side, I attempt to pose like Jesus Christ on the cross, standing up there long enough for a warden to pass by and look in my window. I am hoping she thinks that she's got Jesus; maybe she'll let me go. I'm not that lucky. She tells me to come down off my cross. Then she begins to laugh with the other nurses on her shift.

Peer pressure! Fake, bigmouth, conceited. They didn't realize what I was going through, but on Christmas Eve, Ralph nearly broke my jaw because I was sexually abused when I was nineteen. God! If that stranger hadn't come to Alice, June, and my apartment and abused me! What a setup. If it hadn't been for my German friend, Geisla, who helped me feel better about my abuse, I would have never been abused. Ha! That was my thinking in my crazy state of mind.

I'll remember you, Ralph. How you jumped to your feet, clenched your fist, and yelled, "You what!?"

What a joke. "I had a German girlfriend, and I was abused when I was nineteen." For that you lunge at my face with your fist? I am innocent.

That fist popped me one in the mouth, knocking me hard against the fireplace, hitting my head. A thickened taste of snot erupted in my throat, and painful tears came, spitting triangles from the corners of my lips. He was mad because he didn't like German people and mad at the fact that I wasn't a virgin anymore. He showed his raw neck, and his twisted ogre face turned purple. Mom picked up the golden medieval fireplace poker—like a magic wand with a large pointed hook at the end of it—and struck him over the head. Oo-wee! Yay! She left a two-inch gash in his forehead. Blood spurted from his right eye and made jellyfish-like fingers caressing his chin. Superglue! I wish you were dead, Ralph Sherman. He ran upstairs and began to beat up my brother. The back of my head throbbed as if hit by a bullet. I was slow to react. Gathering my strength, I darted out of the house, yelling, "Help! Help!" I slid underneath Ralph's barbed-wire fence, grabbing hold of the muddy earth, tearing at my arms to break free. Could someone tell me, please, why the neighbors wouldn't help? It's Christmas Eve; they are all in their own little worlds. Police wouldn't listen to me when

I called them up from a gas station. They told me to go back home. I'm glad I didn't. There was sure to be a bloodbath if I'd come back to the house. I guess Ralph was ashamed of me. Ha-ha!

A friend took me with him to my humble pad in Corvallis, an Oregon college town. It was the worst time of my entire life. Christmas morning. "Ain't it strange" (lyrics from "Season of the Witch," by Donovan) and "Paranoia strikes deep" (lyrics from "What It's Worth," by Buffalo Springfield) were playing on the radio. I was still with my friend Sean. We made love, but I didn't care if he touched me, hit me, spit at me, or did away with me. My spirits were damaged beyond repair. I couldn't quit crying, wondering what happened to my poor brother. And could it be that my mother and I bonded Christmas Eve? What about my sister? Is she getting eaten up by headhunters in Australia, as Mom said at the bar earlier? What a mess!

Later, in his white crew cut with a swollen crooked snout, Ralph came up to my place in Corvallis, wearing his dirty boots. He told me he was sorry. But was he, honestly? When I was seventeen, he thought he could get away with stroking my bra straps and kissing me on the lips. I told Mom, and she let him have it. I said it was OK. But was it really? The sneaky bastard. I'll never forgive the asshole. The only thing I learned from that man was how to roll cigarettes. On his fucking rolling machine he was so proud of. Under my breath I said, "What did you do with my brother, Ralph?"

I sat in the hospital waiting patiently. Ralph came by to deliver a pack of cigarettes. I didn't see him again until two years later.

Why did I get my happiness taken away from me? It began when I went out with Ron. No, this wasn't just any Ron; it was Ron Upright.

Ron Upright drove a red Chevrolet with a swastika symbol hanging from his car mirror. When my high-school chums found out that I was going with him, they yelled, "Hey, Sherry Standing, you are standing Upright in a field of tall grass!" They'd laugh.

He ordered a hamburger and asked me out. He had the most beautiful brown eyes, and when he kissed me, I felt like, "Am I doing this right?" Then I sank into his soft thick lips, holding my breath as if to capture the tenderness of the moment as a tingling sensation in my boobs overtook me. He was my hero. Being a Catholic, I was celibate throughout our two years of dating. Petting was as far as it went. He had to show me how to pet in the first place. At the drive-in, he moved his hands over my breasts.

"What in the hell do you think you are doing?" I asked.

He fudged an answer. He crawled his fingers farther down my body and poked me to see if I was pregnant. I was scarfing up a bag of popcorn and a dill pickle from the concession stand. I had my legs crossed and didn't realize what a turn on that could be. I caressed him. He taught me a lot about sex, of which I knew nothing until I met him. I didn't know that being touched on the breast and all over could be so much fun. One time in Seattle, I wanted to spend the night with Ron, but he refused to let me. He said that he was too horny. I thought he always did have pointed ears, and it did scare me, so I stayed with a classmate who was visiting her mom in the area.

Ron and I often had fun dressing up as twins. We dressed up in the style of the day. This time we went for the hippie: burgundy corduroy bell-bottoms, red-orange-brown-violet-yellow paisley rayon shirts. It would make you dizzy just looking at us. We visited the World's Fair site in Seattle and frequented the Space Needle. His passion was electric guitars. As I glanced over at him, his eyes were closed. He brought his right hand up in midair with his fingers, thumb strumming simultaneously. He was actually concentrating on composing a song and playing it on his guitar. He seemed pretty insecure by the way he drew attention to himself. He stuck another cigarette in his mouth. The smell of his nicotine was clouding the air, and as I began to ask him to stop, he lit another one.

He played "Louie Louie," "Pipeline," and "Wipe Out" with his friends on their electric guitars my junior year of high school. The music was intoxicating; I couldn't get enough of it. Immediately afterward, my parents came home drunk and kicked everyone out of the house. In all this chaos, Ralph dragged me by my hair through the grass outside, and I yelled, "You're welcome here anytime."

I thanked Ron for my ride home from Seattle to the Green District, a small suburb of Roseburg, where Mom and Ralph lived. Their plush white station wagon was parked outside. I walked into the metallic smell of puke and the singed cushions of our gold-velvet davenport. I was having my period, and my strength was sapped. To give some insight into the state of mind my mom was in at this time, I came inside the house, washed my undergarments, and hung them up to dry on the shower rod. But I'd left a stain.

My mom grabbed me by the throat from behind. She started to strangle me. She was drunk. "You made love with Ron, didn't you? Didn't you, you goddamn fucking whore!" she yelled.

"No, Mom," I reassured her. Because I hadn't.

She liked to call me a fucking whore every time she got a chance. Sometimes it would be when she was mean and belligerent, and other times it was when she was frolicking around, drunk on her ass, teasing me. I didn't dare tell anyone about this incident, because it was a no-no to talk about your folks at school. Besides, with the petting I did with Ron, I thought I really was a whore.

Society at that time had so many rules. They were strict about petting but silent about parental abuse. The rules of society today allow for sexual talk and teen pregnancy in schools, permitting pregnant students to finish their education, and they have hotlines and clinics for parental abuse.

Ralph hated Ron. He'd say, "Look at the guy, the way he combs his hair. He's the devil, Sherry. Are you going to pay more attention to your brother instead of going with that damn hoodlum?" He thought that I was shirking responsibility and not giving enough of my time and energy to Doug. He evoked a bitterness in me. It gave me the spooks.

I ended up loving Ron for two years. He was in the national guard reserves and was pretty lazy; even though he did do some work in Seattle at Boeing. I got the impression that he wanted me to support us on my Arctic Circle (a hamburger and beverage place) wages, so the day Ralph told me that he'd kill Ron if I didn't breakup with him, I broke up with him.

I couldn't be any more ticked off with Ralph than I am right now. Episodes of the mental distress caused by him and the experiences I encountered as I cruise down the halls of this madhouse peel away my soul, while darkness takes over my being.

But look, just a minute. I found her. The angel of the escape artists. She is another inmate. Down a tunnel we go, without any guards around, and end up at the Oregon State Fair. She has the audacity to call the hospital and turn us in. She really should be locked up. I don't see her anymore, except one day when I look through the thick grayish-glass window of her room; I witness her going through shock treatments. There are electrodes hooked right up to her head, and she is screaming in fits of terror. I think that I am next, so I try to be on my best behavior. I walk to my room slowly, because the Thorazine makes my movements slower than the normal pace. I hide my head and pray so hard to the thick air, but nothing is there. I don't want them to come and get me for escaping.

I walk to the Catholic church on the grounds and pass by two bald men who look like they are in their fifties or early sixties, with huge scars covering the side of their shiny heads. I kneel down on the church steps and plead to God for my life. Inside, I find a confessional. I confess about how I'm not a virgin anymore, whom I like, and my social security number. The penance is steep: three rosaries and ten Our Fathers! Wow! I walk back to my room, wondering in a haze if I even have a rosary.

Then I see a man who resembles my father, and he says, "Let's go for coffee sometime." He amazes me because he knows where everything is on the grounds. I meet him a few times at the canteen. The canteen is about thirty by thirty feet, spattered with metal like Christmas tree tinsel. You can buy a Coca-Cola if you have an aide there, or if you have the money. It is a meeting place for the patients, the great minds, to come and smoke and discuss the nothings that are tattooed in their heads. The conversations go like this:

"Do you have something to say?"

"Oh, nothing."

"What did you do today?"
"Oh, nothing."
"What do you feel like doing?"
"Oh, nothing."
The man sits with me and offers me cigarettes.

I had my first at sixteen with Mom's Bobbsey-twin-like girlfriend, Dell. She and Mom were both stout, wore blue muumuus, and had obsessive plans for me. Dell offered me a suave, debonair Tareyton. I drag on the white weed, hold it in, and pretend that I like it. But I can't get the taste of tobacco out of my mouth fast enough. I got higher than a kite. I showered my hot tongue with cold water, trying to douse it out. When my sister found out that I smoked, she cried.

So every time I take a drag of a cigarette, I feel guilty. The more I talk with the man, the more I am convinced he isn't my father at all. It seems like a month that I've carried around the garbage that he is my father. It is about time I let it go. So from then on, I am friendly, but I don't need to bum any more cigarettes.

My thoughts are missing the track now, and I can't stand the pressure in this environment anymore. My mind is hungry and thirsty for a good shot of sanity. Panic runs like ice water in my veins as I stand in the daily medication lineups here, and while I take my Thorazine pill, I am carried back to the time of my life when I was a virgin. I want to stay a virgin until I meet the right man to marry. I am strong in my convictions as a Catholic, and I think the last thing that I want to do is engage in sexual relations before the blessed sacrament of marriage, which I am willing to die for.

At age nineteen, I completed several courses for elementary and secondary education with a minor in physical education at Southern Oregon College in Ashland and at Umpqua Community College in Roseburg.

I moved to Lincoln City, a coastal town, to room with two high-school classmates. I saw *Valley of the Dolls* and *The Graduate*. (Good movies to heighten my expectations of the events that were going to take place in my life.) June, my roommate with dishwater-blonde, shoulder-length hair and a narrow frame, was aggressive and had a unique drive to correct me and get things done. Her favorite saying was, "shucky dern," a softer word for "drat it," and she used it continuously as she bumped into objects, jinxing them while she went about her day. Her beau was an all-American star football player in Roseburg, who tripped out on LSD and came to visit once or twice. Alice, my other roommate, seemed shy yet had a heart as big as a giant. She and I talked about how we could keep June on the right track.

One time June asked me to sniff glue with her. She was lying on the bed, and I was standing on the knobs of our bedroom door, straddling them as I rocked back and forth. I pushed away from the wall in the kitchen hallway with one hand and swung back to the door of our bedroom closet and caught it with the other. I don't know what got into me. I guess that I just wanted to go on my own "trip." That's the best way I can express it. Alice never intervened about June's problem, but we knew that June was going downhill. Finally, we asked for help from our landlord, but there wasn't much he could do.

I was becoming physically and mentally changed. Songs had a deeper meaning to me, and every note and every word was embedded in my soul. I wore tight denim jeans with pink ribbons braided in the side seams of them, and every time that I heard the song "Sherry Baby" on the radio, I slipped my jeans on to capture the moment of someone singing about me, or so I thought.

We shared cigarettes. Alice and June became waitresses at Pixieland. One night there was a knock at the door. I was downstairs at the landlord's apartment, baby-sitting their baby boy. "Our friend might come by," the landlords had said to me. I heard the knock again. I opened the door.

"Hello, my name is Sandy," the man with charismatic eyes said. I let him in. He said that he was a friend of the "'lords."

He asked me for a drink. I gave him one. After a conversation, he asked me to sit on his lap. I sat next to him, but he sat me on his lap and kissed me. "Do you want to make love?" His voice shrilled from ear to ear, shattering my stiffened body. My face was turning intensely flushed and hollow.

"No!" I shouted. I pushed away his shoulders with my fists clenched, struggling to break free.

He grabbed ahold of my neck and started rubbing it. He ripped off my clothes. I couldn't break free. Sweat pooled in my armpits, and saliva on my tongue was forming a thick wad of paste. My head was throbbing, prancing to the surge of a raging boom box. The next thing, it was morning. Our bodies were pressed together. My virginity had been stolen by the callous thief. Wringing with beads of sweat, I cried, "My God, what did he do to me?" My first thought was homicide. I'd get a knife. No, it wasn't worth it. Why did he do this to me? We'd better get married. I was a virgin, and I wanted to stay a virgin for the man I would marry.

My hair lay thick like stones on top of my shoulders. God, can you tell me what to do next? He won't wake up. On purpose, I thought. I couldn't believe how cheap and dirty I felt. What a fuckin' jerk!

I went to work. I was a waitress at Surf Point Inn, and we were hosting a banquet. That day was the longest day. Paranoia struck me. I thought customers were saying that I was no longer a virgin, and people were talking about me. I glanced out the window, where the waves of the Pacific Ocean met the outer edge of the bar's windowpane. Moved by the surf and the beauty in the sand and sharp rocks, I flashed back to the plush green trees and tranquil scenery that I left behind in Ashland and Roseburg. Sandy took off without saying good-bye.

June's sister, Irene, a hairdresser who graced herself with short skirts, chic blouses, and ratted-up hair, came to visit. She taught me how to hitchhike. Mimicking her, I stuck out my thumb for cigarettes, conversation, and a ride to my destination. She instilled a sense of boldness and courage in me. I hid the rape from Alice and June by putting some distance between us.

With ringlets styled up on the top of my head and false eyelashes fitted by Irene, I caught two rides to Roseburg to see my sister, who was visiting Mom from college. Mom refused to let me in the house, so Diana brought me back to Lincoln City. I might have been able to escape the inevitable, but time was holding me back.

CHAPTER 2

DYSFUNCTION

Three years later, I find myself on Salem's funny farm without a way to get out. I am sane, and I feel that everyone who has abused me through the years is crazy. The problem is convincing the damn staff that I am OK and was OK, and I need to be released to the public again.

Wait! I see Dr. Boyles. He must be my ticket outta here. He is a dentist with boils all over his face. He tells me that I have eight abscessed teeth, and he can pull them all out. I imagine him running after me, naked, with a drill, yelling, "Please let me pull just one more, please!" as he drools all over those bumpy red dots that invade his lower jaw. White pus heads peek over his chin in a soldier-like fashion. I cringe. I concentrate on his expressionless face as I stumble to escape. I slowly pace, dragging my feet to my room.

In a split second, I remember working at a pizza joint called Hokies Pizza Place in my junior and senior years at Oregon State University. I took methods of math, science, social studies, and health and safety to become an elementary education teacher. My employer started hiring men at a wage higher than what I received for the same job. I began work at Hokies at a lower pay and worked up to that wage. When I contacted the labor bureau, the representative came out and talked to my employer, Norm, a tall, insensitive derelict with a sharp nose like a fox. Norm laid me off. He beckoned me with his finger to come there to him. He said, "Throw your apron on the counter. You are done." He pretended to take off his apron and toss it on the counter.

I was holding a heavy tray of dark Bavarian beer, and I had to restrain myself from throwing it at him. He would have made a good target. Casually I asked, "Are you firing me?"

"No, you are being laid off."

I slowly placed my apron on the counter. Coins scattered everywhere.

He knew that if he fired me, he would be in a pickle with the labor department. Then, out of nowhere, he yelled, "Men should be paid more than women."

I lashed out at him. "Cram it up your ass, Norm!" I struggled to smother his words with my resistance.

Outside a dark cloud hung over the cold and intolerant establishment, and I turned to glance at the customers forcing down their pepperoni pizzas with confused and strained looks on their faces. It was worth it. Women do have rights. As I headed out the door, I fixated on the rocks pitted in the gravel before the entrance. I had the urge to destroy the windows of Hokies Pizza Place with the rocks.

This was the breaking point for me. I called Mom and told her to make sure Ralph got plenty of food, water, and bread and butter in his cell (Ralph wasn't in jail). They made my life a living hell. Not only had I made it that way, they were aides to the cause.

I walked to my friend's house. She was a bar and pizza waitress at Hokies also. She helped me fight the case, since she was being affected. When Mom and Ralph arrived, I had already taken eight cold showers, quit college, quit smoking, and started talking to myself. I told Mom that I wanted a sex change. I told her that a guy forced me to give him oral sex. My diet consisted of crackers and cheese. Out my window, I heard voices talking, laughing about a relationship I had with a man named Jack, whom I went out with several times. The voices said that I repeated the same gibberish to Jack as I did with Ron on the night that we got intimate. But this isn't Ron Upright. I loved this Ron more. He was a jock at Oregon State University (OSU) and had a brother named Ralph. Mom couldn't get over the fact that the Ron I was referring to was not Ron Upright, and his brother Ralph was not her husband, Ralph. She harped at me about it.

I couldn't understand why she was acting all crazy toward me, why the mental cruelty, but bits and pieces jar my memory.

Mom was an alcoholic. I got spanked if I told anyone that, though. She issued me mixed messages, periodically saying and doing things she didn't mean. She kicked me out of the house several times when I was a teenager, packing my suitcase and shoving me out the door. At night, I'd sit on the steps of Freemont Junior High School, which was practically in our backyard, wondering where I had gone wrong. I could feel the bruises tighten my skin from the cooking pan and hairbrush that she threw at me in her fits of anger.

My sister would find me and say, "Please come home. She won't remember this tomorrow." So I did.

One day Mom and Ralph took my little brother, Doug, and me on a trip to Disneyland. They informed me that my real father lived in San Jose, and they were going to stop there. I was ecstatic. The thought of seeing my real dad moved me. When we got to San Jose, Mom told me to take the picture that I had of him, which was in my pocket, and she shoved me out of the car, yelling, "Go find your father!"

They took off. I was thirteen, and the streets seemed cold and barren, iced over with despair and loneliness. As I walked down boulevards and railroad tracks, I took the crumpled picture from my pocket and smiled at my dad with love, trying to smooth every wrinkle that had invaded his face with my sweaty, quivering thumb. "I love you, Dad," I said out loud, as I passed by the pool halls, knowing how he liked to play pool.

I was stunned when a man headed toward me. I knew it was he, my dad, whom I had been waiting eleven years to see.

"Sherry?" He studied me.

"Dad!" I cried. I showed some sensitivity toward him, since distance had made us strangers, but I remember how heavy my heart felt as I grieved for the time we had lost. After catching up on our life's experiences, he sent me away on a Greyhound bus to Salt Lake City, and I met Mom and my stepdad there. I think Mom felt guilty, but she didn't show it.

I guess Mom had some good reasons for blowing me off, though. In her youth, she had a sister who died of breast cancer; a brother who set himself on fire and died in a hospital, because he couldn't afford pain medication; and another brother, a teacher, who died of malaria teaching in a village where there was an outbreak of mosquitoes. The tragedies and sadness of her past molded her into a person she did not want to become. She was a proud Brazilian, whose beginnings contrasted with her life in the United States. She came with a sense of fun and a feeling of freedom and acceptance. Her heart danced with the rhythm of the samba. When Mom arrived, she faced feelings of restriction and disapproval brought on by her beautiful black kinky hair, dark skin, and Portuguese accent—traits crying out, "foreigner." She married my father, Jim Standing, a military man who was part Native American, who brought Mom to the States at the end of World War II, but the marriage ended in divorce. Healing was an excuse for another drinking binge. At night, I would listen for my mother, as she cried out for her family with a bottle of whisky in a sack by her side. I felt so sorry for her.

The first time I saw blood was when I was two. Mom threw a Coke bottle at my dad's head as he headed out the front door. Bubbles of red goo ran down the side of his head. You see, she was a Catholic with a temper, and he was a Mormon. No wonder it didn't work. As a kid, I would have recurring nightmares of dragons. When I woke up, I would draw a picture of the dragon and write captions like "There you are. Take that, Mr. Dragon! Don't come to our house again, Mr. Dragon." I wondered if Dad was becoming my Mr. Dragon.

There were other factors contributing to my breaking point that were connected with my feelings toward my mother. I remember swimming when I was about two years old in a fountain in downtown Salt Lake City, Utah, with other children. I started playing with a three-year-old girl with braces. "Be careful of that one," Mom yelled. "She has polio." I didn't know what polio was, so we kept on playing.

The taste of a mixture of catsup and mayonnaise in my food and the feeling of receiving shots in my arm became a part of my memory. Sugar cubes were given to me as something sweet, and a nurse sat by my side, chanting, "Please get better." But strangely, I don't recall wearing braces, using crutches, or not being able to walk, even though the polio crippled me at the time.

When I was coming home from the hospital, Mom was sitting in the front seat of a cab, and my sister was in the back with me. I yelled, "Where's my mommy? I want my mommy!" At the end of a three-month stay in a hospital, I was either mad at my mom for putting me in the hospital, or I was experiencing early signs of my imbalance.

At age seven, I contracted polio again, only this time in the back. Mom rushed me to the Sacred Heart Hospital in Salt Lake City. I had taken the Sabin vaccine, and I was allergic to it. The doctors saw how I vomited and kept me in the hospital for two weeks. Curled up in a ball and packed with some ice, they injected a long needle into my spine. "She has polio in the back," they said.

A boy with polio came to visit in a wheelchair, and we ate sweet rolls together. The next couple of days I felt better, and I jumped up and down on my bed. I knew I wasn't supposed to stand up, but I wanted to get well, and the only way that I could get strong was to do it myself. I don't remember the pain, but I remember jumping up and down in my bed, yelling, "I'm free, I'm free!"

Mom enrolled me in ballet, tap dance, and swimming classes as therapy to get stronger. I got uniquely strong physically and mentally and became athletic and competitive. I defied all odds and became a cheerleader for four years. I was chosen queen of the rally squad in the ninth grade in junior high. However, Mom celebrated my victories with another bottle of booze, and I faced criticism from my peers, who said what a fake I was. Maybe I could have withstood the pressure better if alcohol had never been invented, and Mom had never taken to drinking, and if Connie Funkle, who dumped my things from my locker on the floor, hadn't lit into me for burning a hamburger while I was working with her at the Arctic Circle my senior year of high school. But I didn't think that was going to happen, not in this lifetime.

⸺

With the physical disability weighing on my mind and the mental abuse I took from my parents and Hokies, I wanted to strike out at something in an unattractive way. The purity of my mind and my self-love took a sabbatical. It was a matter of time till I would be a signature on the admission paper for an asylum.

When Mom and Ralph arrived in Corvallis to take me home to the Green District, we ended up in a Laundromat in Albany, Oregon. I made a scene. I said, "I am Jim Standing, a little baseball player." (My dad was the pitcher for a minor-league baseball team, the Darlings, at one time.) I grabbed my imaginary cap, motioning above my forehead with my index and middle finger. I pretended to swing a bat with my hands in a tight grip, one on top of the other.

A person was standing about ten feet away from me. I whispered to Mom, "We have a teacher in our midst." I had no idea who this person was or if teaching was her profession. Never saw her before. Before leaving, Mom struck up a conversation with her, and I found out she was a teacher.

I am following someone's scenario of me back from OSU, and I am being all twisted up with insanity and déjà vu. Someone calls the police. They come, and we take off before they can question me. What Mom and Ralph really don't know is that I've just been visiting a blind, deaf, mentally challenged, and criminal institution to report on for my health and safety class. I am in the middle of going off, and my mind is taking on different personalities.

Mom and Ralph begin to drive me home from the Laundromat and tell me that my brother is going to meet me there. Mom is in the backseat, and Ralph is in the driver's. I spy a rest area and a gas station in the distance, where we stop to tank up. Ralph says that Doug is there; he is hitchhiking home. He might have imagined it, because Doug doesn't appear to be anywhere in sight. I take it Ralph is dishing me a line, and I can't stand his obnoxiousness. My thought processes hurt, and my mind soars, mounting with pain. Ralph gets on his walkie-talkie and says, "Yes, Universal Studios, she is here."

Makes me think that I am a movie star or something. It is bizarre and very damaging, since I'm sick and believing that I have that much fame. It is going to the top of my head. I finally get to see Doug when I reach home.

The strangeness of being home causes me to react to Mom's ongoing intoxication. She drinks more heavily than ever. I'm a ghost in the closet. She can't see me. While she is away at the store with Ralph, the aroma of chicken noodle soup precedes my brother upstairs and floats to my bedroom. He places the bowl of soup on my lap and says, "Here you go, kiddo, eat this." Doug makes a pink champagne cake for Ralph for Father's Day, and I ransack the refrigerator and eat all of the cake.

I say, "Whoa! I'm drunk!" I stagger like a drunk, one foot criss-crossing the other, slurring my words as I brace my hand on the smelly davenport.

When I notice that I have access to Mom and Ralph's cans of paint and paintbrushes, I think I am in the movie *Paint Your Wagon*, and I sing "They Call the Wind Maria." I swing the paint-brush at Doug, dripping white latex paint everywhere, totally and completely off my rocker. I've lost my mind. Checked out. I almost blind my brother by my overreaction. The paint just misses his eyes. I feel awful. I see the psychiatrist the next day.

"Dr. Allred. Dr. Allred, I want to be a boy." I grab the doctor in the balls and genitalia while he's sitting in his chair. "I want to be a boy. I'll die standing up for you," I cry.

I think, "By now, he thinks I am nuts." When I come home from my session, I head for the mirror in the bathroom and peek inside. I see this awful image of me sticking out my tongue and rolling it around. I've visited that mirror once before, as a happy, proud, redheaded teenager in my orange-and-black uniform, getting ready for a football game. Only now, the features are strained, and my eyes are distant and sunken in. I start to grab my neck, pinching off the air in my trachea. I begin strangling myself with my hands, red fingerprints on my throat turning white. Mom sees me do it and frantically calls the doctor, who prescribes Thorazine. Mom picks up the prescription, and I think that I am taking birth control pills, so I willingly go along with Mom as she administers them to me.

I can't breathe. Lying next to my mom in her bed at night, I am gasping for air. My heart is pounding rapidly like Secretariat's hoofs pounding on the racetrack. She strokes my hair. I fall asleep for a couple of hours and awaken in my saturated nightclothes. I want to scream, but I am so sedated that I can't force the air to come up to surface in my vocal cords; besides, I don't want to wake my mom. At six o'clock in the morning, sunlight penetrates the see-through nylon curtains of her bedroom window and casts a shadow where the strands of her thick Brazilian hair lie on my arm. Closing my eyes again, I think of all the hell I put my mom through, and I am saddened.

There is a chance I may be locked up for good. That's the price you pay for the errors you make in life, even if sometimes it isn't your fault.

CHAPTER 3

SIGNING IN

I'm in the bigger building now. Everything is a haze of secretion and deceit. The hospital is playing the song "Abraham, Martin, and John." You can hear Bobby and John getting shot in the record in the background, and you can see the fury in the patients' eyes as they slobber all over their plates of food, latrines, and beds while the song plays on. It isn't a pretty sight. The air is crowded with hate, secretion, and sedation, and I can't stand another minute of it. Tonight will be a full moon.

    I head for the kitchen. Edna and Zelda are working in the dish room. I scrape plates; they pick them up with their long bony fingers and slide their sticky tongues around the surface. They throw up in the sink and continue with the process of picking up, licking up, and throwing up. A very repulsive situation. I have to keep from gagging and losing it. I'm seeing colors of gold, purple, green, and red with corn. This employment is disturbing. Why did I sign up to do this? Time to make another slash on the chalkboard upstairs. (Mark on the chalkboard for stipends.) Ha!

My pipe dreams skyrocket the morning after Mom and I sleep side by side. Someone pours blue grass all over my body and sprinkles golden glitter on the top of my hair. I tell Mom that I want to see the auditorium and Dr. Bonebrake. She asks, "Are you crazy?"

But both are there, just as I dreamed the night before, right in the building where the psychiatrist is. I run from the auditorium on the ground floor up six flights of stairs, and there is a Dr. Bonebrake in his office with a sign on his door, DR. BONEBRAKE, in bold black letters. I say, "Dr. Bonebrake, I won't break any bones for you. Will you dance with me?"

My dear mom climbs the six flights of stairs and finds the truth—that there really is a Dr. Bonebrake in the building. I'm placed in a cop car and taken home. When I return home, I want to sew myself a red velvet dress, but I don't remember why. Mom, who arrives with Ralph, won't let me, so I aim skyward to my bedroom. I take off all of my clothes, reach for a paintbrush, and with red paint, paint over my two favorite Keane paintings (the children with the big eyes with moisture painted in their pupils as if they are ready to cry). Ralph marches upstairs and sees me and hurries back down in disbelief. That's what he gets for stroking my bra straps and kissing me on the mouth when I was seventeen. He isn't even my father. Sure, Ralph, some other time. That's what he wants me to say.

I wrap the paintings in newspaper and try to deliver them to the Whites on Pine Street. There is some hidden meaning to that, but my memory escapes me now. Oh, yes. The Whites were an inspiration to Doug when we moved from Salt Lake City to Roseburg, Oregon, in 1959. I started the last half of my fourth grade at Rose Grade School then. We had a centennial celebration six days away from my birthday at Rose School.

Mom sewed me and my sister pink-and-white flowered dresses and white pantaloons. We wore our curly red hair like pioneers, with smooth spiraled ringlets underneath our matching bonnets.

There were covered wagons circling the school grounds, and children played the parts of Lewis and Clark, Sacajawea, Patrick Henry, and famous pioneers who had made their name in Oregon history. Mom was sweet then and brought us ribbon candy from where she worked at the candy factory. She kept them in a wooden, scented box where the aromas of cinnamon cherry and hickory seeped through the lid and magically spiraled and encircled the air. A big old stick went sailing through my foot as I ran across the kitchen floor after school. She tweezered it out tenderly, splinter by splinter, and treated it with Mercurochrome. She had this odd expression on her face. It was a raised-eyebrow look with a smile that happened at the same time. It created the illusion that you were supposed to know what she was thinking. It took a lot of guesswork to find out what was on Mom's mind, since she was a private person and told us to never open up to anyone about our personal business—or her own. So I took her seriously.

When school was out for the summer, we moved from Pine Street to Maple Street across the steel two-lane Oak Street Bridge, which was nicknamed the "Green Bridge." It connected two sides of Roseburg—the east and west, I believe. It was the only bridge in the city at the time. It got its name from the weathered green paint that was chipping away from its structure, and the ailing impression it left on your mind as you drove across it. I think the floodwaters reached its roadbed when our housing project was flooded out, and we were forced to move in with Ralph, who became my stepfather in the Green District. The only thing the water didn't touch in our tiny duplex was Diana's off-white Catholic prayer book with its gold crucifix exposed, which was lying on an upper shelf beside the top of our Christmas tree.

We lived in a three-room house on Maple Street. The street was covered with maple trees that changed into brilliant colors of rich orange and golden greens throughout the year. One night while I was sleeping, I dreamed that I was riding my bicycle, and my sister pushed me off the seat of the bike. When I awoke we were experiencing "the blast." Our house was tilting to one side.

A truck carrying two tons of dynamite and four tons of blasting agents blew up, killing thirteen people and injured many others, including one who later died. It was the blast of the century. That's the only thing that the people talked about for years, and it was all over the newspapers in practically every city in Oregon. The townspeople were changed, and the mood was somber. The atmosphere was altered and filled with confusion. I was sick-hearted with grief.

There was a rumor that Mrs. White from Pine Street received a message from God just before the incident, and she ran down the street yelling for people to hide under a bed or table or to get out of their houses. It was miraculous, the people she saved. Maybe the blast could have been the reason for my episodes of paranoia, or maybe it was the flood that sent my biological clock walking backward, but whatever it was, I felt uneasy dealing with these things that were beyond my control.

As I remember the Whites, more things come to me from the past.

There was a time when Mom wanted to take Diana, Doug, and me to the nickel mine in Riddle, a small city near Myrtle Creek. It was the only nickel mine in operation in the United States. She was drunk. We were yelling to her, "Slow down, please! You are going to kill us!" as our car swerved back and forth. Three-year-old Doug was in the backseat. She stopped the car and threw the baby seat at us. It missed and slashed Doug's lip, and he began to cry. I ran out of the car, screaming, "Help! My mom is drunk, and she hurt my brother. Look! There's blood!"

She was making up for those nights when we had to care for ourselves alone at home while she stayed in jail, charged with being drunk on a public street. I was lonely. My sister, Diana, wanted me to get back into the car. She didn't want us to be adopted out to someone else, so I got back into the car. I'm happy she made that decision. We didn't need any more complications in our lives. The worst would have been to be split up.

Although Mom's negligence is an important factor in why I got locked up, I don't believe that I can solely blame it on my upbringing.

Severe depression was taking place everywhere. For instance, in 1963, when I was in junior high, I heard over the school's intercom that President John F. Kennedy was shot and killed. I had permission to walk the track by myself. I was hurt emotionally. I walked for about forty-five minutes, holding onto the love that I felt in my heart for JFK and his family. A man of such influence and love for his country, murdered. I wept in pain. The shooting left me with bad memories. Ever since then, my peers called me a loner at activities, parties, and functions.

My life was being reworked at this point, and I began to feel proud and omnipotent as I was chosen Personality of the Month for sportsmanship, an award that helped to eliminate the pain and confusion in my depressive teenage years. My picture hung in the school's hallway. Then Connie Funkle pushed her way through a crowd of students, looked at me with a stern face, and repeated, "You really think you are something, don't you? You really think you are something, don't you?"

I was crushed. "No," I said meekly, trying not to bring attention to myself. It was like being hit over the head with a giant bulldozer. The damage caused me to suffer guilt and low self-esteem, and there was no way to fix it.

I wrap up the paintings and deliver them to the Whites on Pine Street. I get a call from the labor bureau representative about my Hokies labor case. He arrives in the Green District, so I pretty up Mom and Ralph's house and try to contain myself. I'm on a head trip, so we talk briefly about labor issues until I regain composure.

Then he leaves, and I borrow Ralph's car to get a refund for some pop cans that Mom and Ralph have been collecting since I arrived in the Green District. I take Doug with me. I start talking to the cans while I am driving. I make it terribly hard on my little curly-headed brother, Doug, our junior high school mascot, nine years younger than me. He looks down at his folded hands. His expressive blue eyes and incredible long eyelashes are growing tears.

"Well, do you still want a sex change?" asks Allred the next morning in his psychiatric office.

"Yes, I do." I flinch. (The Thorazine isn't working.)

Then he looks at my mom and says, "I think she should go to Salem."

I say, "Yes."

Mom cries, "No."

That night the wind howls, and I think I am on a farm experiencing some tempestuous tornado. Mom's chickens in the chicken coop are restless, and April and Patches, our horses, are stirring about, digging their hooves into Ralph's barbed-wire fence. I witnessed a couple of gray-haired men with suspenders, overalls, and pitchforks on the streets earlier. I wonder if it could be a sign, perhaps, that the world is coming to an end. Has the Wrath of God descended upon us? My brother says, "Hurry, Sherry, I'll help you pack." He smooths his thumb over the palm of my hand where I burned it, intentionally, on a frying pan.

I never told anyone, but I saw Doug's peter under his shorts while he was sleeping, and I almost touched it. That is why I burned my hand. I turned on the high heat of the electric frying pan and pressed the palm of my hand down on it until it seared and sizzled the flesh. Not only that, I started to think that I was Jesus Christ, and it scared me.

I toss two pairs of printed slacks, my white blouse, and denim jeans at Doug to pack for me. Then Ralph says, "Now!" We are running to the car. I can feel another force moving me. I seize Ralph's torn fur-lined jacket. "Ralph, look at me! I'm your dead son," I say, 'cause Ralph had a son who drowned when he was twelve.

Ralph nods his husky forehead. "I know it."

Perhaps I tapped into a ghost in that house. Or is Ralph insane, too? God, if there is one, doesn't want me in Salem. The car swerves relentlessly. There is more wind than imaginable. Uneasy, agitated, and disturbed, I ride in the backseat of Ralph's white station wagon, rocking back and forth and side to side, shaking my knees nervously, with my fingers snapping to the radio. I take a glimpse at the blister that is on the palm of my hand. It is dry, cracked, and sweaty from a clear liquid, like linseed oil, that oozes out into threads of sorrow across my palm's thin lifeline. I dig a hole with my left index fingernail and make a depression in the injured right palm. I try to pop the "carpenter's nail" out, which I believe to be buried in my right hand. I turn to my brother and cry, "I'm sorry."

I sign my name at the courthouse. I write, "Sherry Sherman," my stepdad's last name. Then I am off to the insane asylum. As time goes on, I become Sherry Standing, Sitting, Lying, Understanding, and Outstanding to all my acquaintances in the institution. What a lonely, confined place it is. Oh yes, and we all live for Ralph Sherman, because he sure is a man. Ha! Ha! (I scribble on the asylum papers and note pads.)

A long wiry rod that is attached to a telephone-like receiver is held up to my face. "Have a light," an inmate says as the holes in the receiver light up. I drag on my smooth white Tareyton and get a long buzz.

Another inmate says, "It's called the iron lung." I go nuts as I look in the hall and see someone who I think is my father. We are all in jail, I think. Maybe this is my father's right arm. Is he God?

I'm sitting in the hospital, waiting for someone to get me out. My aunt Deanna comes to see me almost a day too late. My sister is still in Australia with her husband. Perhaps they will come later on. I find a surprise after Auntie's visit. In a brown paper sack, fifty pieces of Bazooka bubble gum and juicy, striped Christmas candy, placed carefully on my bed. I wear the strawberry, lemon, pineapple, vanilla flavors all around my face. A note I find says, "From the kids and me to Sha Sha."

Sha Sha is the nickname Uncle Doc gave me when he was patrolling the Bonneville races, and we shared coffee together. One summer I stayed with him and my aunt, and the sound of the stock car tires broke the stars in half. Uncle Doc had a bald head and a half finger he said was sawed off by the meat-packing plant where he worked. He popped it in my face and said, "Gotcha! Here's lookin' at you, kid!" There was no one like Uncle Doc.

Our dorm is having a baby.

I go to a lily pond on the south side of the institution. I see three white lilies in the pond, fussing about and talking to each other. Two have broad smiles on their faces, and the third looks like she is in a trauma, with teeth chattering and face vibrating in fear. As I bend down to pick one up, the one nearest me spouts, "What are you doing here? You're not good enough for us."

I say, "I don't know, they just put me here."

Another asks, "Did you slit your wrist?"

I reply, "No, it wasn't like that."

The third says, "Why did you make your mother suffer like that?"

I can't answer.

Then she shouts, "You need more medication!"

Sorrow sweeps over my face. I can feel my eyebrows sink in as I see my reflection in the pond. I know it is me in the luminous water, because the tiny dots of film in the saturated air make me squint my eyes. I can feel the corners of my mouth droop down to my chin. I feel trapped and bloated in my body. Bloated from Thorazine. My hair strands shatter the reflection. I feel the urge to waltz around the pond. I sway to and fro with the melody of "Here Comes the Sun," by the Beatles, in my head. I pick out the lily that is soft, that is bursting with color and life—the one that doesn't pose a threat to me. The one that breathes the same air that I breathe and shares the same space that I share.

Because we are having a shower in our room, I want to give someone a special present. I break out with hives as I tug and pull the lily from the pond. At the dorm, I lay the lily gracefully across my bed. I play ping-pong with my friend Maggie outside our cell with a tiny egg of a spider in this big blade of tall grass, and the next thing I know, the shower is canceled.

A nurse's aide named Nora is assigned to me. I think she is the daughter of the head of the deaf institute that I visited when I went to OSU. She smokes with me and gives me cigarettes on her rounds. I never make any sense to her, but I think I do.

I try to be an open vessel, hoping that maybe someday my paranoia will disappear like magic, and people will stop talking about me.

CHAPTER 4

ALTERED

No one knows my secrets or screw-ups from the past that I hide and feel so guilty about.

There was a time when I was young, when my sister held me over the bathtub backward and almost choked me because she was mad at me. I got even by telling her there was a puppy dog behind a bush. I was following the dog and came upon it in a bush. I knew the bush was loaded with wasps. She walked into my trap, and she was stung all over her body.

Then there was the time when my sister, my brother, my mother, and I were riding in a car. We reached home, and my mother moved her finger into the corner of the car door. I opened the door up without looking and closed it on my mom's finger, smashing it. It took my sister to open the door and get it out. I couldn't stand the sight of it. It was turning purple. I was scared I would make her finger worse, so I didn't react to her injury.

Next, my sister and I were taking a bath. Our two-year-old brother opened the bathroom door. We had suds all over the floor, and as my brother walked on the bathroom floor, he slid all around. We laughed and said, "Look at you dance, Dougy."

Mom heard us and frantically came in and picked him up off the floor. We could have crippled the little guy. I felt so sad. And here I was, a cheerleader. My capabilities, strengths, and weaknesses; everything was almost overwhelming.

I slowly walk back to my room. I hang my head, focusing on my belly button. In my room, I sit with a bath towel wrapped around my head like a turban. I hear talk of Freud outside my door; I pretend I am a psychoanalyst.

I come to the conclusion that my two stepfathers had no reason to be cruel to me. I know that Doug's real father, Roy, is still mad at me for locking him out of the bathroom when I was nine. He was going to punish me for not paying attention to him when he asked me to pass the butter to his daughter, Dawn, at the dinner table. I let him know how hurt I was. I ran to the bathroom and braced myself between the tub and the door, pressing my feet against it so he couldn't get in. He and Mom divorced two weeks afterward. I feel I was to blame.

And Ralph, Mom's third husband, who took us to live in the Green District and fed darkness into my life with abuse since I was fifteen, stole my Christmas from me. No one can throw a punch like Ralph, and there must be some psychological reasoning to that. Maybe because Ralph's parents were missionaries, and they punished people who didn't fit the mold.

I evaluate the situation.

Ralph generated hate and jealousy in my sophomore year of high school, causing the first year of my mental undoing. He thought dancing was a sin and tried to punch me for going to a Paul Revere and the Raiders dance at the Armory with my sister one night. Diana and I went to the Armory and shook and shimmied like Elvis. We were having fun. I felt pretty, and the guys thought so, too. They were saying, "Who is that pretty redhead?" Maybe they were talking about Diana, I don't know, but thank God for Diana that night. When we arrived home, Ralph showed his knuckles and twisted ogre face. "So you went to a dance, did ya?" he said.

Diana brought her right arm up to his face to stop him. He backed down. "You'll never be as strong as your sister, so quit trying to be like your sister. Oh, and by the way, only put a quarter of a cup of milk in your cereal bowl," Ralph snapped as I got ready for school the next morning. That day, I was sitting in science class, and my teacher saw me nod off to sleep. He said, "Sherry Standing, wake up!"

I ran into the bathroom and yelled at the top of my lungs, "I'm falling into a big hole, and I can't stand it anymore." I thought everyone was talking about me. I couldn't practice my cheers properly in the house, and I was becoming the least popular girl in high school, ruining my chances of ever being a cheerleader again. I made a lot of sarcastic remarks to everyone, and I hurt other people's feelings.

This was my first bout of paranoia that I can remember.

A year later, I got a call at the Arctic Circle. It was my brother. "It's dark, and I'm alone, and I'm scared. I think someone's in the house!" I left the Arctic Circle and fled home in my crummy 1951 Plymouth station wagon, a gift from Aunt Deanna and Uncle Doc. I waited for Mom and Ralph to arrive. They came home drunk, and I told them that they shouldn't leave Doug alone. "He's only seven."

I didn't want Ralph to get his way with me, but I was blinded by his hate, and I didn't see it coming. I took another blow. I dropped to the floor. The impact of the cold sharp pain caused my upper lip to turn blue and my mouth to swell and become numb. They made Doug go to bed. I cried so much that the following day, my English teacher, Mrs. Ashworth, asked me, "Is something wrong?"

All I could say was, "It's raining outside, and I just got my face wet." A tear drizzled down my cheek. I smeared cherry ChapStick all over my lips. Mom stuck it in my coat pocket for me to hide my fat lip. Mrs. Ashworth bought my excuse, and this left me feeling weak, like Ralph could pounce on me again. No one could possibly have known how I felt.

Due to the strict influences of his parents and the past, Ralph continued to impose his guilt on our dysfunctional family. He played the roles of Dr. Jekyll and Mr. Hyde, supplying Mom with booze, whether she was on a binge or not on a binge, while entertaining a lady friend in a trailer next to our house. When Mom set fire to his field because she was drunk, Ralph beat Doug up for burning his shirt trying to put out the fire. The fire stung like hot wax on Doug's delicate skin. I wanted to take my brother away with me but couldn't.

Not then, not now. Ralph was the cause of my mental problem. There was nowhere to escape. I felt his dominance. His physical inflictions and blame were the true signs of male chauvinism. He caused me to feel insecure and say the things I didn't mean to say. I couldn't be that loving, giving cheerleader I wanted to be. I miss that outgoing person: the special me that I was.

As a result, I want to sink back into a hole and die. My mental system of dealing with the pressure is beginning to erode, and I'm becoming an empty shell of pain and doubt. I hide from resentment in order to find the happiness, but I fall to the voice of negativity that fills my empty shell with despair. I must fill my shell with love and peace to escape my misery. I have a chance to see Nora again and make some sense of all the craziness Ralph has put me through.

⁓

The doctor whom I only see twice, looks like the doctor in the movie *One Flew Over the Cuckoo's Nest*. He tells me that I will have a rough time living on the outside—I guess because I blend in so well. But I keep my head up and play my cards right.

There is a girl here who is a tap dancer. She is tall and skinny, with dark, matted hair. I tap-dance with her. I can tell when she is having a period. It's kinda "lezzy" of me, I know. Guess it's telepathy. I walk over to a circle of women staring into space, probably catching flies in their teeth. I kiss a woman on the lips, thinking that she is a Ron Upright transvestite, not that Ron would ever change his sex. One girl pretends to be my friend, but she sneaks off to my room and steals my makeup and mascara. I look like a homeless baboon. You'd almost have to kiss that whore's ass to get her to lend you anything after she borrows your goddamn stuff. My language goes to the wayside.

Running through the halls on sticky floors, trying to breathe, my face turns beet red, with my tongue a heavy grade of cotton. I finally get redemption. While under heavy sedation, I see my sister, Diana. She appears to be an apparition with an illuminating halo circling her head. She comes to rescue me almost a day too late. I am on Thorazine, and she comes back from Australia with a baby in her belly to fetch me. I itch and jitter all over. My feet and hands are going like the happy motor of a late Toyota engine. Maybe it is the red satin dress I find in someone's closet here that makes me itch. I shouldn't have organized that beauty contest. Teach me to tell others here to get in the drawers of the women of this institution and try on their fancy dresses. "I'm Miss Brazil," I say. Maybe God is getting back at me and punishing me with the hives. Who knows? I am all distorted.

I remember back to our childhood. Diana had scarlet fever, and Mom and I rally to take care of her. Then when she was ten years old, she was waiting at a corner on her way to school. An elderly man had a heart attack and ran her over with his car, dragging her into a telephone pole. I was walking about twelve feet behind her on our journey in the snow, and when I saw it happen, I mentally blocked it and went on to school.

My third-grade teacher forced me to go home. She got a call from my mom saying that my sister had been run over. Fortunately, Diana only suffered bruises and a hurt foot. It was such a traumatic experience for us all, yet we held it together.

When we were young, Diana took a play horse's head from the backyard and got a big board. She nailed four wooden legs to the board and set me on top of it. Then she took a string, tied it around the legs, and gave me the string. She said, "Pull on the string and you can make the horsey walk!"

Like a dummy, I followed her instructions. The horse collapsed, and I landed flat on my little derriere. It caused me to see another side of her: the clever, mischievous side. But she was still so young, curious, and sweet, and she was my sister. How could I stay mad at that sister of mine with such ingenious qualities?

In our youth, our emotions were high and unpredictable. We learned to roller-skate by lacing up the shoestrings of white leather boots attached to our wheels and pushing our feet out in a scissor-like fashion. We balanced back and torso over hips, gliding to the end of the rink. I employed a ripe amount of confidence and bumped my head hard into the cement wall. Bright-red blood seeped through my cracked lips, between my two new front teeth, and down my chin. I began to spit blood into the palm of my hand, but I held the tears back and continued skating. The instructor caught me between her strong arms and heavy thighs and asked me to sit with her while she watered down a handful of toilet paper and stuffed it in my nose. She pinched the sides of my nose and asked me to lean forward. Mom fetched some ice from the concession stand and held it to my cheek and nostrils. Feeling like I had just swallowed a container of Morton's salt, I lay limp in my mother's arms as she unlaced my skates and walked me to the car.

Eventually, we learned to skate well enough to perform routines, one of which was "Teddy Bear's Picnic," which we did in Salt Lake City. Diana and I dressed up in brown jumpsuits that covered our nervous arms and legs. We glided around the rink, keeping beat to the music with our teddy bear ears flapping over our heads. The bears stumbled, but there were no mishaps per se.

Diana and I acquired medals and bars for figure, dance, and freestyle skating. We were proud that roller skating had become the center of our lives. Being on exhibition and attaining stardom was our top priority. Diana was a beautiful diva skater. She had this distinguished Marilyn Monroe mole on her left cheek. In her red hair and green sequined minidress, she skated to "The High and Mighty." Her spread eagles were right on the mark as she glided effortlessly, circling the rink, toes pointed outward, extending one arm up gracefully over her head like a ballerina. Every time I would go to the meets, I'd cry after her performance. She was high and mighty, all right, in my eyes. In a pairs routine, she would cast me into midair by bracing her wrist on mine and maneuvering me with her elbow and forearm. I'd return to her, twirling two 360-degree revolutions. She'd pick me up, without a twinge of hurt or animosity for placing last in front of the judges, as I would collapse with my skates underneath me.

At the end of our last competition, we changed our routines and skated without being sponsored. It was a clean program. I skated to "Flower Drum Song." I completed four double jumps and completed every camel and sit spin. I invented a traveling sit spin, and another person performed it in her program. I felt pretty vainglorious and honored, thinking she might have gotten the idea from me. Diana placed second and qualified for nationals. However, things got strange, and we didn't skate anymore. It was kinda square to be skating in high school, and for a while we laid our skates to rest.

Diana and I became PBX long-distance operators together after high school for Pacific Northwest Bell. We would connect individuals, their families, and business people with a lever, a cord, and a board. Later I would perform these duties as a switchboard operator for Pan American Airlines in San Francisco and Church Hill Hall at Southern Oregon College-SOC.

I was strong in those days. I dropped a lot of pain and sorrow; however, the tapestry that comprised my life put to rest the pain and sorrow only for a short while. After I finished high school and enrolled in college, my more serious problems began. I smoked marijuana a couple of times and took bennies. We were in a war. Diana and I wrote to guys in Vietnam. To goof off, we took pictures of ourselves on top of our cars in our bikinis—Diana with her long red hair and hips like Raquel Welch's, and me with my short red hair, deep tan, and high rib cage. They wrote back. The man I wrote to took a picture of himself stretching out on top of his jeep, leaning on his elbow, propping up his head with his hand as he held onto the photo of me in my bikini. I was impressed. But I never heard from him again, and we don't know what happened to him.

That was a war that killed innocent people and could have killed me, being as sensitive as I was about death and all. It took one of my classmates and damaged two others mentally. It killed many people over there and at home with drugs and violence. It was so sad. It makes me sick just to think about it.

I went to the beach on my twenty-first birthday with a guy who had fought in the Vietnam War. I met him in the Memorial Union at Oregon State University on campus. Jackie, a friend from Roseburg who was rooming with me at OSU, came by and lit her cigarette off his. He asked me out and took me to the beach. He was persistent with me, but I didn't let on at the time that it bothered me. He got me in a choke hold. "You'll do it if you value your life!" he threatened.

I had to do what he said, or he'd kill me. Sex became false and cold. I protested and struggled, and that was the beginning of my worst twenty-one years of life.

I remember how my bad experiences with men started. I was thirteen years old, and I was walking down the street in Roseburg. A man in a VW said, "Come here, little girl." I thought he needed instructions to find a street, so I walked over to his car.

He said, "Do you want this?" His big penis was jutting out of his pants. He was wiping it with a red-and-white handkerchief.

I said no, very calmly, and ran. I called my aunt in Salt Lake City, but I hid the incident from my mom. I was shocked for days, and conveying that incident to my aunt was the bravest deed I could do, I felt. She ended up calling Mom.

When I entered SOC as a freshman, my views of men had changed. I was willing to give some my consideration. I enrolled in classes where male students attended (not exclusively). I took courses in Western civilization, where I learned about the Byzantine Empire; English composition; psychology—the study of the mind and Skinner's box; biology—division of cells and germinations of plants; and art appreciation—learning about the masters of the Renaissance and Impressionist periods.

Suzanne Holmes was my first dorm experience. I was moved from that room, because they were transferring me to Hoffman Hall, which was disappointing. Hoffman Hall was a poor man's dorm on campus that was converted to a woman's dorm, and it had no class. The paint was chipping on the inside and out, and it was sloppily painted pink and white. I got in trouble once or twice for leaving my room with unwashed clothes in my closet and papers scattered helter-skelter. I worked in the dorm's kitchen and felt justified in living the way I wanted to, since I was paying for it. I complained when the housemother told me to leave because of the clutter, but after I pleaded my case, she agreed to let me stay.

That fall quarter, I met a Japanese-Hawaiian freshman named Evien. He was thin and had brown beady eyes. He didn't fit the mold of the male chauvinist type who roamed the college campus. We dated and had an innocent friendship. Because I was insecure, I had my eye on good-looking guys who had been around a lot and had the reputation of looking for beautiful women. It was too bad that they felt that way, because my body wasn't for sale, (and it was a beautiful body). They would come by and drop their dishes off in a compartment of the dish room, and I could tell just what they ate: scrambled eggs for one, cinnamon toast for another. I would fantasize about them grabbing my hand on the dish line and asking me out. But I was dreaming, and it never happened. Sometimes the fumes of fried eggs and cinnamon toast drove me wild, and they would trigger a frozen migraine. I would stand with my red hair lifted up off my head like a troll doll, with a snappy attitude to boot.

My migraines played a crucial role in the development of my chemical imbalance, mainly because I couldn't think or see straight when I had one. Evien was patient and would endure the onset of my hell-raising moods, comforting me as my temples banged together and my eyes pinched back into their sockets. Even though I was being as miserable as I was, Evien and his other Hawaiian friends would faithfully serenade me at my window every night to the song, "Lil' Red Riding Hood," by Sam the Sham and the Pharaohs. I was beginning to wonder if this "red riding hood" would be "everything a big bad wolf could want."

    I could have used a friend while visiting in the Green District that New Year's Eve, though. A half hour before midnight, Mom asked me to share a bottle of wine. The next morning, I woke up on our wet front lawn with her staring at me from about six feet away. We were all hung over. I felt a special bond with her then, but it was a bond of the wrong kind. It caused me to reevaluate my feelings and ask myself why it was so important to drink with her in the first place. I liked to drink, but it was going backward by agreeing with her that it was OK to get drunk.

    I should have known that I couldn't get close to her by drinking with her. Not after what she did to me in the past. Not this way. I offered her a hand and guided her to the front door, her wobbly body breaking my gait. She didn't say much, and I tensed up trying to shake the bad spirits that had been planted in my head by the vin rose. As we parted, I landed a kiss on her forehead, and I pressed onward to SOC with a dancing hangover in my head.

    I enrolled in a Shakespearean theatrical class at SOC and sewed costumes for the actors. I had to chuckle to myself as the thespians moved swiftly across the stage in their brightly colored Elizabethan robes and long English drawls.

    That year, 1968, Bobby Kennedy and Martin Luther King Jr. were shot and killed. I could not believe all the power Martin Luther King Jr. had, and the strength that Bobby and Martin had at the time. They were two great leaders who will never be replaced in my mind, along with John F. Kennedy, my idol. I was saddened. I changed my major to sociology in hopes of becoming a Peace Corps worker. I met Stan: a junior at SOC, very intelligent and good-looking, I thought. I was singing "Born to Be Wild" and "Hey, Jude" to the jukebox in the Britt Union, and he was strolling by with a grin on his face. Stan, being arrogant and egotistical, said that he was an Aquarian. He told me that I was, too, if my birthday was in February. My birth date was February 8, but I didn't think that it made me any more special than anyone else. I thought being special was being a cheerleader, basketball player, or singer, or just being a good person who loved all humanity. I felt uncomfortable attaching a foreign name like Aquarius to me.

At the end of the week, I was at Stan's apartment after classes. We were drinking, and I was wearing a flared yellow-and-white flowered dress that clung to my body. It was a complicated wraparound that Stan had fun playing with. His ex-girlfriend, Julia, called long distance. Julia had baby-blue eyes and straightened blonde hair that she wore in a pageboy sometimes, with the ends tucked under in a pillow-like fashion. She was my competition, but it would have been worse if she were another redhead. We were getting friendly, and Stan jumped to answer the phone. When I heard him say, "Hi, Julia," I cut the bedroom window screen with a bottle opener and left my dress somewhere on his bed, drunkenly changing into other clothes I had brought.

Unwinding like an untangling pretzel, I climbed down the south side of the wall of the apartment onto the street. A couple at a nice home asked me in. I was crying. They called the cops on me, so the police came by to pick me up. I was sent to jail, singing, "I got in my red VW microbus with shovels and rakes and implements of destruction" from Arlo Guthrie's "Alice's Restaurant." The police charged me with being drunk on a public street and asked if I carried a dangerous weapon. I told them no.

I was in jail for an hour, and I don't know who posted bail, but Stan met me at my dorm. He confessed that he loved me—no other girl had ever gone to jail for him. "Big cheese," I thought. Charges were dropped. The following week, Stan told me that we were going to go to Salem, the capital city in Oregon, to meet his folks. Excited, I went to my dorm to pack and caught my roommate, Tamara, smoking a joint.

"May I have a drag?" I said hesitantly, waiting for someone to stop me.

"Sure," she said from behind her brown stringy strands of hair. She held in the smoke till her cheeks were ready to pop and pinched the ends of the white-tinted wet weed. With a long exhale, she handed it to me.

"Just to try it," I said. "My first time."

I held it in, so when Stan came to pick me up to see his mom and dad, I was stoned and laughing. I felt beside myself. He drove me to see his folks in Salem for Thanksgiving anyway.

His mom took us ice-skating, and it was a first time for the both of us. I did a jump into the air, turning 360 degrees. I landed on one blade. I skated all over the rink, and Stan became instantly jealous of me. His mom washed my underwear that I had packed when I was stoned. They were holey and stained. My embarrassment began to antagonize me. I didn't want to take another step.

Distressed, I couldn't shake the feeling of happiness and sorrow of experimenting with grass, and my laughter was not spontaneous. Stan couldn't figure out what was wrong with me, and I told him that I smoked a joint.

He said, "Don't ever do it again."

During our liaison, we became insensitive and closed off to each other's emotional needs. On the cold winter nights, we had a partnership where we would lie next to each other without any clothes on. It put a stress and strain on our relationship, especially during winter break, when we were given permission to stay at Stan's friend's apartment while he was on vacation. I never gave in, and I kept blocking the sexual abuse incident at Lincoln City. Stan and I were ready to explode. We got in a fight, and I took off for a house where my sister was staying. I hid there, sopping my clothes with tears. Stan came to the door and asked Diana if she had seen me. She didn't know that I was there. After he left, I came out from behind her bookcase filled with books in which I could have gotten lost, such as *The Canterbury Tales* by Geoffrey Chaucer and *Walden* by Henry David Thoreau, but time wasn't on my side. I was really disturbed and trying to quit smoking. I thought he was going to dump me. Diana was disappointed in me for hiding. I felt self-conscious, and it was hard to adjust.

After Christmas, Stan told me that he would meet me at a dance at the Commons, but he said he would call first. He didn't call, and I went to the dance, only to find him in a circle of men, thumping his chest. He came over to me and asked me if I wanted to dance. I said no.

I danced and left with a blond guy I didn't know. That was the last of the relationship I had with Stan. He broke up with me. I think he was just looking for an easy excuse and a way to get out.

At the Commons, where Stan took care of the pool tables, I brought him a message. I had a ringlet hanging out of the side of my head. He said, "What's with that at the side of your head?"

I said, "It's my thing. Everyone should have a thing. Sometimes words have meanings, and sometimes they don't mean anything at all."

He bent over his desk and cased the stiff green felt of the pool table out of his left eye. The jouncing eight ball, forced by the pool cue, scattered powder like broken fairy wings along the gullies of the table's rough surface. "Silence is the killer of time," he replied.

Then I left and cried, and after that I was chasing him throughout my college years, but he wouldn't have me.

I recall Mom mailing me tranquilizers to take for my speech classes and my American government class and also sending them during the time Stan and I dated. There was also no limit to the cigarettes, booze, and bennies I added to my system. Must pass those tests. Gotta meet those deadlines. I was a nervous wreck. I'd ask a friend from a ski class about the small white pill he used to help him to study with, and he gave me one to ingest. I followed Stan and kept tabs on him. I became his stalker—hooked, sweaty, and unstable.

At Britt Auditorium I walked on my hands around my sister in a circle and perfected my style of dancing. She snapped her fingers to the ticking of the clock in "Time Has Come Today" by the Chambers Brothers. A girl from my dorm, who was a Janis Joplin look-alike with a multicolored velour dress and fedora, taught me some of the moves. She said, "Snap here when your sister snaps there." How she could emote. There was a good-size audience for our dance class show.

I was on bennies still, but with regard to the pusher, I thought I could function OK. I didn't know what effect this drug would have on me later, but I did know that I had suffered greatly with an inferiority complex by taking the uppers, and I was extremely paranoid about thinking that everyone knew what I was on.

I think Diana understood my problem. I told her that I was the only person in the world who mattered, and people were talking about me and tearing down my reputation. I was suspicious of everybody. After the show I sang "Light My Fire" by the Doors to myself and headed for the dorm. Strange ions entered the atmosphere, and my head aroused another frozen migraine. The next day, I was elevated. I had to argue with myself that I was all right. Paranoia encouraged my madness, and I had just begun to pay for it.

CHAPTER 5

DEATH AT THE DOORSTEP

Mom and Ralph had sent me away to live with Aunt Deanna and Uncle Doc the summer of my sophomore year in high school. I often dreamed about Chipper while sleeping on my cousin Geno's bunk. I wanted to marry him, but the chances of being his girl were one in a million, especially since Diana was dating him at Roseburg High. Diana and her fiancé, Ted, recommended I see Ted's brother, Don, and his wife, Mitzi, in Eugene when Stan and I split up. That is how I connected with my teenage idol. He was driving by in his red Corvette in his sandy Beach Boys hairdo. He asked, "Where are you going?"

I said, "A dance." "Help Me, Rhonda" was playing in my head.

He told me there wasn't a dance at the college that night, and he asked me if I wanted a ride. I accepted, and we went to a party and then to his apartment. We exchanged glances and talked about our experiences, our high-school friends, and about a trip he took to Brazil. I kept my ladylike position, sitting straight like cardboard, upright in his chair with my legs and ankles tangled. My clothes were sweating rivers of stale tobacco and pure gladness that I finally got to sit across from my sister's ex-boyfriend, who had been my teenage crush since I was sixteen. I shyly hid my insecure self and shakiness by bearing weight on my hands. I wanted to leave him with a good impression. He took me to Don and Mitzi's, and the next day he followed me to the freeway. We had the same views about the Vietnam war, the tragedy of losing lives, and the senselessness of it all. His influence overwhelmed me. It left me feeling loved, lucky, and proud that I got to know him. I respected that man so much that I developed a deep infatuation for him.

I moved to Oregon State University in Corvallis and heard from a friend that Stan was going to marry. I thought, Oh, my God, not Stan! I tried jumping in a swimming pool without any water in it to end it all. I thought it was the quick fix. My roommate, Jackie, who was tall and domineering, stopped me. "Don't do it. It isn't worth it!" she screamed as she ran, tearing at my shoulders with her tensed fingernails. I slowed down my steps and pushed away the compelling force that was causing me to act in such a destructive way.

Rooming with my friends, Linda and Jackie, I could feel myself changing. I was no longer a virgin, and I'd have to face it some time or another. The hippies and my religion began to haunt me. We were still in a war in Vietnam. I missed Stan, and I was transforming into a rebel. As I continued to hang out with the hippies, my math teacher from continuing ed. saw me at a hippie bash as he drove by in his car. OSU was a conservative college, and I was leaning toward the radical left. My teachers in the elementary ed. curriculum were taking note of it. This didn't help. For example, I had taken a course in continuing ed. that led me to teach catechism at a Catholic school. I was speechless most of the time, and the children could sense it. It was hard teaching children religion and interacting with them, when I didn't believe in the morals of the Church. I smoked and drank and had no morals. When it was time to receive the Host on Easter Sunday, I did it without making confession to a priest, and I felt like a failure. I couldn't look my students straight in the eyes, walking down the church aisle with hands clenching, body shaking, the pleats of my blouse rising and falling rapidly to the rhythm of my breath. Exposing my guilt, I experienced one of the most difficult paranoid periods of my life. I felt I let everyone down, because I wasn't a virgin and never had confessed it, and the Catholic Church and its teachers were against me. I was convinced they were.

Even though I loved Jackie dearly, I wanted to get away. She got to be overbearing and domineering. She told me not to open up to a priest about my love life. Before my hospitalization in Salem, I needed help. I moved to an apartment on the south side of Corvallis across from Hokies Pizza Place. It was eerie. These bugs would come out of my wall at night, and they looked like the cootie bugs in the cootie game I used to play as a child. They had flesh-like tubular bodies with hairy bent legs protruding out of their trunks and miniature antennas attached to their smiling oval heads. If they could talk, I thought they would ask, "Where did you hide that patchouli oil?" I showered in it every night and hid it in my chest of drawers. I would take the jar out and capture them by placing the jar on top and around them. I would dream of cooties coming out of the woodwork, walking on the ceiling, and fondling my bedclothes. Ick!

Not only that, I was also being uprooted. "I can't quit crying," I said after my sister and Ted's visit with me on their way to another continent. "I don't want you to leave me."

They had just gotten married and were leaving for Australia for good. I had no one—not Jackie or Linda—and no kitchen, just bed and toilet and shower. No one. Living alone, I became more entrenched and more alone; I was scared and hungry for companionship.

I bought two hippie vests from a van nearby selling hippie clothes and other paraphernalia for me and my Aquarian friend Geisla, who moved into an apartment next to me. They were kickin'. Tan leather jackets with long fringes of leather hanging from the chest and armpits. We became official hippies. I drank excessively with Geisla and another friend, Elsie, and made it late to classes. One day, a guy named Jack came into Hokies with his fiancée, Kim. He and I became good friends. He knew my landlady. The landlady had eyes the size of quarters with dark rings around them and was the prototype of a gypsy. She offered me barbiturates, and like a dummy, I took them. I wanted to slap Jack, because I loved him and hated him. He showed me pornographic magazines in his apartment and made me feel guilty about having my period when he asked me to make love with him. He was so insensitive toward my feelings that I wanted to die. I had the nauseating feeling I couldn't measure up to the nude models in the *Playboy* magazine he was looking at. He told me one night that he couldn't be with me; he had other plans. Then Kim came by and said casually that she had gone out with him the night before. I asked him what was going on, and he said, "Nothing."

Thinking they had broken up, I took his Brut aftershave and threw it, shattering his bedroom mirror into a million tiny pieces. Then I peeled out too fast in my Studebaker, and I partially ruined my car doing so.

⸺

Maybe that's why I was locked up in Salem. The hate and bitterness ate me like a disease. I missed the swimming, the sunshine, the parades, the popsicles, and the freedom of my mind and soul. My summer term at OSU was gone. Instead of being a confused, misguided college dropout, I became a paranoid schizophrenic trapped in an asylum. As time went on, I made several attempts on my life outside the institution, because I lacked the necessary medicine and therapy that could have helped me to control my disease.

Diana came from Australia to get me out of the institution, so I could live with her and Ted, but I slept a lot. In a small city near Ashland called Talent, where we lived, I quit taking my Thorazine, and my sleep became regulated. My strength came back, and I worked three jobs. At five o'clock in the morning, I'd get up to work in a pear factory, peeling bad stuff off pears on a conveyer belt. At three in the afternoon, I was a main chef at Omar's, a small restaurant located near SOC. And after that, I pulled a shift as a barmaid at Omar's, also. The schedule lasted three or four months.

I went to a group meeting near Medford, Oregon, after I had stopped the Thorazine. Diana and Ted took me there. It was a mental health outpatient meeting that I had to attend because I had been hospitalized and given the psychotropic drug called Thorazine. There were about nine crazies—people who acted like they didn't know why they were there and where they came from—and I was getting messed up talking to them. I vowed never to go to a group meeting again.

Diana tried to get me to see a psychiatrist, but he was real crummy to her on the phone, saying that I had to take Thorazine the rest of my life, so we forgot about therapy, and I decided to never take Thorazine again. I picked walnuts with Diana, and we laughed about the good times. I tried to get out of her way, because she was close to giving birth to her first and only child, Justin.

Before I moved out of her house, I was at the house of a stranger who smoked grass. One day I wanted to experiment with LSD. He said that his roommate had LSD and would probably give me some for a price. When I took it I got on his roommate's drum set and played through a song, everything on beat. His roommate was about to flatten me, because he wanted his sleep. They wanted sex for drugs, and I didn't feel like delivering it, so I sped home and discovered that I didn't like that drug at all. Next day all I could do was to stare out of Diana and Ted's kitchen window with its shiny blue-and-white-striped curtains.

I was singing "One pill makes you larger," the lyrics to "Go Ask Alice," by the Jefferson Airplane and crashed on the counter. I came to work too stoned one time. I did marijuana and vomited all over myself. After I visited a friend in Corvallis, I vowed I'd never do grass again. Since my bout with LSD, I have never been able to concentrate while on illegal drugs. I'm thankful. Some people's systems are just different.

In December, Diana gave birth to Justin, a beautiful baby boy with chocolate-brown eyes and a contagious smile. His sweet grin was irresistible, and it was hard to go about my day without being touched by his impact on me. I went out with a guy I knew in high school named Leo, and I moved to Eugene to be with him. We had a wonderful time, but he stood me up. "You can stay here. I'll come back," he said.

I read a letter from his girlfriend that was on his dresser. Pride put itself to the test, and wet tears dropped like blankets upon the sheet of paper. When he came back, he told me that he was seeing someone else, but I could stay at his apartment. I was crushed. I wanted to take a stiff drink and bang my head against the wall. I could have used a therapist then, but I thought working things out the best way I could by myself and avoiding being laughed at was the best solution. I found out I was wrong. I changed environments by checking into a motel. It was called the Kennedy Motel.

I pretended that I was sitting with Jack and Bobby Kennedy. In my motel room's chair, I would light my cigarette and put it out in the arm of the chair. At night, I ran through the streets, thinking I could control their— John and Bobby's—spirits and make them run through glass. A policeman yelled, "Hey where are you going to?" as I rushed past him.

He seemed suspicious of me, as if I were a candidate for an arrest. A guy who attempted to run with me said that he just saw someone go through glass. The cop took the bait somehow and looked oddly at me for some reason.

I traveled to Corvallis and went to a dance. I saw Ron, the guy I loved, one night. He was a jock. I wanted to, but I couldn't tell him how ashamed and embarrassed I was to have become mentally ill. But would he please forgive me? We had an excellent and sensual experience. I'll never forget that night, seeing him again. We just stared at each other, wondering what the other one was thinking. That was my night in Corvallis. He was with a girl and danced with her, and I danced with a guy and left.

When I returned to the Kennedy Motel, a topless dancing agency called me out of the blue and told me they wanted me to work at a topless club named La Mars in Eugene. I thought it was a golden opportunity to dance and make a living at it, but my mental illness got worse. I shaved my crotch and stayed with a couple of men in town. I chose a bright yellow-and-orange two-piece set with orange sequined pasties and an orange fluorescent G-string. I danced on tables and on a platform that was about twenty-five feet long and fifteen feet wide. I sewed a black velvet patch to cover my right eye to sympathize with my brother-in-law's mother, who had eye surgery in Coos Bay and was wearing a patch.

As I was walking home from work, a man in his sixties shouted, "Hey, don't I know you?" He was behind me with a large black bag tucked under his armpit. He saw me wearing the patch over my eye and asked me to dinner and then to a motel. I slept a couple of nights with him and hated it. He had a big belly and little or no empathy, and afterward he followed me everywhere. He wouldn't let up.

At La Mars, the old man was throwing money at me. I cried on stage while dancing to "Riders on the Storm." Diana had sent me a letter that day saying that our grandfather in Brazil had died, and suddenly I got really depressed. I never knew him, but I had heard wonderful stories about our grandfather. He was the only tailor in the village where Mom grew up in Brazil. This was the wrong time to die. My boss said, "It's time to go upstairs and do a nude act."

I said, "No! Nothing doing!" I got fired for crying on stage and not dancing nude.

As I walked down the streets of Eugene, I was having my period. Prior, I was thinking I would never make love again, so I stuck my house key up inside of me. Thinking I was some supernatural creature, I took my Kotex out of my pants and dropped it on the sidewalk.

As I walked the streets, two hippies, thirtyish with long dark hair, followed me and asked, "Can we stay the night?" I said that they could. I felt so useless and confused for sticking that key inside of me, because one of them had to take it out of me. I offered my affection to one of the guys one night and to the other the next day. I told them to get lost. One did, and one lingered on.

I was questioned by the police about who I was and where I came from. I wore overalls two sizes too big for me, and I was walking the streets again. I ran to my apartment and moved my couch, which I had taken out for the hippies to sleep on, back to the wall. I lay down. I took a green screwdriver, which Ted had given me as a going-away present from Ashland, brought it to my chest, thrust the tool down, and stabbed myself in the chest and right breast. The attempt on my life was futile, and I kept the incident a secret from everybody for a long time. My nipple and my chest burned in the place I thrust the screwdriver. My heart pumped and would tweak every once in a while, but I wouldn't tell a soul. I felt so worthless.

My concept of religion was very hazy, because at the time the Baptist and Catholic Churches influenced me. A girl named Lona, in Ashland, who was working as an assistant chef to me at Omar's, brought my soul to the Baptist Church. She said, "You're not interpreting the Bible right, and you need to learn more."

She dyed my hair blonde when she had a handful of Baptist friends over. They were talking about a baby and how ugly it was. They said someone should drop the baby on his head to see what happened. I was sick, and this influenced my thinking at the wrong time, the worst possible time.

About three minutes after my attempt, Diana, Ted, and Justin, their son, showed up from Ashland. They had written and said that they were coming, but I never got their letter. They said, "We are going to get you out of here."

They put down some money on another apartment. It had long folding closets, a gas stove, and chips of plaster peeling from the walls. I had no money to pay my landlord, and I was a mess. I didn't tell them what happened to me for a long time. While we were at the apartment, Diana and Ted asked me to hold their baby, because they had to go to the car for a minute. As I held little Justin in my arms, I nearly dropped him on his head, but I had more strength than I knew.

Holding my beautiful nephew in my arms, ready to drop him, I threw Justin on the bed and cried, "Oh my God, what is wrong with me?" I looked over at my little nephew and sat him on my lap. I was crying, and he smiled. I think that my sister and Ted were gone less than a minute, but I just felt totally bad about it.

My sister and her husband came back and took Justin and left. I thought somehow they knew. Now I walked the streets more than ever. I called myself Bobby Kennedy, a name I took when I dyed my hair blonde. I couldn't stand what I had almost done, and I couldn't stand myself. God, I'm a monster! I punished myself for it.

A close friend of mine, a counselor, told me that some people have those thoughts. If they act on them, they are criminal, and if they don't act on them, they aren't. "What will help is to write down your faults or what you are thinking. Then talk them over with a friend, a sister, a doctor, or a therapist when you are in that situation. Call a crisis line if you need to. There is a way out. There will always be someone there to care and talk with you."

Because I was sick, I continued to attract the wrong kind of people. I continued to live in Eugene, and I was sodomized after that experience. A guy from a truck ripped my clothes off and disgraced me. Too painful. I pleaded, "Please stop!" I never saw him again.

A fire burst out in my pan of wax when I decided to make candles in the broken-down apartment that Ted and Diana had rented for me. I managed to run out the door with the pan, fire and all. It made a small fire, and then it went out like a light. I lay on the ground, my head cupped in the palm of my hands, expecting to be stirred by what I had imagined to be a big explosion. I picked myself up and went back into the apartment. There was smoke all over the ceiling.

From my Catholic beliefs of two powers, God and Satan, and the strict Baptist beliefs, I came to the conclusion that my God is a good God. He is all-powerful, and there is no power beside him.

He doesn't throw people in a fire to burn forever, because he is a loving father. He does not test, trick, and run people through the mill, as some would think. He is everything, and he is heaven.

He is everything.

This theory stuck in my brain, and I was able to accept my mental problems as well as others in my walk of life. I finally began to cope with my paranoia.

CHAPTER 6

SETTLEMENT

I'm in Salem now, not the Oregon state hospital, but Salem where the attorney general takes his seat. "My name is Sherry Standing, and I am standing up for myself and fighting for my rights as a woman. I want to see results!" It is 1972.

A group of women's libbers would march to the state capitol building in Salem three weeks after I created havoc there.

Roger Brown, the labor commissioner who came up to Corvallis to talk to Norm and me about the case, told me before I went to Salem (the state hospital) that the attorney general would make a decision on my equal pay case. I didn't know what was taking so long, so from Eugene I traveled to Salem, the city where the asylum was located, to start the ball rolling. I thought if I didn't act, there would be more cases like my own, and more women would suffer.

At the capitol building, I barged into the attorney general's office and said, "I want to see the attorney general and get back pay for my equal pay case against Hokies Pizza Place in Corvallis."

A secretary with a brown bouffant hairdo said that she would talk to the attorney general. I waited. Then I asked, "Is the attorney general free?"

"Just a minute." She asked my name.

"Sherry Standing."

"Have you been hospitalized?"

"No, and what does that have to do with a sexual discrimination case?"

In a sharp manner she remarked, "You can't talk to the attorney general, because he has an appointment."

"I'll wait."

"You need an appointment."

I was getting mad. I asked, "Why are you giving me the runaround? Why do I need an appointment when you acted like it was all right to see him? I'm entitled to my money. It's against the law to discriminate in the workplace."

The secretary called the police and then my sister in Ashland. I don't know how she got her number. I think she called the asylum and checked my records. The secretary told me to go to the phone booth and talk to my sister. Everything was confusing.

"What's going on?" Diana asked on the other end.

I said, "The police are going to arrest me if I don't go home and leave the attorney general alone. They've denied me my rights because I had an episode of mental illness." Then we were cut off.

I had thought it was time to express what I believed in by supporting equal rights for women, since I wasn't getting any reaction by pressing my equal pay case against Hokies. But my plan was defeated, and at that point in time I had to settle for nothing. I might have been ill, but for once, I knew I was right.

I don't know how Diana got on the phone that day, and I never asked her, because I thought not knowing could have saved me from making things worse. I was certain that it was not in my best interest to make a scene in front of the policemen. So my moment of protest fizzled out, and I went back to Eugene empty-handed.

In Eugene, my life got so bad that I stooped to calling my mom to help me out. The sixty-year-old man I met while dancing came back in my life and said, "Leave your car at a garage, and I will buy a new one for you." He didn't give me a car, and I never heard from him again. I lost my stereo and my guitar that had two miniature white feet painted on it by Ron Upright. I lost other things, and of course, my car. How stupid to think that I could just dump my car off at a garage and instantly get a new one from someone I didn't know or trust.

I went back to Roseburg and stayed with Mom, Doug, and Ralph for a week and worked at Ralph's Shell station, pumping gas. Ralph had become a proud owner of that gas station in the area. Doug bought me records: Carole King's *Tapestry* and Andrew Lloyd Webber's *Jesus Christ Superstar*, lyrics by Tim Rice. I memorized the words to the albums. It seemed like Doug and I were more inseparable than ever. We'd exchange T-shirts, and he would come to town with me.

My mom's friend, Dell, asked me to stay with her when I called her up on the phone. Mom couldn't stand me after one week at home. We got in a fight, and Mom kicked me out, hair dryer and all, yelling, "There you are, you white trash! Go live with Mama Dell!" So I went willingly to live with Dell. I didn't see Doug for about three months after that.

I arrived at Dell's house after walking several miles across the freeway. "Jeepers, Sherry, what did you do to your hair?" she asked.

"It's apricot gold," I replied.

"Is it a wig?" She was very inquisitive.

"Nope, I dyed it." I stroked the soft curls.

"Oh, no! All that beautiful red hair."

"Yup, it's gone, I guess."

She sat down at her petite dining-room table. It was the table where we smoked our Tareytons and dragged out all our experiences of our lives. Dell made me feel comfortable. She took an interest in her house with great ambition and enthusiasm. A different shade of wallpaper would go up every month, and I'd say, "Gee, Auntie Dell, not another one!"

She teased my memories as she circled my head with another wreath of smoke. I made sure that I didn't say too much about Eugene, because I thought I would screw myself over.

"There's a dance tonight. I want to go. Can you fix my hair?" I asked.

As she began to dab blonde dye on my hair, we ran out of bottles, and I panicked. So we jumped into an old fixed-up Studebaker that I got from a junkyard and floored it to a drugstore, singing "Bye-bye, Miss American Pie." It was exciting. Dell got the owner of the store to stay open long enough for us to purchase the evil potion, light ash blonde. We sped home, and Dell finished bleaching my hair. I loved Dell as a person. She was sweet. She helped me get a job as a waitress at the Umpqua Hotel and Single Tree, just by being there with her in Roseburg that summer.

Her husband wasn't there all the time. He never stuck around. He was a long-haul truck driver, and when he came into town, he would call on the phone first. If I answered the phone, he would ask, "Are you wearing a bra?" I had nothing but pity in my heart for him. Yet I was a princess in his castle, and he made me feel like the world revolved around me.

I met George the evening we bleached my hair. He was a Mexican singer with thin black hair and bedroom eyes. He sang and played the guitar with a band at the Umpqua Hotel, better known as the Indian Room. He sang "Heart of Gold" by Neil Young and "A Horse with No Name" by America. The girls went ape over him. George was always trying to get me to smoke a joint in his room after hours. I protested but gave in once. I was sleeping with him one night, and I had a dream that Satan had started scratching my leg.

I woke up and George was scratching me there on the spot of my leg where Satan had scratched me in my dream. I got an infection on that spot and went to a doctor. The doctor told me what to treat my infection with, and I forgot what it was. In a couple of days I called the doctor again, and the nurse said that the doctor was dead. He died of a heart attack. I quit smoking cigarettes again, and marijuana, because I was frightened, and I thought I had some control over what happened to people. I never have touched marijuana since.

When George's gig was up, I became a cocktail waitress at the Umpqua Hotel. I missed George, but this was one of the best jobs I ever had. I wore short black shorts, a black silk bodysuit, tan leather moccasins with felt pastel leaves decorating the top of the shoe, and a long strawberry blonde wig. As a cocktail waitress, I relished the time spent mingling with the customers. I would sing along with the bands as I delivered drinks. "A Horse with No Name," "Barefoot," "I Gotcha," "Diary," and two songs by Carole King, "Smackwater Jack" and "You've Got a Friend," were played by the bands and on the jukebox. Each song illustrated the piecing together of my experiences during this era.

That summer, I received a call from a man working for the labor bureau. "Will you come to testify for your case about Hokies Pizza Place in a court hearing in Salem?"

We had a date and time to appear, but I settled out of court, because I was afraid I'd have another breakdown or something would happen to my family. Someone had put a bullet hole through Ralph's truck window. I received a $500 check, and with it a note from the attorney general stating there would no longer be discrimination in the work force.

But I question how many sexual discrimination cases are still standing these days? Quite a few, I think.

During my employment with the Umpqua Hotel, my sister, her husband, Ted, and their son traveled to Roseburg and brought me to Coos Bay to see Don and Mitzi, who had moved from Eugene. I grew close to Don and Mitzi. Don tuned pianos up and down the coast and became the pianist at the Sawdust Theater, a melodrama type of theater where they held vaudeville type plays with ragtime music and skits. It was a thrill to see him perform. Mitzi wrote two books, *Made in Japan and Settled in Oregon* and *From Here to Everywhere*. She was confined in a relocation center during World War II, when she was growing up. Don and Mitzi were great parents and good people. Don took me on motorcycle rides, and Mitzi would have incredible crab feasts. They gave me their backpack to hitchhike with. They wrote their address on the back of it, in case I should get lost.

I thought that I had everything that I wanted in life and more. My experiences in Eugene were behind me now, and I had won my case against Hokies. I had my backpack. Nothing would ever bother me now.

On my day off, my sister's friend Wayne, who looked like he was from some hippie commune, took me to Crescent City. He had long brown hair that hung to the middle of his back, a rusty-colored mustache the shade of weak tea with short yellow hairs sticking out of it, and a dark Ho Chi Minh beard that came down to his collar bone. I curled up on the soft sand next to a tree. I could feel and hear the ocean roar, because I fell asleep resting close by it. "Cast Your Fate to the Wind" was playing in my head. Why I wasn't swept away by the majestic tide that night was beyond me, but I wasn't afraid. Hitchhiking into town the next day, I met Wayne, and he took me to the beach where I had slept. He said that he and his wife were making a burial for me, thinking that I was taken away by the tide. We shocked each other when I arrived at the beach, because I was alive. I had Roxanne, his wife, worried for nothing. A tsunami couldn't have shaken me from my nest.

After Wayne and I picked up two hippies and had a good time riding in his van, we reached Ashland. That summer, I met my redheaded friend, Alanna, with whom I was in high school. We shared a singing part as a nun in *The Sound of Music,* our high-school musical. She asked me to come to her wedding, and I said, "Of course."

It was to take place in Oakland, California. On my day off, I drove to San Francisco, in my old Studebaker with flower decals on the roof and the sides, to attend her wedding. My car was a heap of junk, but everyone enjoyed riding in it. Every time I took my car places, it broke down—flat tires, dead batteries, out of oil, and the like. At nine o'clock that night in San Francisco, I happened to be in the wrong place at the wrong time. My "Stude" stopped on some trolley car tracks. The trolley car driver got out of the trolley and helped me get off the tracks. After he helped me off the tracks, I took off and ended up at a gas station. I had gotten lost when I tried to make it to Oakland. A gas station attendant asked me to stay with him for the night. While I got my car fixed, we went to his house. He said, "Take my bed. I have another room to sleep in."

He took a shower and approached me, saying, "You are not leaving here before you have sex with me, are you? What did you think? You'd get a bed for nothing?"

I dashed to his living room. He cut me off at the pass. He turned off the lights. Fear rushed to my heart like the angel of death. It shook the walls of my soul and frightened the shadows of my innocence. It left me petrified and inept. However, I was the stronger one. Stretching my arms out, I felt for the door and pushed my way through the screen, carrying myself to the station. Out of nowhere, a tall, beautiful, ebony-skinned African American man, who gave off an air of graceful beauty, asked me if I needed help. Would I like him to fix my car?

He said, "The battery has got to be charged overnight, so would you like to come to my motel with no strings attached?"

I said yes and took the opportunity to be with him. That night we sat side by side on a bed, drinking King Alfonso on the rocks, and discussed our families, his wife, and children, and everything in general. He was precious. I think we must have slept two hours in each other's arms. In the morning he fixed my car and pointed me toward the church in Oakland where the wedding was held. I never saw him again.

I went to Alanna's wedding. Her carrot-red hair was astonishing as her aura glowed with simplicity. She was a beauty. There was a gathering of family and friends embracing each other with freshly picked pink and yellow flowers in their hands. Alanna's sisters read poems that Alanna wrote, and Alanna wore a veil, which she said looked like a baseball catcher's mask. I could feel her big blue eyes winking at me through the face guard as she said, "I do."

On my trip home, I decided to quit the Umpqua Hotel and go to Coos Bay. Don and Mitzi's arms were open to me. Don asked about employment and I remembered the pretty outfits I wore when I danced in Eugene. I thought it would be a good thing if I could dance again and receive a decent wage, but this time I could do it right. I thought real hard about it, and the light went on in my head. Yeah, I could go to Portland to be a topless dancer and lead a great life now. Dell and I decided it was best for me to leave, so I packed and left her house.

CHAPTER 7

HIGH ON PERFORMANCE

I joined an agency that placed topless dancers and started working at Mary's Club, the Palm Gardens, and the Carriage Room in Portland. It was the peak of all my experiences of employment. On the rebound from working long hours at my job at the Indian Room, I was proud of this new form of art and beautiful way of expressing myself. I was petite, with a tight abdomen, long waist, attractive rib cage, and alluring back. As shy as I was, I could dance up a storm. It was the early seventies, and I had quit drinking, smoking cigarettes, and doing drugs while working at the Indian room. I think I was the first dancer who didn't drink or smoke or do drugs. I never engaged in relationships with men during that year. On occasion, I would reminisce about my trip to Eugene and what went wrong with me. I could have died trying to take my life that day, but the past was behind me, and I couldn't let it interfere with the new dancing job. I was grateful to be alive and loving every minute of it.

At first, we dancers had to pass a talent contest. I wore black velvet knee-high boots, black short shorts that I had worn at the

Indian Room, and a light-blue T-shirt. I took off my top and shimmied to the song the jukebox played. I wanted to dance to Marvin Gaye's "What's Going On," but I wasn't that lucky. I did dance to "Mercy, Mercy Me," another Marvin Gaye song, though, and that was appropriate. The guys liked me regardless, and I passed the test. Mark and Eddie called that night and said that I could dance for their agency. Mark was tall, sort of a bully, with a crew cut and blue eyes that weren't that noticeable. He made me feel uneasy when I was around him, because I had the feeling he was hitting on me. Eddie was a short, gray-haired man who was sincere and sweet to all of the dancers. Unlike Mark, he seemed to have morals and took the initiative to make me feel at home.

I rented an apartment in Southeast Portland. It had an old tattered Persian carpet on the floor, a small kitchen, and a big bathtub. I was now Sherry Dancing, instead of Sherry Standing (dancing to the radio and jukebox throughout the day and night). I danced to the songs "Freddie's Dead" and "Shaft." It was cool under the black light wearing a gold uniform—a G-string and arm cuffs with orange fluorescent fringe. I had to remember: *"Don't forget the pasties."*

I called up the labor bureau about why we had to wear pasties and Band-Aids on our breasts. Someone in the establishment said it was a law to cover your breasts while dancing at clubs. I thought there were men laughing at me. So the next day, to rebel, I took two ocean shells and taped them up to my nipples with a Band-Aid. I was given the choice: Band-Aids or pasties. I got in trouble.

The air possessed a strange odor of coconut oil, sweet milk, chestnuts, and Marlboros the day I walked into the Palm Gardens, the topless club on Southeast Powell in Portland. Bottles of booze and palm trees embellished the atmosphere, and a strobe light gyrated around in a circle above the dance floor, casting a spell and drawing me in like a magnet. The performance of the dancers was electrifying, sending out vibrations to the men, who were proud to be sitting there, waiting to be engaged in an act of sexual seduction proffered by the artist.

It was the best job I have ever had, but dealing with the hard personalities of the dancers while my mind was still somewhat offtrack was a bit confusing, since theirs were offtrack, too.

First was Kiki, "Kinky" for short. She was a drop-dead gorgeous blonde with incredibly green eyes. Her face was beautiful, but she seemed hard and empty at times, as if the wind had sucked the air right out of her lungs. Her body was desirable to the men, with sharp accentuating curves in proportion to her tall physique. As she smoothed a special cream over her tiny stretch marks, massaging it into her long thighs, she revealed a life of promiscuity. She had married, had a baby, and been around the block a couple of times, or so she boasted. The men adored her skinny waist and the way she tantalized them as she stood in front of the metal bar that encased the dance floor, separating the dancers from the men, who were sitting in their chairs behind it. As she pulled a long blonde hair out from underneath her G-string, she teased the guys with it and attempted to give them a feel or two when the owner wasn't looking. Being ahead of the times, she danced posed, bending from the waist with her head held high, hands resting on her knees for a period of about three to five minutes. Then facing the bar, she squatted with knees bent apart, undulating her stomach, swaying her buttocks to and fro to the music. She managed to arouse the men, and they respected her just as well.

Mar was about my height and could have passed for a beauty queen. She had a widow's peak, long straight black hair, and crystal-blue eyes gleaming above her high cheekbones. Her arms were muscular, and her calves were generously shaped, like those of a gymnast or a long-distance swimmer. Because of her widow's peak, I thought she was a demon, and I didn't bother to associate with her much. I was afraid of her presence and conceit and thought somehow it would mar my personality being around her. She exuded bad luck, so I gave her the nickname Mar.

Only once did we get together and watch TV in her small apartment, located on the south side of the freeway from me. She smoked two cigarettes and wasn't too sociable. She was more interested in what was going on on the tube.

In the dressing room, she brushed her black crotch with a bright-pink oval hairbrush that had thick white fur covering the body of the brush. As she met the stage, she exposed two inches of her crotch above her black velvet G-string concealing the remainder of it underneath, waiting to be brushed again after her performance. She would dance barefoot with her proud carriage and her hefty thighs. Her barefooted blisters made beat to the percussions and vibrations of the song, "Dance to the Music," by Sly & the Family Stone. Flinging her long black hair around from side to side made her popular.

Zule, another dancer, was in her midtwenties. She was tall, with a slender figure and beautiful enticing brown eyes. She could have passed for a teenager. She danced the "swim," stretching her arms out in front of her like she was doing the breaststroke, moving one hand over the other in a circular motion. Then she would bend her elbows back and surprise you with a chest lift. She gave me a smile as I entered the small dressing room. She would comb out her long brunette fall, which wasn't attached to her head, fasten the jewels around her neck and in her belly button, and adorn her face in the mirror.

"How is your day going?" I'd ask.

"Fine, thanks," she said as she puffed on her cigarette. She snuffed it out in the ashtray, flicking it between her middle finger and her thumb.

She was being polite. If she had a bad hair day she would let you know it. Offsetting your routine, she would stomp over to the jukebox and strike the songs "Back Stabbers" by the O'Jays and "Let it Rain" by Eric Clapton. I had to let it roll off my shoulders. I was there to dance and not get mixed up with other personalities or competition. I was there for my freedom. But I called her "Jewel" because of the precious jewels she wore when dancing and the accessories she lent me at the club.

Every guy was waiting to see this flasher named Pert. She had a round pallid face, small hazel eyes hidden by slick dull-brown hair, and a slim body. She flaunted herself, testing the waters with every male spectator and every performer she had made ties with onstage. She was dressed in shiny white cowboy boots and tassels. When the music started, she began prancing, carefully touching one foot on the stage and then the other. After the prancing had ceased, she rocked and swayed to the music with her boobs bumping together and her tassels jouncing simultaneously. Before you could exclaim "Ouch!" or "Oh my God!" she was reaching for her G-string, pulling it down below her thigh while she danced. She made the owner nervous and on edge when she slipped down her tiny blue G-string and exposed herself. I heard that she ended up paying fines for the sake of the reputation of the Palm Gardens, and on different occasions the bouncer escorted her out. I thought for a moment that she was a plant to see if we would succumb to her wild fantasies and sexual tactics, but the truth is, I was wrong. She wasn't really that hot, and she had less effect on me than I thought she would. I was strong to say no to her advances. Girls like that didn't last long; in order to live up to their reputation, they had to repeatedly prove and outdo themselves, and they generally took the wrong avenues to do it. She eventually was jeered off the stage.

My first day at the Palm Gardens, I danced in front of the owner and other drooling men. The owner was fantastic. When I met him, I was enticed by his smile and his blue eyes, which were framed by his white hair and white beard. I fell in love with him, even though we didn't touch once. I danced to the tunes "Put the Lime in the Coconut" by Harry Nilsson and "I'll Take You There" by the Staple Singers. When I saw him, I got excited on the spot and then moved in a different direction on the floor, feeling embarrassed.

The next time I saw the owner, I had made a G-string with white feathers and did a Sharon Stone with all the men there. Vernon said, "Your thing is showing." Having been brought up with backward Brazilian ways, I didn't know what he was talking about.

I had sewed and macramed my G-strings and tried to keep up with the trends of the times, but the only entertainment I had besides work was listening to the radio, because I had no TV. I missed not having other types of media to resort to. I had been worn thin by my dancing days. My red hair had lost its luster. I decided to quit the agency, because I didn't want to put a wedge between Greta, the owner's wife, and the owner, Vernon. Greta was a stunning person, with a Barbie doll figure, a big bust, and innocent blue eyes. I thought the world of her. She was a bartender at the club. During my last days of dancing at the Palm Gardens, she requested songs on the jukebox for me to dance to. I would punch songs that weren't on her list and dance a ballet routine to them. She couldn't figure out what was going on. When she asked me why her songs weren't being played, I told her I didn't know. One day I walked off the stage, grabbed my things, and headed for the exit of the club. Greta stopped me and begged, "Please don't leave."

I was crying, and she was crying, but I explained, "It is time for me to go." I didn't say anything about my crush on Vernon. It would have torn her apart. Even though she didn't want me to go, I left anyway. I was becoming very sick again.

As I think back on it, it was all the tension that started to build inside of me that ate me away. For instance, at the beginning of my employment, Mark and Eddie warned me, "You have to pay for your uniforms. They aren't for free." I didn't think it was fair to pay for something that was part of the job. I began to develop uneasy feelings toward the agency then, and as I worked, I couldn't stand the thought of being manipulated. I was being paid a decent wage, but I had to pay the price of men blowing on my butt and telling me to get down on them for money. I wanted the man with the smiling blue eyes, white beard, and white hair. Vernon was Greta's, and if I ever went out with him, I'd have to pay the big price of respect. I made the right decision. I left. I was off my medicine and taking birth control pills instead, because I wanted to take precautions, and my illness slowly caught up with me.

That winter I visited my real father, whom I had found on the street in San Jose when I was thirteen. He had married three times.

Mary Jo was his third wife. They met in San Jose and moved to San Bruno, where Mary Jo worked as an English teacher. She had sent strawberry blonde switches of her hair to wrap around Diana's and my ponytails when we lived in the Green District. It was Christmas. I was trying to relive my past in a good way and must have suffered from flashbacks then. Mary Jo and Dad were invited to their neighbor's party, but they didn't go. Mary Jo, busy making fondue for a party of her own, casually mentioned that she and her first husband were married by the Prince of Persia and that she had taught English and music in Mosul, Iraq, and Beirut, Lebanon. I was impressed. That morning I drove to Half Moon Bay to see if the scenery had changed from when my dad had taken me there on a break from college. He had written to Mom in my later teenage years and invited me to come for a visit when my spring semester had ended. I took the Greyhound and lived with him and Mary Jo during my sophomore break, when Stan and I separated. I worked at Pan American Airlines as a switchboard operator at the San Francisco Airport. Mary Jo took me to work and on excursions throughout the city, shopping at Ghirardelli Square and visiting Fisherman's Wharf, so I could get acquainted with the area. Dad worked part time as a used car salesman. I had the opportunity to see the Doors at the Cow Palace in Daly City near San Francisco, with a date with whom I fought and struggled the entire concert.

When I got back from Half Moon Bay, my dad was angry with me for coming in and out of the house. I went to the neighbor's party that night, and when I came home from the party, I found I had a flat tire. The neighbors helped me out and paid for a new tire to be put on my car. I thought for sure my dad had let the air out of my tire. My half sister was there, but I think that she didn't want to get involved, because she didn't say a word. I drove to Ashland.

I stayed with Diana for five days until New Year's Eve. I had cut my ties with the topless clubs in Portland and theoretically kissed Eddie and Mark's theatrical agency good-bye. It was foggy outside, and I was wondering how the moisture stayed in the clouds and how birds stayed up in the air so freely. I was driving from Omar's to celebrate the holiday. I was in a state of confusion and mentally sick. I had been reading books on the corruption of government, one by Jeanne Dixon, and I got in a little trouble for making a protest of my own against Watergate. While I was driving down the road, a cop stopped me for driving in the fog without my glasses. I was shouting things against Nixon, things that didn't line up with reality, and I was held for a while. Charges were dropped for political reasons after I fasted for five days in my cell.

As I was held, I tried to invent my own intellectual satisfaction. I was yelling, "President Johnson has died of a heart attack." (Come to find out later on, President Johnson really did die of a heart attack.) And then I was really getting paranoid about it and thought the FBI was following me. The night my sister brought me home, she made a cheese-and-tuna casserole dinner, and we got in a fight. She called me Satan, and then we weren't on good terms at all. So I left with all my dreams shattered. I held out my thumb and began my quest for Huntington Beach, California, at midnight, on foot, in the middle of winter.

I utilized my time walking and meditating on how to work through the abuse from Mom and Ralph, what to do with my experience with the men from Vietnam and Eugene, and the sexual abuse in Lincoln City. I had a chance to pray the rosary, which I imagined to be in my jeans pocket dangling next to the duffel bag that Don and Mitzi had given me. I accepted defeat and walked on.

CHAPTER 8

HITCHHIKING JOURNEY

Where was I going? I had no idea. I was alone. It was like being in the desert, and no one was there. I was wondering if I would come out of this alive, and when I would get my next cigarette.

Was I still smoking cigarettes?
Yes.
Was I feeling guilty about it?
Yes.
Was I feeling guilty about my suicide attempts?
Most definitely.

On my way, I was trying to make some sense out of why I tried to take my life. Four days before my Watergate protest, I was lying on the freeway waiting for someone to run over me, because I was mad at Ted. He had told me I needed to find a place to live. We had a senseless quarrel, so I took to the freeway and lay in the middle lane to get back at him. A man from a nearby gas station picked me up bodily. He was crying. I asked why.

He said, "Why? My daughter was run over by a truck on Christmas Day."

I felt his painful breathing brand the life back into me. His heavy teardrops fell and dampened my starving skin. That man saved my life. He really did knock some sense into me. I didn't realize how precious life was until then. Maybe by leaving my sister when I did, I spared her the grief of my suicide. I was learning a valuable lesson in life: how to communicate.

On my journey, a man in a car stopped. This was my first link to reaching my goal of getting to California, even though in the back of my mind, I was thinking of Oregon. He picked me up and stopped at a motel. He let me out of his car and took off, not saying, "Do you want to make love?" or anything. How strange it seemed. Each day as I walked, I begged and pleaded for someone to pick me up and perhaps take me back to Oregon. I didn't mean to hurt Diana and Ted's feelings. I cried even more. I was teetering on a dangerous seesaw between life and death, and I knew it. Nothing balanced out. I so wanted to put this screwed-up life of mine in order. Why did I do such horrible things, such as trying to take my life and living so carelessly?

A married man named Curly picked me up. I didn't know if Curly was his nickname, or not, so I assumed that he was named Curly because of all the long flowing curls on his head. He was headed for Downey, California, to meet his married friend named Sal. Sal was feminine-looking and in his forties. When we got there, I danced for Sal and Curly on their kitchen table, and they took me to topless clubs. They were nice to a point, yet they were searching for sex to satisfy their male instincts. The orange groves near their motel were abundant, and I would hike to get the sweet juice from a succulent orange while they worked. I had sex with men who picked me up while I was walking to the orange groves.

Curly wanted me to dance one night for him and Sal. I didn't want to, but I danced anyway. He accused me of teasing them and going out with other men besides them. He said, "Put on your fluorescent G-string and dance," so I did. Then he bit my nipple. The pain was so intense, it almost knocked me down. I packed my things, and then he bodily threw me out of the motel room.

My nipple began to swell and throb. It stung like someone had just jabbed me in the breast with a safety pin. I wanted to scream, but the pain overrode my emotions and suppressed my tears. All I brought on this journey with me was a duffel bag, my dancing outfits, and my toothbrush. He kept my toothbrush, and he made me mad. Outside his motel room was his red vehicle. I wanted to deflate the tires of his car but didn't. Again, I relied on my thumb to get me out of Downey, and I took off for LA.

A young man with a rugged-looking face and pit marks in his cheeks picked me up on my way to LA. He led me to a broken-down shed he used for a guesthouse. Boards were torn from the roof, with splinters jutting from the wood. It was sore to the eye and touch. He turned on all the burners of his stove in his shed and said he wanted to share his life with me on his tan leather couch. He said he had a wife, so that brought things to a halt. I had a dream of this experience before: the burners, the stove, the couch. It seemed that the more mentally ill I was, the more déjà vu I experienced.

His grandfather lived in a house next to his shed. The grandfather was an alcoholic, and he threatened me. He kept unzipping his pants in front of me and drooling all over himself. His gardener was a sweet African American man, who took me out of LA on a trip to get the grandfather alcohol. "Bring your things," he said. I grabbed my backpack and ran quickly to his car. He gave me a ride to LA and said, "Here." There were a couple of dollars pressed between his two delicate fingers. I'll never forget him for that.

I met a man named Jack who took me to Azusa. He was a combination of Stan and my idol, Chip. He had Stan's beautiful blue eyes, Chip's blond surfer hair with bangs that he so arrogantly tossed over to one side of his head, Stan's sharp, handsome dimpled chin, and Stan and Chip's sensual lips.

Azusa was a Spanish-speaking town, and I knew a little Spanish from a two-year course I took at Roseburg High. I got a job in a Mexican bar as a bartender. The clientele was all Mexican. I slept next to a Latina who worked at the bar. She didn't know any English. She had a friend named Rosa, and she was more than friendly with her. Rosa came to the apartment one day and looked through my G-strings with her friend. I hid behind her couch, and I could hear them giggling and trying on my outfits, saying "Que bonita?" How pretty? "Este mucho bueno." It is very good. "Vamos!" Let's go!

This little Spanish metropolis was confusing to me. No one spoke English. The people and the place were enigmas. For example, I wrote a postcard to Don and Mitzi saying that I made it to LA. I borrowed a stamp, and as I shuffled away from the post office, a car slammed into another car, and I thought it was my fault. I was experiencing some extreme paranoia. The glint of my red hair was reflecting the sunlight, and I thought I could have caused the wreck.

I intended to go to San Francisco to get away from Southern California for a while, because the lyrics to the song "San Francisco (Be Sure to Wear Some Flowers in Your Hair)" kept going through my mind, and I was spellbound. It was mesmeric.

I couldn't shake fate. I left my dancing outfits behind in Azusa. I had no choice. A couple of guys had given me an ultimatum. "Your outfits or your life." I found fingernail polish in the refrigerator at their house. They told me there was a woman who lived there, but she was murdered. I chose the latter, my life.

A man picked me up and wanted to know if I had seen Disneyland. My biggest dream in the wide world was to get to Disneyland. He drove by it, pointed to it, and said, "There it is!" And that was that.

I wondered what his intentions were. Then he drove on and asked if I wanted to go to Huntington Beach, so I said yes again. He took me there and dropped me off and yelled, "Good-bye, sucker!"

But this is where I really wanted to be—sunny California in the wintertime. It was January, and there were lots of surfers, and I felt safer there. More than I did in San Francisco, I convinced myself. I ran into the ocean with my coat on. I shivered like a dog shaking its fur after a cold bath. My teeth were chattering. As I began to walk, I thought of establishing myself a base and parking myself there. I was out of cigarettes, money, toothbrush, toothpaste, clothes, and food (half of the things I wished I had started out with when I left

Ashland). I drew a sign on the sand: GOD, PLEASE HELP ME. Before I knew it, I turned around, and there was Gene, a good-looking hippie with eyes as blue as Christ's and clear as the waters. He was standing with what I had envisioned—strips of strawberry Christmas candy melting in his hand.

He asked, "Would you like a piece of red licorice? I'm Gene Joiner. What's your name?"

"I'm Sherry Standing, but I'm sitting, and I'm broke right now."

He was with a friend, but I didn't want to be pursued by his friend, so I glued myself to Gene. He and his friend said that they were going to baptize me in the ocean, so they walked way out in the water, carrying me. I was confused and fighting. I protested, yelling, "I've already been baptized."

I brought Gene into the bathroom and started attacking him sexually. His friend left, and we built a fire with some wood on the beach from a broken-down lifeguard stand. I thought, "Am I dreaming?" We called a restaurant to ask if we could eat barefoot at their place. One place said it was all right.

When we went to the restaurant, I thought I was being followed by two FBI men, because there were men in uniform who appeared to be FBI to me. They sat down in a booth at the same time we arrived, and they said, "See what she does next." I was sure they were watching me. Come to find out it was just nonsense in my head.

Gene is younger than me by two years, and he is attractive and sweet. He had been married to a girl named Dawn, like my stepsister, and his middle name is Roy, which was my brother's middle name.

We went to church on Sunday. I wanted to get my outfits from Azusa, so Gene took me there. When we arrived at the main hotel in Azusa, it was under construction, with doors missing and floorboards torn up. I asked the desk clerk, "Where is the man who has my G-strings?"

A man in the lobby spoke up. He knew exactly who and what I was talking about. After following directions, we found the man's car, and Gene jimmied his way into the trunk and got my uniforms and overalls out.

The next day, Gene took pictures of me on the beach. I thought that I must have a figure like an hourglass. I thought I could be a movie star and that every Hollywood agent passing by in his car could be looking at me. It's crazy thinking, I know, but I remember Mom always told me there were two cities in the world: Salt Lake City and Hollywood. My dad had an aunt, Gloria Viola Standing, who was a popular opera singer in New York. I was very proud and happy, thinking that someone might choose me to be a celebrity. It didn't dawn on me, the seriousness of this thinking, because one of my distortions of reality is fame, and it was a determining factor in my hospitalization in Salem.

Gene had a sense of humor. You needed one if you were going with me. I quit smoking for three months and went down the false crusade of life, trying to convert everyone, so I made Gene stop. On a date, I didn't let him smoke, and he said, "Well, just let me get my cortisone pills for my eczema in my glove compartment." I ran out of the car ripping all the silk off of my red dress that he bought me for my birthday. I climbed a three-tiered tree, and Gene couldn't get me down.

When I came down, a stranger stopped and asked, "Do you need some help?"

I went to his place. I was intrigued by the aquarium. It was nice to watch the fish swim back and forth.

Then he said, "You are pretty hooked on this guy, aren't you?"

Trembling from my psychosis, I said yes.

He took me home, and Gene was waiting at the door for me. He apologized. I apologized, too.

When I'm settled in, I try to continue my faith. I walk to the Catholic church in Santa Ana for evening masses and security. Something is lacking in our relationship, and I want to demonstrate my love for Gene by kissing him on his chest. With a quick reflex, he slaps me across my face. I am hurt, so I take off walking to the church, trying to seek solace and understanding from a mass or a priest for what I've done. I can't talk to a priest, but there is a mass in session, so I stay.

I decide to come back to the apartment and try to patch things up. Gene and I make a pact that if one of us is going to get mad with the other, we'll stay and talk it out. If we want to leave, we'll tell the other one where we're going. Gene is worried about me and feels bad about hitting me. I forgive him and brush his apology aside. With my outfits with me, I pursue a stripping career.

The night I begin stripping, Gene's religious sister and her husband want to meet us at a Pat Boone concert at Melody Land, a large performance venue near Disneyland. After the concert, I have Gene take me to the Shangri-La in Anaheim to audition for dancing. I show my figure to the owner, clothes off. I think the real reason why I am popular is because I match. I'm not real busty, but I can create rhythm with my body. I dance to "Jesus Is Just All Right" and "From the Beginning." I make ten dollars an hour, and get twenty dollars in tips.

Next, I am scheduled to dance at the Briar Patch for an agency called Foxy Lady. I wear blue jeans and a beige-and-pink cotton blouse at the nude dancing contest. A dancer, whom I don't know, gives me a long elegant green silk dress to wear. It is soft and smooth. It clings to me and makes my body sparkle. When it is my turn to dance, I punch the tune "Respect Yourself," by the Staple Singers, on the jukebox. I can't undress all the way because I feel nauseated, so I leave the stage. The bouncer makes me go back onstage. Taking all my clothes off, I receive an overwhelming round of applause. They yell, "She matches." What a joke, huh? I look pretty good with my red-haired patch and red wig. I have blonde locks underneath (the blonde job Dell did with my hair two summers ago, and the hair dyeing I had done since then). I am a bronze Brazilian redheaded beauty, and my darkness shows everywhere. I win the contest.

Gene makes me quit the Foxy Lady agency, because when he comes to pick me up at the Briar Patch, he sees me dancing nude with all the guys yelling for me. He says that he has never been so embarrassed in his entire life. My health starts to decline. We plan a vacation to go to Oregon, but my sanity unravels. The day before our trip, I move his humungous walnut grandfather clock, which his father made with his bare hands, out on the balcony of our apartment. I am worried about never being able to dance again. I think I am in an Alfred Hitchcock movie named *Premonition*. I think that Gene's father gave Gene the clock for a heart, and he is like a robot.

Strange things are happening to me during this time of my illness. For example, I like to play Yahtzee and card games while Gene is working. I hope that if I play Yahtzee long enough the die will disappear, and I can scare Gene. I shake the dice all day long. When Gene comes home I ask him if he will play Yahtzee with me. He says yes.

We play, and as I shake the cup of five dice only four appear. We look all over for the fifth die, but it was nowhere to be found. The next day, I fart. It's not a brain fart, although I wish it had been, and the die appears on the floor underneath the chair that I am sitting on. I call Gene and tell him. He thinks I am possessed.

Crazy as it sounds, the next day I start down McFadden Avenue in Tustin to walk to Santa Ana, and I pick up a pipe on the road. I swing it around my head as I parade down the middle of the street, holding up traffic for twenty-five minutes. I think to myself, "It's a full moon, and I don't want to go home and start smoking cigarettes again with Gene." I know something is wrong, and I need help. I just can't control it.

I make it to a Catholic church in Santa Ana where I go for mass. I go up to the altar. As I kneel at the altar, the priest giving mass clears his throat and asks me to sit down. I stuff the pipe in my pants and walk out of the church, making believe that I cause all the Hosts to disappear. I think that I am Jesus Christ and have some supernatural powers.

A policeman stops me on the corner of the street. I begin to dub him over the head with my magic pipe and say, "I'm Jesus Christ."

He says, "All right, Miss Jesus Christ, you are coming with me." I willingly go to the station.

"My name is Sherry Standing Jesus Christ." The cop laughs with another cop. "We are going to take you home. Where do you live, Miss Christ?"

I don't tell them. It is a wrong move, because unfortunately, I'm sent to a mental health facility before I can contact Gene. I'm at a switchboard desk, and a warden lady says, "See if she will do something for Burt Reynolds!"

I will do anything for Burt Reynolds, not knowing him. I slam my hand on all of the keys on the board, thinking she is talking about me. The nurse and two attendants throw me bodily into a room, tie my hands to my bed, and administer shots of Thorazine to my thighs—the thighs that I worked so hard to keep in shape by walking to the zoo and bicycling all over Tustin's orange groves when I first was living with Gene.

I yell, "I'm allergic to Thorazine!"

The needle stings my tender legs. It pierces and breaks open my skin. I feel the cold intense pain as it digs into me. Feeling like I have been injected with a hundred earwigs all greedily eating away at my legs, I scream and cry. I twist the leather straps that scrape my wrists and rub them raw. They continue to shoot me up. When I try to escape from all the misery, I fail miserably.

Once again I am nude, only this time they take my clothes off. I tell an aide to hit the wall. "St. Peter would like it." He knocks on the wall just to humor me.

I am ordered to transfer to Bellflower Mental Institution. I am also ordered not to tell the doctor who would examine me anything except that I have a chemical imbalance. They are covering their asses, because they tortured me in their hospital with restraints and shots. I almost died.

When I open my eyes in the middle of the night, there is a Spanish girl looking over me. She says, "Que bonita, Mama," as she begins to kiss my lips.

I think it is my aunt Deanna and her daughter. Then, realizing that I don't know them at all, I begin to cry. Deanna wrote to me before the hospitalization, but all I could do is hallucinate on her letters, interpreting them to mean that my sister, Ted, and Justin Loftus have passed on. I scream silently, my raw voice sticking to my stomach.

It is a murky day, and the sun seems to reek of urine; the sky drains itself of hues of cobalt blue and alizarin crimson. A lawyer reaches out to me as he walks through the door of Bellflower Institution in Bellflower, California. "Where do you live?" he asks. "Do you have any relatives? How can I contact them?"

Gene is called. He drives all the way down from Tustin to meet us in court: a one-to-two-hour drive. I am placed on the stand in court, which is very foreign to me. The room is twisting and spinning, and I don't know anyone. The doctor is there. He has to be present to testify in my case and give an evaluation, so the judge can pass a sentence. He asks if I take pills or anything in the nature of drugs.

I say, "No. What is the question?" He repeats it, and I ask, "What is love?" (Meaning do you love a person by giving a person psychotropic drugs when they are allergic to them?) But I don't get a chance to finish saying what I mean, and the judge bangs his gavel sharply, a cold piercing sound that I would never want to hear again.

He says, "OK, one month in the facility." I break down and cry.

I am locked in my room at night, and the smell is so strong, it's like someone pissing down the walls of my room. As I wake up, there is a man urinating on my bed. I charge up the hall. "That damn motherfucker is pissing on my bed," I yell.

The wardens don't budge. "Welcome to the real world," they say.

I befriend a girl who was drugged at a party and stuck her hand in some battery acid. She is as pretty as a pale-green melon. She has big dark eyes. A watery crystallized blister covers her entire hand. We say the rosary as we walk down the halls. I am forever singing the whole album of *Jesus Christ Superstar* with her. "I Don't Know How to Love Him" is my favorite song from that album, and I can't quit singing it.

I am given Thorazine, but I spit it out at the water fountain. The new doctor introduces himself and asks me to try a medicine called Stelazine. He is built like a hunk and appears to be part Latino, with sleek black hair and mystic brown eyes. His warm approach is genuine, and he seems to be interested in his work. I put my faith in him. The warden injects the Stelazine into my system with a needle, because I was caught spitting the Thorazine out. Later on, when they finally trust me with my Stelazine medicine, they give it to me orally.

The ward has a picnic and we, the patients, play volleyball. A nurse asks, "How come you are here? There's nothing wrong with you!"

"Everyone looks so familiar," I tell the nurse. "I think they are trying to trick me by putting people here who look like my brother-in-law, the superstars, and my stepmother."

I go along with the program: smelly bodies in the shower, walking on my hands, and doing pirouettes and arabesques as I hold onto the railings along the hallways. Gene brings me cigarettes and a psychedelic dress. It is a bright paisley design—red, orange, violet, blue, and green—colors that might not harmonize on any other type of garment. A blonde girl is trying to throw her weight around, waiting to get my Gene away from me. She whispers to me that she and Gene are an item, and she tries to hold his hand. I block her out and pretend I don't listen to her.

Soon I am released. I find the key that opens the place; that is, you need to "act" sane to get out! So then, having acted sane enough, I get out, and Gene and I take our vacation.

On our trip, our van breaks down next to the freeway. I am in a fantasy world. Gene's van has a wooden bumper. I tell him to bend down and kiss the wooden board on the front of the van, and it will start. I am thinking that he is Christ. He does, and the van starts. It runs for at least a little way. I fixate on the Christ, and in my mind Gene and I become the Trinity. I can't shake the damage that the hospitals have done to my mind. Salem and Bellflower sent a shock through my system that is irreconcilable with my sanity.

We visit my aunt and uncle in Deer Island, Oregon, and also, my mom, Ralph, and Doug in Roseburg. Doug, Gene, and I take in a movie at the Pine Drive-In. The name of the show is *The Poseidon Adventure*. I cry and sympathize with the minister, Frank Scott, played by Gene Hackman, who goes down with the ocean liner. Then we sing and wail, "There's got to be a morning after," some of the lyrics from "The Morning After" song as we drive home.

Subsequently, when we return to California, Gene doesn't want me to work. That cuts all my ties of being sociable and talking to anyone. I think he wants to protect me because I am a dancer. I take to the orange groves with my bicycle. He finally convinces me to take birth control pills, and I agree to take the pill—if he will marry me. After three months of living with him, I give in and take the pill. I bloat up like a balloon and eat baked potatoes and Three Musketeers bars. I get hooked on watching soap operas. We take trips to Disneyland and Knott's Berry Farm, but it is no longer fun. I am itchy, depressed, fat, and miserable from my Stelazine and being shot with Thorazine. We go to a drive-in movie, and he brings out an aluminum ashtray that looks like the one that I used to smoke with in Bellflower. It resembles a glass mirror and reflects my image, the frightened and distorted face that turns hard and distant.

I am outraged because it is a reminder of being in Bellflower. I get anxious, and my head is filled with sick crazy thoughts. It is difficult to adjust. I jump out of the car and walk eight miles from one drive-in to another. I stub my toe, and it bleeds. I have feelings of being a witch or one of the apostles, but I am afraid to tell anyone. The blood symbolizes the suffering and the supernatural. After the movie is over, I call Gene on a coin telephone, and he comes to pick me up. He writes me a poem and an apology.

⌒⟶

I can remember going through a healing journal I kept while living with Gene. How fun it was before I was hospitalized. There were great memories of great times we shared when I was living in California, despite my mental condition. I wrote, "I dreamed of me and Gene traveling to Hollywood and having a flat tire. We didn't have any money to change it, and a gas station cashed our check to fix it." The dream came true when we got a flat in Hollywood and didn't have cash. I asked Gene to cash a check at a gas station, and even though he thought I was a crazy lunatic, they cashed it on the spot. Then one day we were invited to a promotional speech and dinner for San Diego Country Estates. I had dreamed the whole speech. And you know, when we went to the dinner, everyone looked like movie stars, and the speech was given verbatim as in my dream.

After Bellflower, I had the opportunity to learn to paint and enrolled in an oil-painting class so that I could let out my frustrations. I began working through my problems, escaping to my canvas, and Gene finally consented to let me work as a telephone solicitor for San Diego Country Estates.

But one morning, he pulled out the rug out from under me. He said, "I don't love you anymore."

I was crushed. I couldn't push the tears away fast enough. We packed my things and took our last trip to Ashland, Oregon, together.

I stayed with Dell in Roseburg. Gene moved to Illinois. He wrote and wanted me back, so I took the Greyhound to Illinois to be with him again. It took five days to get there. I didn't sleep for three of those nights. On the Greyhound bus headed for the East

Coast, I was having multiple migraines and couldn't think straight. I arrived at a station in Iowa, next to the Illinois border, at midnight.

The driver said, "There are no more stops. You have to get off."

"But where do I go to? I have a ticket to DeKalb," I cried.

"Sorry," the driver replied and left.

I thought it was a conspiracy—all the Greyhound bus drivers throughout the country were on a mission to stop me from getting to Illinois. I got my suitcase. My head was pounding. A tall, friendly African American security guard from a hotel down the street offered to escort me to the hotel. I had no money. My bus would arrive in the morning at six. I tried to sleep, but the security guard came to the lobby and halfway woke me up. He said, "Your bus is here."

It was five thirty in the morning. Trying to make sense out of all this, and realizing that I had slept some, we walked to the bus depot together.

I made it to Illinois. Gene picked me up, and we stayed with his parents first. Later we stayed with Joe, his wife, Eileen, and their three children, Cathy, Becky, and David. Joe and Eileen had a barbecue that night, and I fell in love with Joe right off. He was tall, dark haired, and handsome. His wife, Eileen, was a strawberry blonde with oval-shaped hazel eyes. She told me I could sleep on the sofa. Then, in a backstabbing manner, she started talking about me.

When I woke up, I could see a vast area of cornfields and this huge flatland. In the distance, the towers of Northern Illinois University were reaching for the clouds. I asked myself, "Is this the path I'm supposed to follow, or is there another episode of psychosis lurking in the wings?"

CHAPTER 9

THREESOME

Since his birth, Gene had eczema, a skin condition that causes rashes and dry, cracking skin. Over the years he had been treated by several methods, including cortisone injections. Finally, even that didn't give him relief, and as a result, his skin became incredibly irritated. Soon after arriving in Illinois, his entire body became engulfed in itchy rashes so severe that he had to go to the Mayo Clinic for treatment. His mom and dad thought I was to blame for Gene's skin problem, because I was a dancer. They thought this was morally wrong. The stress of living with me must have caused his violent outbreak.

I got a job at Northern Illinois University in DeKalb as a kitchen helper at Lincoln Hall. I checked students' IDs as they came through the food line for their meals. I also prepared salads and desserts for lunch and dinner.

I was thrilled that someone like Joe's wife appreciated my artistic skills. She would hurry up the stairs to where Gene and I took shelter and compliment me on my work. Downstairs you could hear her record, *The Sea* by Rod McKuen, playing, the sound of the ocean and the waves crashing to shore. It was my favorite music of all time.

I missed my period and a pregnancy test proved positive. The song "Having My Baby" by Paul Anka was playing on the radio. I considered all options, but I came to find out I wasn't pregnant. I had a cyst on my ovary, and it finally was shed in my next menstrual cycle. I had to talk to Joe about it. I wanted to know his opinion. I certainly did not want a baby while I was taking medication. Joe was very consoling. Gene had come from Mayo, and before my cyst passed, he was ecstatic at the news that he might be a father.

He said, "They wrapped me up like a mummy. I finally found some relief in the hospital."

I told him about shedding my cyst. He was disappointed because he wanted to father and parent a child. I said, "Maybe sometime later, Gene."

Joe had purchased the house we all were living in from his grandparents, who had lived there for many years. Gene and Joe's parents had told them that there was an old chair somewhere behind a wall in the house. On Joe's day off, Gene and Joe decided that it must be hidden in a chamber behind a set of dresser drawers, which were in the wall of the upstairs bathroom. They pried and banged around until the set of drawers came loose, and they pulled them out of the wall. Through the opening we could see an old chair. When they wrestled it through the wall and got it downstairs, the chair resembled a recliner chair with an adjustable back and leg rests. It wasn't padded like a modern recliner. Later, we found out it was called a convalescent chair. What a sight to behold! Eileen took off with the treasure.

Life was good, and the Christmas holiday was electric. I got together with Gene's mom, and we took cardboard boxes and covered them with butcher paper. Next we took felt and cut out trees, candy canes, and snowmen (just about everything Christmasy we could think of), and glued them to the boxes for Joe and Eileen's children.

Gene's mom was tall with a sweet, childlike laugh and twinkling light-blue eyes behind her feline-frame glasses. On Sunday she taught Sunday school to hundreds of children at her local Baptist church.

Their dad, Vivian, had short, thinning white hair separated by the front of his forehead. His smart inquisitive eyes kept me on guard as he asked me questions like, "Have you quit smoking yet?" and "When are you and Gene going to tie the knot?"

I misread his intentions toward me now and then and perceived his questions to be tainted with sarcasm, instead of carrying an honest message or innocent connotation. "Sometime soon, Vivian," I would tell him. I felt as if God would move the earth out from underneath my feet if I gave him a wrong answer.

His specialty was making grandmother and grandfather clocks, benches, tables, and candlestick holders for his family and other people. Even though his hands were rough and rugged from hammering so many nails in his shop, his disposition was soft and good. I invariably would hear him say "Oopsie Daisy" as Becky or David would run behind him and grab him by the knees or "Upsie Daisy" when he would grab them by their hands and pull them up to rest on his shoulder.

There was a fight brewing between Joe and Eileen Christmas Eve. I think if Vivian had been aware of it, he could have prevented it. Eileen told me to go to the Sears Tower in Chicago with Gene and Joe. That is where they were planning to celebrate. Gene insisted that I sit up front with Joe, and then he made the mistake of falling asleep. With Gene in the backseat of Joe's ACM Hornet, I daringly grabbed Joe's genitals. He said, "I love you."

I was amazed. My eyes grew big and chills ran down my spine and into my stomach, making a 180-degree turn. Me and Joe kissing like crazy, while Joe was driving. When Gene woke up, we stopped at a few bars in Chicago. Returning to the car, Joe mistakenly drove us to Wisconsin, and we ended up without any money for the tollbooth. Joe had made a wrong turn, and we had gotten lost. Luckily we got a pass to go through. We paid it when we reached home.

Prior to this mental escape and going to the Sears Tower with the two brothers, which began to mold and shape my life, Gene took me to the hospital again. I had a terrible migraine, and the intake person committed me to the psych ward, because there wasn't a doctor available at the time. I was having psychotic thoughts.

There were people walking around this small place asking me, "Have you seen my butt?" This was the winter of 1974, one I'll always cherish in a way and never forget. I had been hospitalized for the third time. I was sick again, but I was developing a bond with Gene and Joe, and I thought it was something special. On the ward, I created a clay sculpture of pears, apples, and other fruit in a wicker basket, but I left it behind. I concentrated on getting my release papers, not knowing why I was hospitalized in the first place. I was ecstatic to get out. I grew paranoid about the idea that someone at Northern would know I was hospitalized, so I tried to make believe that I wasn't committed. It was a vicious cycle that circulated in my brain. When one part of me said to go and speak the truth about what had happened, the other part of me begged me to stay and say that it hadn't. I said and did funny, off-the-wall things and had ill psychological mannerisms due to the side effects of being locked up, but I had to trust my judgment. Besides, I was in love with Gene and Joe, and that was all that mattered. I ended up telling the truth.

My fragile world was becoming unchangeable. The trip to Chicago's Sears Tower with Joe and Gene had caused my head to swim. Christmas Day we met at Virginia and Viv's, and Eileen bought me some black nylon underwear for a gift. We ate a turkey dinner with fresh lettuce leaves and green beans we shucked from Virginia's garden. She lit her oven and baked cinnamon-sugar cookies and a tart apple pie. Then we all went home. I had a bottle of Kahlua. I told Gene that I was going downstairs to see if my Kahlua was gone, since I didn't put a cap on it. I knocked on Joe's door. He answered it and threw his warm arms around me. Eileen came out of the bedroom and dashed upstairs to get Gene. Eileen had a boyfriend on the sly, and I was thinking she didn't care. As Joe and I lay in bed, we offered each other our passion and swapped our affection. I loved him. But my God, he was my brother-in-law, so to speak. Someone was bound to get hurt.

I went to a counselor with Gene, but the counselor said, "I can see you and Joe together. You and Gene could have a relationship for a long period of time, and if you could move away from Joe your relationship might work." On the contrary, Joe moved out of his house, and Gene and I found an apartment around the corner from Joe's apartment. We were too close together. One night I would visit Joe, and the next night I would see Gene. Together we remained friends. The brothers got a tape from their sister saying that I was corrupting them. I thought that they didn't like me anymore, because Gene and Joe were agreeing with parts of the tape. I went out of my mind and in a fit of rage threw a Coke bottle at the window and ran out of the house barefoot on the snowy, icy gravel. Who knows where I was going? Then I came back, and they asked, "Now don't you feel silly?" I did.

We frequented the topless clubs in Illinois. While we were in Aurora, we were stopped by the police. We were in Gene's broken-down green Ford. Gene was driving. The alternator had quit, and we were driving without our lights on to try to save our battery. The officer said to me, "Who are you with?"

Joe got mad when I pointed to Gene in the front seat, because I was supposed to be with him. Joe was in the process of a divorce, and I didn't want him to get into trouble because he was with me. The officer ordered, "Get out of the car." They put Gene and Joe in the paddy wagon and they put me in their cop car. I felt a meltdown coming on, somewhat like the experience I had with the police before, but I managed to pull it together. By being cooperative, I was willing to accept the unwanted pressure and heed the call of the officer telling me to get into the car.

Off to a restaurant we went. The police asked, "Are they the ones?"

Everyone shook their heads. "One guy had a bruise and a tattoo on one of his arms."

We were mistaken for people who fit our description, and our car was mistaken for a car that sped away with its lights off, because we had our lights off. Gene and Joe thought that I was going to cause a scene, since I had been held in jail before, but I was quiet. The police let us go and told us to fix our headlights.

After we had numerous adventures in the topless clubs, I went to their mom's house to see where I fit in. I think I was searching for an answer to decide whom to go with. I was confused by going with two guys at the same time, especially brothers who looked alike. Both had dark hair, kind blue eyes, bushy mustaches hanging over their upper lips, and dimples accenting their cheeks. One was taller, thinner, and older. He parted his hair to the side but looking at their images in the mirror, Joe looked just like Gene. Their mom told me to go back to Oregon, so I granted her wishes and boarded a Greyhound. Joe kissed my cheek, and Gene saw me off on the bus. Loving the two brothers at the same time was the hardest part of my life. Sometimes I think harder than my stays in the mental institutions, but losing one of them was the hardest.

Dell welcomed me back from my journey to Illinois. I hadn't left on good terms with Dell the first time I had come to live with her, and I was afraid that I had worn out my welcome. It took courage for me to live with her and her mom, who had come up from Arizona, because they filled the air with their smoke, and I struggled to find a space to breathe. Dell meant the world to me, but there was a mean streak in her, and I couldn't quite put my finger on it. Maybe because I thought that everyone was against me at that time. For a couple of weeks, I made my topless outfits, and I became strong enough to go back to Portland and dance, hoping that I could decide whom I loved more—Gene or Joe.

Before I left I saw my brother, Doug. He still lived in the Green District and was a senior in high school. He was the main actor in the play *By the Skin of Your Teeth* by Thornton Wilder. He played the part of Mr. Antrobus. I helped him with some of his lines, and he learned every line by heart. He was a true performer and personified his character. When it came to the part where Mr. Antrobus was asleep, it looked as if Doug was actually asleep. I unwillingly rejected his good vibes as my head succumbed to pounding and nausea. After his act, I lost it. I cried and cried but never told my brother that. I was just excited for him and impressed with the way he played his character. Dell went to the hospital with me because the pain in my head was intense. I turned into that frustrated and cross troll doll again. I think I was worked up over Doug's performance and wanted to get involved in his lines, so I developed a severe migraine. The doctor told me to drink lots of Coca-Cola and eat chocolate. Then he sent me home.

After tearing up the chiffon dress—yellow background with blue and pink pastel circles—that my sister had purchased for me for my high-school banquet, I made a wrap to dance to the "Moonbeam" song. I drove up to Portland to work in the topless Mary's Club and the Carriage Room for Mark and Eddie's theatrical agency again, and to my surprise, the clubs had changed. The far-off smiles of the strangers, the lost looks of the crowd, the tantalizing of the bartenders, and the fear imposed on the dancers by the agents created an unsettling atmosphere.

At the Carriage Room, I liked my bartender, Sonny. He called me Sher. He was friendly with all the dancers, but I had this feeling inside that he was sweet on me. I was lying on the stage, dancing to "Nights in White Satin," and he came by and kissed me. Then hasta la vista, baby, that was it. He didn't talk to me again. I continued dancing with my clothes half-off.

When I was working at Mary's Club, I was shimmying my hips and boobs, and I gazed toward the audience. I spotted a familiar face. There was Sandy, the man who sexually abused me when I was nineteen in Lincoln City, sitting next to some assholes. He said, "I'm sure glad that I made points with her."

They dropped their jaws. I was humiliated. I cried and turned my body to face the wall so that all the men could see was my backside. I wanted to kill and kill and get it over with once and for all! I jumped off the stage to my dressing room and called the police, but the cops couldn't do anything about it, because I didn't file a complaint in Lincoln City. What a letdown.

I was honestly considering a James Bond tactic and taking out a contract on Sandy's life. A nice African American man saw me crying onstage and asked if he could bump Sandy off for money. I almost made a deal. The black man was most kind and sensitive, and I wanted to spare him. So I said, "It isn't worth it."

There was this stripteaser named Star dancing that day who did the Chinese splits. She had an acrobatic routine, with purple glitter streamers slithering down her throat to her voluptuous breasts. Another dancer was an African American stripper named Violet. She moved her feet the way Michael Jackson did, only with golden bracelets around her ankles. She would reach over her head with her right arm, bend backward, and touch her heels with her right hand. She was extremely flexible and graceful—a true artist. I wanted to befriend her but didn't get the chance. I wanted to reach out to the dancers, but I was shy and suspicious of anyone who was friendly to me. As I perfected my dancing on the stage, I felt the urge to heave, so I ran down the steps to the bathroom and started upchucking. An agent happened to be there. He was yelling at me, trying to rough me up with words, but one of the dancers said, "She's sick. Leave her alone." She asked me what happened.

I said, "There is a guy out there who sexually abused me in Lincoln City." She kissed me on the forehead and left. The next day, I started smoking an amphora tobacco pipe and got in trouble for doing so onstage. I guess that's why my agent was after me, because I couldn't do anything right. Who knows? As I see it, we were artists who were way ahead of our time, and the agents couldn't quite catch up.

The next night, I went out with a jerk who gave me a bladder infection in the course of making love. It stung like fire and burned my inner thighs. After I saw the doctor, I purchased my bladder medication. I danced at a small club that attracted very few customers. I followed a woman who twirled tassels attached to her nipples to the songs "The Great Effect" by David Grusin and "Wipe Out" by the Safaris. She was an older woman—brunette, dark eyes, and stretch marks. I guess from twirling those tassels for so long. After her gig was up, I put on a show dancing to the Beach Boys' songs and music performed by the Temptations. I went home early, and my boss bawled me out and told me not to go home early again. With my feet full of blisters and yellow callouses peeling at my heels, I quit Mark and Eddie's theatrical agency for the second time. I joined the Arthur Murray Dance Studio and learned to teach people how to dance ballroom style.

My shoes were profoundly tight for my feet, but I persevered over a two-week period. I wobbled trying to maintain my balance, but later, my coordination took command. The instructor said, "Meet your partner eye to eye, watch your posture, don't slump." I quickly got the knack of performing the intricate dance steps with a partner. I did the cha-cha, tango, and waltz with grace and ease, my toe and heel pointed to the beat of the Latin music. Looking my partner in the eye, shoulders upright, I sidestepped and shuffled on cue. Our partners were other dance members, but I decided not to pursue teaching the customers because of the state my mind was in.

I applied for welfare and received food stamps, but I didn't have a fridge. An old resident at the apartment building I lived in told me to leave my bologna outside on my window ledge, and that would keep it cool. Was he crazy? I tried it and lay down for a nap, and I had a nightmare of a guy in San Francisco with blond hair and piercing blue eyes eating the meat with demons by my window.

A guy who wore black-and-red dancing shoes took me out the next day to see *The Exorcist*. I could only see half of the film and went home alone. The guy left a note on my door, and I read one line. It said, "I thought you were stronger than that."

Oh, how hard and cruel life really got for me. It hurt my mind to think. I was suffering from insomnia, and my landlady was going to evict me. I was having nightmares of hell—a hell that I envisioned and dreamed of when I was a Catholic going to high school. It was becoming a reality to me, because I was being approached by a group of Hare Krishna people while I napped at a park. A couple of them showed me a picture of a red fetus, and after that I couldn't eat right. I suddenly lost my sanity and my ability to rationalize again.

A dancer took me to the unemployment agency. I stayed overnight with her, and she stole my best velour pants outfit. There was a lady at the unemployment agency, whom I met the next day, who took me to Deer Island to live with my aunt. I told my aunt my predicament and moved my things there, but she didn't have room for me to stay, so I came home to Roseburg. My mom said that I needed to go to the hospital. I couldn't sleep because I was hallucinating. I brought Dell to Portland to help me pack, so I could go back to Roseburg to live with her. Dell saw the mess my room was in and didn't understand. Scrungy cigarette butts, clothes strewn on the floor. Containers of yogurt and packages of spoiled bologna plastered on the dresser. After packing, we chain-smoked, traveling on the winding roads to her yellow-painted house in the heart of Roseburg. Dell tried her best to be accommodating to me, but it didn't work. I was too far gone.

I had problems in Portland that led to chaos in my mind. For instance, I couldn't reach Joe. Gene was getting married, and I was receiving hate mail from Gene's fiancée, Joanie. I took a psychological test and saw a counselor twice, but he said I was perfectly sane. I memorized most of those psychological tests, and I knew most of the answers, so I wasn't surprised when he said that the results were OK. I was sane. But I knew down inside that I wasn't sane. I was far from it. This time, for once, my mom and Dell could tell it.

When we reached Dell's house, I said that I was going for a jog. I started running and couldn't quit. A guy driving by rolled down his window and yelled, "Go back home, you goddamn whore."

I started to regress to the criticism that I had taken in my high-school days. How undeserving I was to get all of those attacks! I felt a hard, cold pain in my head. Every movement of my legs perpetrated more meaning. I pounded my feet into the ground. My mind ached. If you were given a block of metal that had human properties like feeling and aching, and then you hammered on it for an hour and then threw it into a fireplace and quickly doused it out with a pitcher of ice water, my brain would feel the same sensation.

It was the cold, hard pain of emptiness that occupied my mind as the mental anguish took over.

I reached a mobile home park where I thought my girlfriend lived and knelt down and began to cry. A man with one arm and his wife came to my rescue and asked me to come inside. I thought he was Dr. Allred, who had committed me to be in Salem, because he also had one arm.

The man made a few calls, saying, "I had a baby boy," over the phone. I thought he was talking about me, because I had told Dr. Allred that I wanted a sex change some time ago. Then he asked if he could call my mom. I gave him a number that my mom told me never to call, because she didn't want me to bother her if I was sick. She and her friends came by to pick me up. My judgment was put to the test.

CHAPTER 10

SAN FRANCISCO

One of Mom's friends from AA drove me to Mercy Hospital in Roseburg. It was my fourth hospitalization. I was hospitalized for three days, and then I was released without medication.

As Mom drove me away from the hospital, she had an outburst. She yelled, "You asshole, why don't you go to San Francisco?" She opened the car door and kicked me out.

We had not discussed San Francisco before, but Maria certainly did think it was an option, maybe because Dad and Mary Jo lived near there. She probably thought I could live with them again. I was hurt and losing respect for Mom. My own mother didn't care if I was alive or dead. I walked to Dell's and picked a plum from someone's yard and handed it to her. She was watering her pansies and petunias, and the roses on her trellis.

"Auntie Dell," I said, "I'm going to San Francisco."

She handed me a hundred dollars for a ticket, and with two suitcases I took the bus headed for San Francisco in the middle of the night. That would ironically turn on me once I got there. There were guys traveling to San Francisco from the Job Corps on the Greyhound. We sang "One Tin Soldier" and other songs on the way down. When I reached the bus depot, I had no money, no ticket to return to Roseburg, no car, and two suitcases. I began my journey to hell.

A man picked me up and said he knew of a hotel I could sleep at, after I got a room for free. I went with him to a place where there were bloodstains all over a bathtub. There we slept. I wanted to wake up before him, so I could escape, but suddenly we woke up together. He started beating me, pounding on my thighs with his fists because I wouldn't give him sex. I swear he could have murdered me. I grabbed my bags and ran heavily down the stairs and into the street, my heart knocking at the walls of my chest and throat. There was a woman with a half-shaven head in East Indian garb motioning me back. As I ran farther, a man from a clothing store held up his thumb to me and smiled. I thought, "Hmm, maybe this is someone I can trust and have a relationship with sometime." I thumbed back. We got to know each other fairly well, and he told me that I could live at his place until I got settled. He would sleep on the floor, and I could sleep on his mattress. He had gross pimples all over his back.

Each day (without my medication), I put on his dusty old cowboy hat and placed a wine-colored crystal rosary around its crown. I dressed up in his boots, two sizes too big for me, and in his baggy clothes and hat, I headed out the door.

One day in particular, I went to his friend's place. She stayed in her apartment, and her husband worked with my roommate at a clothing shop. To get to know her, I said, "I'm going with Gene and Joe and who knows who." I wanted to get close to her and let her know me a little bit better. But those were the times when I was sick, and I had to pay for others being sick all around me. She said, "See ya later" and closed her door.

My roommate and I did have some good times. We went to dances at a place called Dance Your Ass Off, and we rode trolley cars. He showed me his motorcycle, which we would ride sometimes, and when I thought I was pregnant with someone else's kid, he told me how to get to General Hospital to find out. The test was negative, but I didn't quite tell him soon enough.

One day, I was sick and queasy. I couldn't quit vomiting. Brian, my roommate (for lack of a real name), forced a horse pill down my throat. All I did was hallucinate. I wanted to move, and I couldn't. I finally got the strength to walk around to different shops, and someone gave me money for a beer. I bought one at a convenience store that had a narrow entryway adjacent to a park with wooden benches. I lay on a bench and placed the can on my forehead.

I thought, "Where is my concentration? Why can't I talk, see, hear? What am I doing here?" I found my way to Brian's. When Brian went to work, I took all the pennies out of his stealthy money jar and bought some rich chocolate ice cream with them. I started regurgitating and couldn't quit. I left a small amount of puke on the floor. When he came home, he said, "Just a minute, I am going to get some baking soda to clean this up." He came back and asked if I wanted a back massage.

I said yes. I lay on my stomach as he straddled me.

He asked, "You are going with Gene and Joe and who knows who? What about me?" He grabbed my neck and began to strangle me.

I screeched, "You are killing two people instead of one, because I'm pregnant."

He finally let go and said, "Where is my gun? I want my gun now!"

I cried, "I'll get my bags now."

He said, "Get the hell out of here."

As sick as it seems now, I yelled, "I love you."

I wasn't pregnant in the first place. I just said it to spoof him, and I could hardly talk.

A couple of policemen stopped me running down the street. "Get in," they said. I told them what had happened, and they replied, "Sounds like a fish story to us. Are you a cop harasser?"

They said that they would drop me off at a station, so I could stay there overnight and file a complaint. They dropped me off at midnight, but there was no station. They said to remember 666. I got taken! I ran to a hallway that I saw in a distance and remembered all the songs from *Jesus Christ Superstar* and belted them out inside this towering cement structure that looked like a Broadway theater. As I came out of the building, someone took a picture of me. It startled me, and I kept walking. There was a person with black hair and a widow's peak sashaying about, looking like Satan, but I think he was Alice Cooper. He wore a knavish, black silk cape and slacks. His thin hands and sharp fingernails were fixed in his pockets. Even from afar, I could feel his breath freeze the frightened lines of my brow and the corners of my mouth, penetrating my mortal soul. There was no such thing as Satan, I was telling myself. I was trying to rely on my philosophy of life I had adopted in Eugene, when I got out of Salem. And strangely enough, the reality of it all had saved me.

I headed toward a Lutheran church and sat on the lawn, singing Mary Magdalene's song, "I Don't Know How to Love Him," from *Jesus Christ Superstar* again. A stranger came by, and I walked with him to his apartment, which had a gate at the entrance, locked with a padlock and chain. He brought me upstairs, where it smelled like vomit. "A limousine is waiting for you." He spoke with a spiked hairdo.

I teetered down the stairs like I was walking on a high wire with a perverse sense of timing. Someone caught my eye, got into the limousine, and took off. I couldn't make out who he was. Another stranger unlocked the gate for me, and once again I made a quick dash up the street. Churches were akin to each other, located on every block, it seemed. My next camp was a Catholic church. I went to the rectory and rang for a priest. No answer. I walked to a corner of the rectory and left one bag full of my clothes on the curb. Hopelessly, I walked back to the rectory, very tired, cold, and confused. I even tried to get ahold of the nuns. I told them on their intercom that I wanted to be a nun and that I was pregnant. How I longed to talk to someone. I was weary and had no medication. I sat and waited on the rectory steps all night. The sun rose and shone so bright, casting a shadow on the congregation as they entered the church while the priests unveiled the statues. I went to mass and received the Host, swallowing it slowly down my mangled throat. I told the priest I was in trouble and needed someplace to sleep. He and another priest showed me where a bed was, so I could rest. They woke me too soon out of some bad dreams and said, "You have to leave." One priest gave me a quarter for a bus and told me where to get off. He said that it was a haven for pregnant girls; I would fit right in. But I wasn't pregnant.

The bus driver refused to let me off at the right place. Instead, there was a jagged street about twenty minutes away. The driver got irritated at me and told me to get off the bus. I did a lot of walking and thinking. My link to the real world would be in five days. I never found the people or place the priest had in mind. A mysterious-looking man picked me up, and I traveled with him until he took his pants off and told me to make love to him. I only carried one bag, since all my material things were gone, and I no longer possessed a need for survival. While he was driving, I jumped out of the car without the bag and yelled, "Get away from me, Judas!" I called him Judas because he was wearing a tiny gold earring in his right earlobe, which is how I imagined Judas to look. Besides, I still had the misconception that I was Christ.

During my stay at the Catholic church, I had a dream about two girls riding a miniature trolley. I jumped on and off the car. Also, I met a black girl in a phone booth with stuff all over her pants. The dream came true not only for me, but for the girls in the trolley cars and the girl at the phone booth.

I staggered from walking for so long. There was a tunnel, and above it there was a beach: sunshine, small bombs going off, music, people having fun. The tunnel could only be approached by a certain place. I couldn't resist temptation and began to walk through the tunnel. People were nude. As I walked, my feet became like lead in my shoes. A naked man with his son came out of the tunnel. A hard lump developed in my throat, and my face burst red hot, causing me to raise my heels and speed out of there as fast as I could. This was the ultimate fate I was to meet—with death and the bout with psychosis that was to follow.

As I made my way through San Francisco, I walked through a black community. The people of the community were truly harmonious. No one approached me. I went to a telephone booth, and I saw the girl in my dream. I asked her for a cigarette, and she gave me one. In an instant, I saw what appeared to be the tip of a black man's penis on the ground. It was an enigma to me, so I ran for my life.

Exhausted, penniless, starving, wearing my long red dress that Gene had bought for me not long before, I fell onto the grass on the campus of a community college and made snow angels in the wet lawn, using grass instead of snow. My mind was very sick and dancing with craziness. I went to the street corner and began crying.

A nice African American man came up to me and said, "Don't cry. I'm your boyfriend."

I asked, "Which way is the freeway?" He pointed. I really think he was my boyfriend in another life. I thanked him, and I began to run.

Signs were telling me to go to LA or San Bruno. A man headed for San Bruno picked me up and told me to try on his red jacket. I felt safe with him. I thought, I'm going in the wrong direction, but I would do anything for a hamburger. He called himself Sonny Schmidt. He took me to a bar, and people gathered around him. Then he took me to his apartment, which had golden floors and a long silver spear in his bedroom. It was barbaric. I told him that I wanted a hamburger, and he took me somewhere to eat. To my imagination, it smelled like souls burning, so I couldn't eat. Sonny took me to a friend's house. His friend had an unbelievable blond, braided beard that hung to his knees. I shook his beard, and he introduced me to his wife. There were dogs and cats everywhere. The guys went to get some ice cream for us. Sonny and I went upstairs, and I fell asleep. Somehow they mentioned the name of my idol. I don't know if they meant my Chip in particular, since that was a popular name at that time. Sonny had a picture of a guy on his wall.

I shared my affection with Sonny. His friend came into the room unannounced. I was feeling uncomfortable. Someone had kicked out his friend's teeth, because they were in when I first saw him. I remembered the number, 666, that the police told me to put in my consciousness. Morning peeked through Sonny's window curtain. It was six o'clock and my sixth day in California. I called Ted from Sonny's phone when he went to work. I told Ted that I was alive.

Ted said, "We were worried about you. You didn't stop by Ashland before you went to California."

"I'm all right." I started singing, "You got to take good care of business." We laughed and then hung up.

I fantasized all day long. When Sonny came home and asked me what I did, I fudged it. The silver spear still bugged me. Was this Satan I was sleeping with? I put on his robe and ran down the street—robe only. I seemed to fly, and Sonny ran after me. "Please come back and get something to wear!" he yelled.

I came back, afraid. I slipped on my torn red dress, afraid, and headed out the door.

He said good-bye.

I closed the door and said, "Good-bye, you goddamn fucking-A Satan!" I took off for the Catholic church nearby to talk to a priest before I hit the streets.

"Father, I think I'm sleeping with Satan," I cried.

The priest said, "Look for a white van on the side of the road. He will take you home."

How did he know? Lucky guess, I should think! The Hunchback of Notre Dame in a white van pulled to the side of the road and picked me up. That's the name I called my ride. He was thin and had a hunchback. His tilted chest and camel's hump gave the appearance that he had been sleeping flat on his stomach on a table for the majority of his life. We had a falling out when he stopped the van and brought out a rubber. I hadn't seen one till then.

I said, "You hit me in my colopsiosololitude," which I called the end of my sanity.

His condom threw me off psychologically. I said that Ashland was only two hours away, when it was actually eight or nine hours from San Francisco, I talked him into bringing me to Ashland. Reluctantly, we made it to Ashland, and I said, "My brother-in-law will pay you for gas." No one was there, but the door was open when we arrived at my sister and Ted's house. With an extreme case of schizophrenia, I told him to leave. "Your car can run on nothing," I promised. He left for good.

Diana, Ted, and Justin came home, and we traveled to Coos Bay to stay with Ted's relatives: Dorothy, his mom, Don, Mitzi, and their children. I told them a slice of what happened. Mom came up by herself to visit with us. I was mentally off. In fact, I thought all the Loftuses, my mom, and I were going on an ark, and the world was coming to an end. My mom and I took a short breather in her car. My brother couldn't make it, but while I was out for a smoke with Mom, we heard a cry.

Someone yelled, "Oh, my eyes!"

My mom turned to me and asked, "Why did you hurt your poor brother's eyes?"

I said, "I didn't." Then I thought I did. I thought I had the power of God. Something was awfully strange. I had surrendered to the illusion that drew me into my insanity and was left hanging over the edge of the cliff of my unpredictability. Mom's visit was short. She gave me twenty dollars and said, "Go live with Don and Mitzi." She didn't want me anymore.

At night, I lie down and count to ten as I begin to breathe deeply, first relaxing the tips of my toes. Then my instep, next, the balls of my feet and my heels. I reminisce about how beautiful the world is as I place all my confusing thoughts into a box. I wrap that box up with a string in my mind and send it off into midair. I continue counting. My calves are relaxed. Breathe in and out. My knees are rested, and so are my thighs. Then I kiss San Francisco goodbye as my box dances beyond a fluffy white cloud with the string trailing behind, and then I can see the string no more. For these few moments, I let the positive in. My past is gone. My divine intellect records only what has been given out and then gives it away to the universe. There is nothing to be afraid of. When I wake up, I count to twenty and relax each part of my body. I can change what has been done to me. Hips, deep breathe; stomach, breathe; back, breathe; breasts, breathe (my organs are in good working condition); shoulders, breathe; arms, breathe; elbows, breathe; wrists, breathe (I let go the need for this condition in my body); hands, breathe; fingers, breathe (the sun comes up in the morning and the sun goes down at night). Back up to collarbone, breathe; neck, breathe; chin, breathe; cheeks, breathe (face-to-face, cheek to cheek, side to side). I am so relaxed. Ears, breathe; nose, breathe (my eyes are deep in their sockets); head, breathe; and hair, breathe. I think of a happy place. This is my special place, the happiest place I've been. I will embrace it now, own it, and remember it when I count back down to my toes.

I stayed in Coos Bay several days. Mom couldn't get rid of me so soon. My illness had overreached its peak. No one in Coos Bay could understand me. I began to hitchhike to Roseburg, and Don drove by unexpectedly and said, "I have your suitcase." It was the bluish-gray striped metal case where I kept my roller skates, high-school clothes, and orange-and-black uniform. It was a present from my mom that I used for long-distance trips. We sipped a smooth chocolate shake, and he dropped me off at the highway. Bruises were formed on my swollen legs from the fists of the stranger in San Francisco, and my throat was tender from the strangulation. I was so sick, and I didn't want Don to know. Catching two rides, I returned home to Roseburg.

At Mom's, I told her about my San Francisco trip, and I asked her if she would please see a priest with me. She didn't believe me but finally conceded and came with me to see Father Murphy. He was a stout and jolly middle-aged priest, who was the epitome of one of the friar advertisements you'd see in Gifts of the Spirits Catholic stores. He wore a large wooden rosary draped around his waist with a sculpted wooden cross that hung below his navel. He asked, "OK, why are you here?"

"Mother, do you love me?" I asked.

"No. I wish you were never born," she replied.

The priest exclaimed, "Maria!" Then he said a prayer of understanding for my mother and me.

I liked the priest, even though I had some emotions still stirred up about the Church. He was a good priest, regardless.

Doug was in another play, and Mom and I went every night to see him. Mom got me a mattress from the AA members. Doug slept uneasily on a cot next to me. He couldn't figure out why I wouldn't sleep on the mattress.

I said, "I was strangled on a mattress."

Mom wanted me to go to counseling, but I didn't want to. I ended up going anyway, against my will. After therapy she'd ask me, "Did you take your pills?"

So to make her mad, I hustled to the bathroom and took twenty 10 mg tablets of Stelazine. The day that I overdosed on Stelazine, Doug and I were going to Diana's in Ashland. Doug brushed and braided my thick, coarse red hair, tugging from my scalp. I was lethargic. Doug's car broke down on the freeway as we drove through Grants Pass, and I told him to take it to Ashland anyway.

By luck we made it there, but the transmission was all screwed up. Diana paid for our bus ride back home. All I could do on our bus ride was hallucinate blue chicken. Confused, I reached over to Doug, grabbing him by the shoulder, and said, "Doug, the dogs next door to Mom's house are Satan's friends, Mark and Eddie from my theatrical agency in Portland."

His heart sank. "Oh, Sherry." I really did scare him.

My best friend, Linda, and her husband, Jeff, asked me to move in with them, so I did. I called Joe while I was living there to find out if I could stay with him in Illinois and asked him how he felt about me. He didn't want me to come back, because, he said, "Gene and Joanie (Gene's new wife), are arguing about you coming back to Illinois. I like you fine, but Gene and Joanie are afraid that you will break up their marriage." The chance of Joe and me connecting was out of the question.

Christmastime was nearing. Doug, Diana, Ted, Justin, Mom, and I celebrated our last Christmas Day together, 1975. Mom and Ralph had divorced, and I began working as a volunteer with children.

CHAPTER 11

KISHWAUKEE

My pride was stretching and unfolding like a fruit that had just ripened and blossomed on a tree. I was being included in helping to promote the emotional, physical, and intellectual development of children, and I was becoming a new star on the horizon. After I completed holiday activities with the kids, Mom dropped by Linda's for a visit.

She walked through Linda's cherrywood front door all fidgety, shaky, and unsure of herself. I could sense the uneasiness in her quavering voice, and I was left without words to ward off her negativity. She looked in my eyes with her hazel-green blank eyes and asked, "Why are you accusing me of going to bed with Joe?"

I asked, "How and why? He's fifteen hundred miles away. You must have done it by remote control, Mom."

Hurt, she grabbed her purse and staggered out the door. She sped away in her broken-down white station wagon. I felt sorry for her and cried.

Two hours later, Joe called. "I'm sending you a hundred dollars to take the Greyhound to come back to live with me."

I was ecstatic. I had a feeling inside that Illinois was where I belonged, so I let the facility where I volunteered know I was leaving. In a couple of days, Doug took me to the bus depot and said to me, "I hope you know you are doing the right thing!"

I was less hesitant to travel all that way to be with the one I loved after hearing my brother's words. I brought my blue metal suitcase and a Catholic Bible called *The Way* that Linda gave me.

The Greyhound made a stop at Boys Town. I bought Doug a postcard with a picture of a statue on the face of the card. The picture was of a boy carrying a smaller boy on his back. It read, "He ain't heavy, he's my brother." Mom wrote a letter and said that my brother was hurt when he received my postcard. That made me feel sad! It's really hard to think about it now. On the other hand, it was a right move, and my brother couldn't have sent me off to be with a sweeter man than Joe.

When I arrived at Joe's in Illinois, I was having a painful bladder infection, and there was every indication that the medication I took for it was interfering with my psychotropic drug, Stelazine. I notified the doctor, and he told me to stop the Stelazine for a couple of weeks. My chemical imbalance, with all its hallucinations, fired up in full force again. Episodes of my onset grew too intense. I will relate them here.

I enroll in a sculpture class at Kishwaukee Community College. Out of pine and walnut, I make a table with the help of Joe. It has a swerved stand done by a lathe machine and a box foundation with a polyurethane top with playing cards all round it. Out of clay, I concoct a set of miniature bowling pins with a blue glaze, which are dried in a kiln with clay thumbs on the sides of the pins. They fit on top of the table.

I work with alabaster rock and have to file it down. In addition, I take a drama class and play a role opposite a character named File. I make a dollhouse, and I am touched and hurt when one of my dolls breaks her foot. I am bewildered when the bread I am making at home won't rise. I direct the play *Man of La Mancha* for our drama class, and I play the part of Dulcinea, while File and another guy costar with me as Sancho and Don Quixote. Something doesn't seem right. I am getting too much variety of activity.

It is when I take on the role of Charlotte in the play *Marat/Sade*. My partner is to be the actor who played File in my first play. I have my lines memorized. While we are rehearsing, File takes off his shirt and his back is loaded with those gross pimples, like the guy who tried to strangle me in San Francisco. I thought, My God, that's him. Why did he follow me all the way here from San Francisco? He even came to my house to rehearse!

The next day, when it is time to say our lines, I let someone go ahead of us. The teacher says, "You can be the monitor, Sherry."

I keep yelling at the actors, "Line!" at the most inappropriate times. Hurt and hurting everyone else, I stop yelling.

The teacher then says to my partner and me, "We don't have time for yours today." My partner and I are disappointed in not doing our improvisation of *Marat/Sade*.

I try out for *Summer and Smoke*, and I stop smoking prior. I get a small part in that play and can't take any more pressure. Trying out, memorizing lines, and dealing with pill pressure, I snap. I get anxious to go back to Oregon to Doug's high-school graduation. I take wooden boxes in our apartment and place Joe's Newberry's photo machine pictures and paste them on the box. Every time that Joe talks to me harshly, I put a penny in the box. I think he is a priest, and I confess to him.

Next, my voodoo hut with toothpicks. I manage to put them in front of the door when Joe walks in from work. He gets hexed—that's what I think. I sit out on the balcony and take off my clothes. A child sees me, someone says later. I'm thinking everyone is ganging up on me. I tape a *Playboy* picture of a redhead on Joe's bedroom wall, thinking it is I.

Joe is calling my counselor and Dr. Kirts, the psychiatrist, telling them how I do each thing, but since we aren't married, he can't have me committed. Legally I have to physically hurt myself or someone else before Dr. Kirts can force my hospitalization. Joe's kids come over Sunday for visitation. One Sunday, before my hospitalization, I make a chicken dinner with thin slices of boiled eggs and corn on top of the chicken.

Cathy says, "Daddy, do we have to eat this?"

They do eat some, just to be polite. We are nearing Easter holiday, so I am more or less off the hook. I macrame Becky a purse and Cathy a wall hanging. I paint Snow White and the seven dwarfs on the kitchen cabinets for David, but this is for their birthdays, and I am giving their presents to them for Easter two months ahead of time. Yuck!

My mind is speeding, and my body is slowing down. I can't sleep. Way too much stimulation. My bladder hurts, I am peeing blood, and still I am off the Stelazine. I macrame a witch and glue a sign, SCOPES TRIAL, on the back of its head. Joe tells me, as I am looking at his nude magazine, that there is a girl in there for whom he will drop me like a hot potato if she ever shows up on his doorstep. He goes to work, and I burn the picture in the sink.

Two days later, my next-door neighbor, who is always keeping me up by making passionate, painful noise with her roommate, causes me to lace up my roller skates. Then I retaliate by rollerskating nude in the apartment.

Jim, one of Joe's brothers, who is the landlord at the time, knocks on the door and asks, "What the heck is going on there?" He tells me to keep quiet.

I call the cops on myself. They don't do anything about it. It is two o'clock in the morning, almost Good Friday.

We are getting several calls a day. They wait for me to answer. Then they hang up. Joe thinks it's Joanie, and I think it's Eileen, his ex-wife. So I walk to Eileen's house to take a bubble bath in her upstairs apartment, where I lived with Gene. Then I tiptoe downstairs and wait for her to come home. When she comes home, she sees me sitting on her couch, and she says, "You took away my husband."

I say, "I want that picture I painted for you that's on the wall."

She steams. "You can't have it!"

"Stop me!" I stand and leap toward her.

I unhook the painting off the wall and take off with it. It is of the ocean. I knew she liked the music of the sea, so that's why I had painted it for her. I walk to Gene and Joanie's and knock on the door. Gene opens it up, and I shove the painting on him. He shoves it back on me.

"Do you want this? I don't want this." I throw it at him.

The air is thick. I can physically feel my body—blood, muscles, and bones—twist and tangle up so that there isn't an ounce of sanity left. I come back to the apartment, and I say to Joe, "Gene and Joanie put acid in the orange juice I bought at the store."

Joe is frantic on the phone. I scoot my table and dollhouse downstairs outside the apartment. I proceed to drop my Stelazine bottle, which I hadn't touched, behind a counter at a corner store. There are two guys there, and I almost take off with them. I entertain the thought in my mind.

But then something happens to me, something like never before. I'm not going to run anymore. I know I need help. This is a new twist for me. I am sick, and I am shooting for an IQ of 20, and I know it. It is like I'm at a senior citizen's center, and all these elderly ladies are sinking their hooks in my head, trying to crochet a coaster out of all of the follicles of my brain. What is real is no longer real, and what I call my sanity remains a vacant lot in my hard cruel world of reality. I run upstairs, this being a big nightmare. I see him, the one I love and the one I care for. No more running and hiding from my problems.

I go to Joe and say, "I need help! I'm ready to turn myself in." Joe drives me tearfully to Kishwaukee Hospital.

As I come through the door of the hospital, I say to the receptionist, "I'm turning myself in."

An aide from downstairs comes up to get me. The psych ward reeks of sterility in an iced-over atmosphere, and there is no turning back. Geraldine, the RN with white hair spinning out of control and beady green eyes beneath horn-rimmed glasses, meets me and shows me a room. She asks me what happened.

I say, "I'm having a chemical imbalance, and it is out of control."

"Is that right?" she retorts coldly.

I tell her that I am having a nervous breakdown. She opens up her hand, with its hard creases and lines, a hand that has pushed pills for years. In a harsh voice she orders, "Take these pills."

Being intimated by her, I take the two little blue tablets of Stelazine. That ends my restless streak of psychosis and sheds all of the life that I know of the past. Five minutes later, I rip off my clothes and start down the hall. It takes four attendants to put me in a double-door rubber room that I believe consists of walls made of rubber surrounding the room. I run to the window, tear down the curtains, and expose myself. The attendants come in the room, slap me down on a bed, strap both my hands and ankles to the sides of the bed, and inject me with more medicine. They lock both doors and leave me there for almost two days, coming in and out to administer medicine.

I scream at the top of my lungs, singing songs from *That's Entertainment,* and *1776.* "Sit down!" I yell as I look at the small glass window and see only darkness. I have the premonition that someone like Satan is coming to fetch me.

I fall asleep. It seems as if I am unconscious in the torture chamber for two days. It is worse than the hellhole I went through in San Francisco, Bellflower, and Salem. When I finally awaken, I am in another room. A male nurse is in the room, taking my straps off minute by minute. It seems like it takes hours to get them off. He can't work fast enough. My wrists and ankles and body are racked with pain. He is smoking a cigarette, and I ask if I can have one. He gives me a smoke, and I am in seventh heaven. He can possibly pass for Brad Pitt in *Legends of the Fall!*

My stay in this mental health facility is three long, regretful months. Why am I here? Will God ever quit screwing me over? It should be a one-week stay at the most. But three months?

Joe comes to see me. I embarrass him saying, "You smell like sex and have bad breath!"

But he keeps seeing me. I let loose and cry out, "Please let me go home!"

I can feel him mentally crying out, too. His children write me a little story. They even do a talk show for me. Joe tapes them doing a talk show interviewing him. On the recording, they call him Mr. Clean. Giggling, they ask him how many sinks he had cleaned and why he didn't grow some hair. His kids mean the world to him.

Their stories include "There Was an Old Lady Who Swallowed a Fly," which later links me to my sister and the way she cared for me and my disease. They draw the old lady with a fly in her mouth on a piece of paper, and Joe grades their paper. It is such a reward.

One day at Kishwaukee, I get a break from a man named Skip. He brings me out of the hospital to a place named Reality House, a halfway house to facilitate assimilation back into society. He tells me I will learn to cook, write, read, and sing all over again. They have a newspaper called *Insights,* for which I learn to be their typist. I write my articles in *Insights* and send copies everywhere. One time I make sloppy joes with corn on them, and everybody at Reality House eats them. I have a thing for corn—maybe this is the Brazilian in me. I wonder if they are too nice to say they know the difference.

Things get better at Kishwaukee, but the institution—as I called it in those days—makes me pay for the bad things as well as the good. I tell Dr. Kirts that I am ready to leave, and he says no.

So I call Joe to come and get me anyway. Two hours later Joe asks me where my meds are. I tell him reluctantly that the doctor discharged me without pills. I am hallucinating yellow flashes of light. We drive to the hospital, because I need sleep and rest, but they won't give it to me when I get there. Geraldine threatens me with straps. She is one of the biggest assholes who walks the face of this earth, next to Ralph. I finally sleep and continue to be locked up.

It is getting near the time of Doug's high-school graduation. I set my heart on seeing Doug graduate from high school, and I am in a race to get out of the hospital in time to get there. I make a calendar for the duration of my stay. All the games, hurts, mental anguish, and criticism the staff of the psych ward impose on me convinces me that I will never be the same, and I am not going back again. I am smoking cigarettes, and my trips to Reality House help me to become stronger. I decide to try to quit smoking, and I recall writing a cigarette schedule for myself. Geraldine gets into my drawer one night, takes my schedule, and accuses me of hiding things from her and the facility.

Burt, a crazy friend of mine, does all kinds of acrobatics with me. We stand on our heads in the rubber room and do handsprings in the hall. At night, he is having trouble. His room is four doors away. I get out of bed, lie on the floor, and listen for him. The next morning the nurse asks me why I slept on the floor.

I reply, "How would you like to sleep on a bed that you were tied to and can't relax yourself on? I don't understand."

A couple of days go by, and I am shoved into the locked room. I recite my role as Charlotte, which I know by heart from my improvisation of *Marat/Sade*. Funny thing, after I am done, they let me out of that room. This could have happened the first day I was there. There wouldn't have been a hassle!

I walk around Kishwaukee psych unit twenty times a day to get out of there. They transfer a woman who likes women to be with me. But that's not my preference.

She approached me one night. I don't think they knew what she was like. I made an attendant stand by our door all night to protect me, because she made an advance toward me. You see, I told Dr. Kirts in the morning when he did his rounds about her. I was released the next day. Before I left, one of the aides said to me, "You are a sucker."

I said, "I like lollipops," and that was the end of Kishwaukee. I left for good.

I was released in June 1976, and Joe and I made it to Doug's graduation. I was in a state of elation to be with my brother for his special day. I gave him the card table and the bowling pins that I made for a graduation present. I had been receiving disability checks from my stay at the Oregon State Hospital in Salem, and I got my job back working at Northern Illinois University in

DeKalb that fall, working five days a week, five hours a day. It was one of the greatest gifts I could have received, besides having Joe as my partner. Three more months at Reality House were in store for me.

CHAPTER 12

SOUTH AMERICA

Mom, Diana, Justin, and I took a trip to Brazil the following summer. I was still depressed and quite jittery. I can remember my psychiatrist saying, "I can't help you if you are depressed. Try to change your thinking."

That was Dr. Kirts for you, so kiss my grits if you please, Dr. Kirts. What that doctor didn't realize was that I was manic, and when it came to mood swings, I needed all the help I could get outside of the institution. When I had the swings, I was up laughing and down crying. I didn't belong in some damn hospital; I needed medicine.

Before I left for my trip, Joe made me go to Reality House. I didn't like the feeling of being there, because I had expectations of being treated for two mental illnesses, but I had to go. No one tended to my disease of manic-depression. As far as they knew, I was a paranoid schizophrenic. I know that Skip and the staff were only trying to help, and they did the best they could with the tools they had, but the patients and I were all sick. It was like visiting an ash can that stood in the hallway with everyone's dead cigarette butts and ashes. Voting on whom we liked and whom we didn't like and what we had to eat. How I suffered in thought. We went to field museums, threshing bees, the circus, pottery houses, and the like for therapy. I struggled with my sanity. I was depressed, lighting the end of my cigarettes with the butts of other members as they drifted off in a fog. Something had to kick the mania I endured.

So I got my shots and my passport, and I packed for my trip to Brazil. I'd always wanted to visit Brazil. It was Mom's country, but I didn't know if my mind could take it. Joe was staying in Illinois to continue his work at the printing factory, and traveling without Joe was like having my right arm disconnected.

I weathered the storm, and one rainy night on a slippery runway, Mom, Diana, Justin, and I arrived in Belem. The plane we boarded was a rickety contraption with paint chipping at the edges. It was amazing that we got up in the air and stayed there. Belem's airport left much to be desired. It was small, approximately one hundred feet by forty feet, and rustic. The walls had an eight-inch base of concrete with plywood walls extending from a six-inch base. We took off from Belem, stopped in Fortaleza, and then on to Sao Paulo. Mom's sister named Leo, who died of breast cancer, had a daughter, Myrna, who met us there. Throughout my life, Myrna wrote sweet letters, and Mom translated them for me. She and I were close, even though I lived a continent away. Myrna pointed to the street and gave me the Portuguese word for it. Then I told her, "Street." She repeated it.

Mom had been high on the bottle during the trip, and she hid most of it from her sisters, who were nuns in the convent. It would be a long time before I'd see my relatives again, and the opportunity moved in and made a sour spot in my stomach. I tried to use transference but didn't get anywhere. She insisted on having her bottle of booze with her.

I found time to rest in silence on a swinging hammock at Aunt Paula's house in Sao Paulo. Aunt Paula was Mom's youngest sister. As I concentrated on getting well, all my distresses and hospitalizations were swept away by the rush of ocean air swaying the colossal palm trees outside. Diana woke me from my nest, and she, Justin, Myrna, and I strolled, arm in arm, to the beach, with the warm sand squishing between our toes and on the bottoms of our feet. We cautiously avoided the sting of the jellyfish near the ocean waves. Diana was so infatuated with this bowl on the beach that she had Myrna pose with it, while she took her picture. The white sand and blue water accentuated Myrna's olive skin and turquoise-colored eyes. It was inspiring.

    We met my aunt, Sister Beatris, the head nun, and her assistant, in San Antonio near Brasilia. Aunt Beatris ran the convent in San Antonio. The people of the town called her "Mama." She had an assistant who brought her Coca-Cola and goods. The Coca-Cola was a stronger taste than the cola I tasted in the States. There seemed to be these little particles of caramel floating around in the bottom of the bottle, so each time I drank it, I was wondering if I was getting the real thing. We had an extension on our visit, and because we stayed past our time to return home, my aunt took me to the dentist. As I was sitting in the dentist chair, she asked the dentist for a prescription for Stelazine, which he gave to her after talking to me in Portuguese. It was hard figuring out what he said to me, but all I needed to do was nod my head. We picked up the bottle, and I took my medicine. Fears and paranoia subsided.

    Mom became mellower, and I couldn't wait to get back home. Before we left, Aunt Beatris had a play for us. The children of the village put on *Little Red Riding Hood* on the dirt floor of the church. I remembered the time when Evien and his Hawaiian friends sang "Lil' Red Riding Hood" to me next to my dorm window at SOC. Those were the sweet special times. So much had happened since then. That evening, Diana played her record *Locomotives* that she bought from a street vendor, on Auntie Beatris's record player, and I sat back and enjoyed my sanity. If Elton John had been singing "The Circle of Life" at that time, it would have been truly appropriate.

CHAPTER 13

A MOVE TO OREGON

Doug caught me in a moment, and I laughed, spitting my drink of Tab through my teeth and making a wheezing noise in my lungs. He flew in from Eugene to visit Joe and me in Sycamore for his winter break from the University of Oregon. I had just come home from Brazil, and we spent quality time watching the game shows, smoking cigarettes, and viewing the flatland with cornfields.

Doug had an infectious laugh and the sick sense of humor that ran in our family. I was guilty of the same thing. We'd joke about things that other people wouldn't necessarily joke about, such as this contestant on a game show who stuck her tongue out at the host as a nervous habit. She seemed to be wanting to impress the host by trying to get attention with it. Doug said, "Hey, Sherry, look at this girl. See the way she is sticking out her tongue?" We got worked up in stitches over something that seemed ridiculously humorous.

It was a short visit, not because of our crazy antics, which we recognized, but because he needed to make it back to O'Hare at a certain time, so he could return to college. The snowy weather was horrific. We never discussed Salem and my mental breakdown. He was sensitive. He didn't want to bring it up and hurt my feelings. He said that we would have to take a trip to Brazil sometime, but we never got the chance to. I loved that kind person.

After Doug left, Joe and I planned a trip to Ashland with Joe's kids to visit Diana and her family. We went to the Jacksonville Museum, and Diana made tuna sandwiches. We did some doodle art on the lawn. It was fun exploring all the memorabilia and artifacts of the Wild West inside the museum. I learned all about the struggles other people went through just to eat, live, and survive. Somehow my pain didn't quite serve itself; it couldn't measure up to the pain that the people went through in the eighteen hundreds and earlier periods of time. I sometimes wonder what they took for their mental illness. Vitamins perhaps, or healthy food? Or were they just locked away for good for something that wasn't their fault? It must have been very difficult for them. I had so much to be thankful for.

We went to see my friends Linda and Jeff, who now lived in Medford. We swam in her pool, which was seven feet deep. I climbed the plush yellow-green carpeted stairwell of their two-story house and played "He Ain't Heavy, He's My Brother" on their jukebox. I was thinking about Doug and missing him. I would close my eyes and visualize him and me in the gleaming reflection of the two figures etched into the crystal-blue Saint Christopher's medal around my neck. The saint carrying the prophet on his back. I thought to myself, "I will carry you, dear brother, through all eternity for everything you've done for me. Thanks for walking the mile in my shoes. You ain't heavy, you're my brother."

We camped out at KOA campgrounds at the coast near Lincoln City (close to where I was abused in 1968), and we mapped out a stopover in Portland. All I could remember were the fun times I spent with Alice and June, my roommates there, roller-skating, fishing, and dancing at the beach. The ocean has a strange way of healing our wounds. The air can be so encouraging. I felt happy and in ecstasy at this time of my life. I finally got to do something with the children, especially Joe and Eileen's precious children. But my ecstasy burned a fuse as I reminisced about how hard it was when I took a couple of trips by myself from Illinois to Portland to visit Mom. I had been in inner turmoil over incidents that happened with my mom and me about Joe and the kids and my visits with Aunt Deanna, who lived in Deer Island. It was hard to be happy and stay happy.

The trips my mom would lay on me were like this: "Joe doesn't want you, Sherry. He's just using you to see what he can get." Or after I saw Aunt Deanna: "Deanna couldn't care less about you. Nobody likes or wants you Sherry. You are a nothing, a nobody."

It left an imprint on my brain. I had to stay on top of these remarks and just say, "She's an alcoholic and will never change."

Even though her words were piercing and sank deep, I suffered with manic-depression, and I thought at that time that I was going to fight my mom to her grave. I wasn't going to think her way. So on my vacations and in the time spent with my relatives, I took very little initiative to be with Mom.

On the brighter side, at one of the campgrounds I was setting my hair with rollers, and I called Becky "Little Miss Organization," because she was picking things up and putting them in places of her preference. All of a sudden I was dropping my rollers everywhere like a clumsy juggler on an off day.

She came back to me in the bathroom and said, "Hello, Miss Organization."

Later at a restaurant, Becky and I were laughing so painfully hard at each other over what Joe had said that he had to separate us. It made our stomachs sore just to look at each other. And those were the special times.

It was a month before I returned to work at NIU. A girlfriend of mine from Reality House, Jeanne, had moved to Atlanta. She won a trip to Atlanta for a two-week stay on a radio contest. I went there for the two weeks as her guest and learned how to water-ski and ministered to her about life and her boyfriends. I had gone off one of my Stelazines and called Joe about it. He said that it was OK, since I had told him that I was getting dizzy. We agreed that I needed to talk to Dr. Kirts when I came back home. After arriving home from my trip, I had a session with Dr. Kirts, and he said, "You cut back on one of your Stelazines. That's not OK." He was mad. "That was an unwise thing to do. Go back to taking your regular dose."

So I did, and I never went off my medication again. I hate to admit it, but I must give Dr. Kirts credit where credit is due. He is one of the reasons why I kept taking my medication on a regular basis and decided to follow my doctor's treatment plan for the duration of my life.

But there were downsides to the effects of Stelazine, and because of my hospital experience, Joe was getting fed up with me for sleeping a lot. So he asked me to please read *Your Erroneous Zones* by Dr. Wayne W. Dyer, which had just come out on the market. I thought if anyone needed it, he did, but I was wrong. I read it and loved it. It was just like a parallel to the life I chose (my hitchhiking excursions) before I reached Joe. I followed my instincts without hurting anyone, and I was successful in finding someone to love. I relearned a lot of what I already knew of life and about my choices, but mainly, I became more independent by reading the book.

During the four or five years Joe and I lived together, we had an emotional strength, and our chemistry was intact. I didn't think I could ever possibly love another man or let another man into my life. I remember Joe asking me, "OK, what do you like to do for fun, Sherry?" So I told him that I liked to walk. We walked all over DeKalb and Sycamore till our muscles gave out, and we could walk no more. I could never get tired of walking with him. Exercise was such a help in strengthening my mind and getting in touch with my spiritual, mental, and physical needs.

I took up oil painting again, and learned how to oil paint in the basement of a ninety-one-year-old artist, Cora Minor, who had taught Joe's mom when she was a girl in school. She was a master in DeKalb and Sycamore's world of art. Her brushstrokes were so fine and firm that it was difficult to interpret her painting process in one take. I would drive through the blizzards just to take a class from her.

Our plan was to get out of Illinois because of the blizzardy winters and move closer to Eileen and the kids, who had packed up and left for Las Vegas. I felt sorry for Joe. He cried because Eileen had left without telling him. He had invested his love and time in raising the kids and honored his visitation rights. It didn't seem fair. The only way to strengthen communication with them was to head for Oregon, where my family lived. Mom sent Joe an *Oregonian* newspaper. He contacted an employer for a printing job through a want ad, and the employer responded.

On our way to Oregon, ironically, the first city we drove to was Klamath Falls. It was snowing in the spring. Here I was in my Rabbit driving to Oregon! Who would have thought it?

Our trip to Oregon took five days. There was a never-ending stretch of flatlands through Nebraska and a scary stay in Nevada. I was drinking Tab at the time. We stopped at a store near a gas station in Nevada. It wasn't open, and I needed a Tab fix soon. Joe was losing patience with me for delaying our getting on the road. In frustration and anger, I accidentally backed into the gas pump and put a dent in my fender. Joe got out of his truck and literally cussed me out. I wasn't going to fight him at this stage of the game, so I followed him. Later, he stopped at a rest area, threw his arms around me, and apologized. "I'm sorry Bunky," he said. I felt bad, but at other times I would have taken off and gone the other way.

My cousin met us at the Oregon Health and Science University (OHSU) located on the top of a hill in Portland. She had friends who were moving from Beaverton who were renting a house. We stayed there, since they were on vacation. When their landlord happened to call up to check on his place, I answered and said, "We are your new renters." He had a fit. How dumb that was of me! Joe got on the phone and wiggled his way out of that one. I would often stick my foot in my mouth, saying and doing inappropriate things that I didn't mean, especially if I was going through a lot of stress or my meds were off (most likely my meds were a little off). It took poor Joe to get me out of those situations.

We ended our search for apartments and settled down in a house on Mason Lane in Portland. That weekend we traveled to visit my brother in Eugene. He broke the news to us that he was gay. I said that I was going to be a topless dancer again, so if he didn't mind that, I didn't mind that he was gay.

I sought help from a therapist named Jim Friesen. I said, "No, I'm not comfortable with Doug's choice of sexuality. I want it to go away. I have a hard time sleeping. I want to cry, because I think Doug will die."

Doug introduced us to his boyfriend, also named Doug. We stayed at Doug and Doug's one night and heard a popping noise in the morning. Mount St. Helens blew her top. Mount St. Helens, a volcano located in southern Washington State, had erupted and spewed ash all over the streets of Portland. It was sad to hear the reports of people fleeing from their campgrounds around the mountain, getting singed by its fires. A man named Harry Truman, who was warned to evacuate, said that he would go down with his mountain. Later, when I became a certified nurse's aide, I received a vial of ash from his friend—my patient Cecil—who mined with him.

I started working for Mark and Eddie again and thought I was smart to smoke Now and More cigarettes. I had become quite the nicotine addict. I was stressed and challenged by Titanic Tina, who had a big blonde hairdo, a knockout figure, and big boobs. Because I was thirty-one years old, the pressure and competition that went with the career was detrimental to my mental health. I decided to bag it and never returned. Besides, there were better things waiting for me around the corner.

Joe and I traveled to Las Vegas to pick up Becky and David for a visit. We stopped to see my dad and his wife, Mary Jo, who moved to Middletown, California. The trip had a damaging effect on my personality. Dad was impressed with Joe's political views and the world. He asked us to come dancing at the country club. I told him I was a topless dancer, and he said, "Good."

Later that night I said, "I have been hospitalized." He felt bad for me and was empathetic toward me. "It would make me nuts to be strapped up and treated like you were," he said.

I told him that they had no choice. When the time had come for Joe and me to leave, I said, "Dad, I don't want to go to Las Vegas."

He said, "Your stepdaughter, Cathy, is graduating from high school, isn't she? Isn't that what you said? It will be fun. Go and have fun with the kids."

Worried, I lingered. "But Joe's ex-wife will be there."

He reassured me, "You'll be all right." Joe and I departed.

We met Eileen and the children at Eileen's house in Nevada. David found something that scared the living daylights out of me. It looked like an atrocious demon with miniature horns—a horny toad he captured in his backyard that he wanted to bring back to Portland with him. It was important to let him keep it, since it was one of David's many security blankets, though I felt hexed by it. Cathy was as pretty as a picture with her strawberry-blonde bob tucked under the blue silk graduation cap that matched her blue eyes. She had been sweet and supportive of Joe and me. She had kept the kids in line most of her life and cared for them as a mother would, even when she lived with her mom in Illinois.

On our trip, Joe, David, and I went to Pahrump, Nevada, to be with Eileen's folks. The mystic country had enticed me. It was weird. I strolled around the sunset-shadowed pathway with Eileen's mom, and we talked about Eileen. I had to hold a lot in. It was embarrassing. I could tell that I wasn't welcome there. I realized how much they loved their daughter, Eileen. I had heard stories about Eileen's relationship with her father from Joe and Eileen herself, although I didn't realize how close they were. I tried to conceal my thoughts about my medicine and dry mouth, because I knew how she felt about my Stelazine. I wouldn't let her think she was part of my mental problem, for fear she might rub it in. In my mind, it would mean that she had won. So I suffered. With my mouth as dry as it was from my buffer, Artane, I could have caught a thousand grasshoppers with my tongue. She asked Joe to fix her car and rewarded him with a six-pack of beer. Then, shortly afterward, we left.

We arrived in Portland with bittersweet memories. The company I worked for granted me a vacation before I left for Vegas, and when I returned for work, they fired me for no apparent reason. It was a phone-soliciting job, and the work wasn't very steady. Nevertheless, I had my heart set on working to prevent a crisis, which I was anticipating going through with the children. Now I had no job.

Becky, age twelve, and David, age eight, were typical adventuresome kids. I took them swimming every day, but they wanted to watch soaps afterward. Thinking with rocks in my head, I said, "You can watch an hour of television a day." Sometimes I'd turn off the TV if they ran ten minutes over the hour. Now I understand why they rebelled. Becky looked for jobs in the paper for me, and my goal was to work as a nurse's aide after they left. She found a strawberry-picking job, so I agreed to work with her, picking strawberries side by side in the crisp mornings. She'd spend all her money on M&MS.

"Don't you think it would be nice for you to spend it on gifts?" I asked her.

"No," she replied, furious with me.

I really underestimated the logic of a child, and I harped at her about it. Oh, how I wish I had those days to do over again!

We went to the airport every night to see Joe while he worked as a printer. They counted how many cigarettes I smoked going to and from the airport. They asked me how many cigarettes I smoked a day and why I smoked, and I said, "I don't owe you any explanation."

Things got to be real messy, and I wanted to go on vacation. I'd had my fill of kids. After strawberry picking, Joe wanted me to get a full-time job. He kept telling me I needed another pill.

One day when my car wasn't working, he fixed it. "How does it drive?" he asked me.

"It doesn't sound quite right," I answered.

He miscalculated my feelings and said, "That pisses me off. Eileen gave me a beer for fixing her car, and you tell me yours doesn't sound right."

That was the worst thing anyone could have said to me. To bring Eileen into the picture like that was the wrong thing to do. Becky began bad-mouthing me, but I wouldn't hit her. I vowed never to hit a child. Joe began another argument, and Becky stepped into it, mimicking me. Joe told me to shit or get off the pot. My relationship with Joe, the handsome, sweet, sincere intellect whom I loved for five years, with whom I came all the way from Illinois to Oregon, was unraveling before my eyes. Brazil, Kishwaukee, visitation rights. It was a matter of time, and it would be all over.

I said, "OK," and grabbed my purse and drove six hours to Diana's in Ashland with eight dollars in my wallet.

My friend Linda and her husband Jeff were in the midst of a divorce. She moved from White City to an apartment not far from Ashland. She would give me a place to stay. My sister and I went to a Goodwill store and bought clothes for me so I could apply for jobs. Diana bought me a work suit for two dollars. Because I filed for mental health disability, I also became a happy recipient of welfare and food stamps, and I was issued financial aid. I connected with Linda to arrange for my belongings to be brought to me at her apartment.

Harry & David, a huge fruit and candy factory, became my employer. I cut chocolate squares and kneaded dough for cakes. It was fun seeing the little old ladies—or should I say big broads—with their hairnets on, cutting candies, eating fudge, and samplings sweets as they went down the conveyor belt. Linda and I met over coffee on my break. We bumped into a guy whom we went to high school with. He told me he had been living with someone for ten years. That night we had an affair that would haunt me for the rest of my life. He was married. I didn't know about it. Later, I asked him if it was just a one-night stand, and he said yes. I was relieved and hurt at the same time—relieved that I wouldn't end up with a jerk like him and hurt that I got intimate with someone so soon.

CHAPTER 14

PRESSING ON

Linda left a message on the machine saying, "Meet me at the club. I have someone who wants to see you."

There was Joe. "Maybe I'll be going back to Portland with your stuff," Joe said as we hugged and kissed repeatedly. Joe had just arrived from Portland, and I had gotten off work from Harry & David.

I didn't know what to do or say about my affair. After all, Joe and I had broken up. It was at Linda's that I talked to him about my mistake, and he cried. I wanted to jab myself in the eye thirty thousand times.

"Has my little girl gone out on me?" he asked.

"I went out with a *married man*," I cried.

Joe sobbed. Tears concealed his handsome face. I couldn't sleep, so I called the crisis line. Then at three in the morning, I drove to Ashland to vent to Ted. When I came back to Linda's, Joe made a decision to leave and took off for Portland the next morning.

I stayed at Linda's till August then moved to Roseburg. Dell always had her arms open for me. She was amicable in that respect. While staying at her house, I applied for a Head Start job and took a certified nurse's aide course at Umpqua Community College. I learned about the circulatory system, the brain, the skeleton, the muscles, and nutrition. I learned how to lift, wash, and feed patients, and all about decubiti and dying. I resisted holding on to things that were sensitive to me, and finally my world began to rock.

I found myself in a spontaneous place. I learned from a friend where Chip, my teenage idol, lived and impulsively called him up. I didn't realize how much he cared for me. He joked about how I'd left him, and I reciprocated by saying that he'd left me, and then we laughed. It was forty years since we'd last touched base. We decided it was too late to do anything about it. He was married and had children, but he could still elevate my feelings. When we hung up, I wrote him a letter as a means of healing and sent it to him.

Socializing with guys became hard on account of my mental illness. I had sworn off drugs quite a long time back and didn't want those back in my life. It was a struggle to say no to the weed imposed on me. I ended up falling head over heels for a guy I'd graduated from high school with, who was paralyzed from the waist down from a motorcycle accident. We dated for a while, but I couldn't participate actively in parties that we were invited to. I couldn't do the socializing he wanted to do. I was just coming out of a relationship, and if push came to shove, I wanted to be with Joe, because he was there for me emotionally. So we parted and went our own ways.

Children were my main interest, and I volunteered at a Head Start center to read and sing with the children. It was a warm, genuine experience. Linda moved to Roseburg, and I'd come over, and we'd drink at the mansion she worked at. I didn't realize what alcohol was doing to my chemical imbalance. Somehow, I thought it was all right to drink, but it wasn't. I started to use alcohol to give me a lift, wipe out my circumstances, and sleep. I was becoming the shadow of my mother, and every time I looked into the mirror, all I could see was a monster of a face looking back at me. I was feeling guilty about drinking. I started making excuses about the way I was. I felt like a louse.

I went to AA once or twice, but I couldn't quit mixing booze with my medication. I couldn't find much help. The group told me I was just an alcoholic. Mom had called me from Portland, which complicated things. She told me she had been mugged and was going to find the guy who did it. She was crazy drunk, so I drove to the big city, bringing Dell with me. We met Joe and set out to find her. We drove to the town square and into the heart of Portland. There was Maria with her pants half-down and a bottle in a sack in her hand. I felt so bad.

After taking care of Mom, I went back to work. I was living in a studio about twenty-four by twenty-four feet that Dell had rented for me. I was cramped. I went to bars often. One day I was surprised by a visit from Joe. Bob Seger was singing, "We've got tonight. Who needs tomorrow? We've got tonight, babe. Why don't you stay?" "We've Got Tonight" became my favorite song. Joe's timing was good. We went to a bar and then home and got intimate. I picked up on his cues and slept in his tenderness. He went back to Portland the next day, and I cried.

Mom sobered up and traveled to Roseburg on the Greyhound. She came to my tiny apartment and told me to play "Sunrise Sunset" from *Fiddler on the Roof* on the record player. She said, "This little separation from Joe is a good thing."

"Mom, do you ever dream?" I asked.

"Not much, why?"

"Because I met Joe on a mountain in a dream when I was a teenager. His eyes were crystal blue, and his hair was coal black. His arms could carry my weight and two cords of wood in gold. He swirled me around the Green Hills with his strong back, towering over me by nine inches. He was electrifying. We danced under the falling stars to the Dr. Kildare song, "Three Stars Will Shine Tonight." He took me away from all my suffering that night on the mountainside. I didn't tell you that dream, because I thought you knew, but I did tell my sister, so it was safe. She has probably forgotten it by now."

Mom had me run around the track at the park five times. I'll say one thing—Mom was a pretty good influence on me at times.

I was lucky to have broken up with Joe for a while. I learned that I could make it through life without him, but I was lonely and felt deficient in some ways. My old roller-skating teacher, Steve, opened up a new rink in Roseburg. After hearing his name on the radio, I hurried to the rink, holding my white boots and precision wheels, and greeted him. He asked me if I wanted to teach tiny tots. I said, "I'd love to!"

Then there I was with ten little toddlers following me to the middle of the rink, wondering which foot to glide with next and where to put their skates down. It was a wonderful rejuvenating experience. I found my niche for the first time in a long time, and I felt like I belonged. My mind was full of sunbeams.

Teaching skating lasted three months. Because of my insecurities and my shakiness, I put my skates once again to rest. I was giving off an air in such a way that people and friends seemed to be afraid of me, and it caused me to worry excessively about myself. I understood that I couldn't be best friends with everybody, but because I was going overboard in sharing myself with others, people formed negative opinions about me. I was asked to join religious groups, but the logical sensible portion of me told me, "Don't do it. Don't get involved." Maybe it would have helped, and I wouldn't have been so awkward. One day, two doors away from my studio, a girl with stringy black hair wanted me to come to her apartment to see her picture. I went over to her unit to see what she had done. It was a drawing of Satan. I gasped. It shook me up, but I didn't let her know. It had horns, a pitchfork, and a big belly. I just turned to her and said, "That's nice." I left.

She borrowed ten dollars from me. I didn't have money for my pills, but I gave it to her anyway. She never paid it back. Another day, she and a friend came by and knocked on my door, but I didn't open it up. They left me alone, but I called a priest and said, "Father I need to have an exorcism done."

The priest made an appointment to see me. He was a charismatic priest with earth-brown hair bordering his heart-shaped face and hypnotic blue eyes that invited me to confide in him. Underneath his clerical garb was a physique that women would die for. I came to the church, and he showed me all the food that the parish had brought for Thanksgiving. He placed his hand on my head, and said a few words, and I was done.

The following week, Linda invited me to her mansion with her new boyfriend and his friend whom she'd met in church. Her boss was out of town. My date looked pale and aloof—somewhat like the Pee Wee Herman type. He made me want Joe more. I asked Linda, "Do you still have the book you were reading called *Dynamic Imaging* by Norman Vincent Peale?"

She said, "Sure." She handed it to me, and I walked down the mansion's long winding staircase and began to read it. I excused myself and said to everyone, "I have to go." I got into my Rabbit and sped home.

It was nine o'clock. I had been separated from the man I loved for a year and a half. I reached for the phone. "Joe, can I please come back to live with you?" I said.

"Well, I don't know."

"I'm going to become a prostitute if I don't come back!" I persisted.

"OK, two weeks, and you can move up here," he relented.

"Thanks, Joe. I love you so much." I hung up and yelled at the top of my lungs, "I'm going back. I'm really going back to Joe!"

I was singing octaves higher than any note ever sung by an opera singer. After two weeks of fussbudgeting about, I moved in with Joe in Portland and touched base with my counselor, Jim. Sometimes I saw Jim once a week to keep myself intact and to relax. I let go of all the bad that happened to me. We talked about my symptoms and the side effects of my pills. Some people thought this consistency of seeing a counselor weekly was a weakness of mine, but I listened to my inner voice, and it told me it wasn't so. I kept up with my sessions.

Shortly after I arrived in Portland, Joe was talking to the owner of the Laundromat. He was an old and decrepit man and seemed like he didn't have a care in the world. I was reading a *Newsweek*. I went over to the owner and asked, "You look like you have been around a long time. Do you know all the names of the presidents of the United States in order?"

He seemed flabbergasted. "Not really."

I couldn't believe I said that. Joe had a shocked look on his face, as if he didn't know me. He changed the subject with the old man, and I sat back down. We laugh every now and then when we think of it. But I hadn't been able to continue it long. I knew I needed psychiatric help.

I was hired by Mount St. Joseph convalescent center on the graveyard shift to take care of the dying and help the living to live comfortably. At the beginning of the employment, I had been drinking in my spare bedroom. Joe happened to be outside my door. I opened it up, and he was crying, "Sherry, you can't mix alcohol with your pills."

His face was pale, and I could tell he was holding back his nervousness by making a dent in his thumbnail with his index fingernail. I felt his emotion. One look at the expression on his face rid me of my thirst for alcohol and got me out of my rut for good. Realizing how much he cared for me stopped me from drinking. I never have touched liquor since. It's hard for me to fathom what I would have been like if I had continued to take my medication with booze. I might have ended up in the hospital again or worse.

Joe's brother John died that year. I dreamed of his death a couple of nights before it happened. He had fallen off a Ferris wheel in my dream. He was holding his head, saying, "I didn't die." Depression filled my head with fear. Joe asked me to explain to him what had happened, so I revealed my dream. We were called two days afterward and told that John died of a heart attack. John's face was so real.

Several weeks later, I took Mom out for lunch and dropped her off at the bank. My negative premonitions stayed active in my mind, and I couldn't force them out. I couldn't change my line of thinking. Why couldn't I have premonitions of good things? Was it my imbalance or my medicine that was making me think this way? I was having dreams of things that would happen the next day. I was thinking I caused them, because I thought of them the night before.

Mom was not an exception to the rule. So when I received a call later that day from Eastmoreland Hospital telling me that my mom was there and in a coma, it didn't faze me. It was exactly what I thought had happened. The doctors found out she had diabetes. I bought a notebook with a mama cat and her kittens penciled on it and wrote her poems about herself. She showed her appreciation, and in her spare time, she drew pictures of beautiful floating butterflies and butterflies smoking cigarettes with the caption, "You've come a long way, baby," in the notebook.

Before she was admitted, she was into some positive religious groups like the Infinite Way. She traveled to Hawaii with friends and then stayed at the YWCA to beachcomb. "The monarchs are in season and they are all over here," she wrote. I had cut ties with her, but in one letter she sent a picture of her on a surfboard holding a ukulele, with a wreath of flowers around her head, riding the surf on a big wave. That was so like my mom. She really did have a sense of humor, and I'd like to remember her that way. When I took her home from the hospital, she started going to diabetic classes to see what she could eat and drink, but she started drinking alcohol again. She said for the hundredth time that she was going to give up alcohol. She struggled so much.

I was experiencing painful periods then. My family doctor said that he needed to perform a hysterectomy, because I couldn't take the pill that could treat my endometriosis. I wrote Mom and told her that I was having surgery. I had been trying to be secretive about my existence. I knew if she saw me, she would go on a binge, even though I told her that I was having the operation and where and when it was going to take place. She visited me before my surgery and went to my room after it was completed. When I awoke from surgery, the pain was horrendous. It was like I had been jabbed in the abdomen a thousand times. My belly would tweak and throb. I glanced over at Mom. She was hunched over in her tan overcoat, sitting on a chair near my bedside. I asked her for a cigarette. She lit a Virginia Slim for me. (It was 1984.) Then I asked, "How are you doing?"

She twisted her hands. "I've been getting drunk every night. Isn't that what you want to hear?"

"Please leave," I insisted.

"Why?" she asked.

I pointed to my abdomen. "I don't want you to see me like this."

It was terrible for both of us. She called the next day to see if I was all right. I couldn't keep anything down. The pain was stifling. It worried her. I told the nursing staff that I didn't want to see her again. This was just one of the games Mom and I played with each other. But I stopped myself from creating a scene. I wasn't going to get mentally ill over it, and I wasn't going to let her get to me. I would call my sister or talk to my brother, my brother-in-law, Joe, or my counselor, Jim.

⌒

Becky and David lived with us during this critical time. My hysterectomy had an unsettling effect, and Mount St. Joseph was stressful. The kids were trophies to Eileen until they became typical teenagers. Then they were pawned off on us to deal with. It caused us all to be on top of each other in a small house. Although Becky gave me a bad time, she had a heart of gold. She'd ask me what to do about her boyfriends, and she would confide in me as much as she could about her mom. She played the flute beautifully and filled our small hut with dancing melodies. She would do needlepoint and gave me her homemade Christmas gifts. I was still smoking cigarettes, and she let me know that it was not acceptable.

No matter how much trouble I gave her, she graduated from high school. Becky was weakened by my talking about her on the phone when she could listen. I'd tell people she was just like her mom. But she prevailed. It became a give-and-take situation with us: the adolescent moods would invariably irk me, and my resentment of her mother calling us would irk her. I took an aerobics class with her and her friend and tried to make the rough times smooth.

One day Becky was feeling bad about her boyfriend. He was treating her wrong. When we came home from aerobics, I tossed her a pillow and said, "Here, kid, throw the pillow."

We threw pillows at the wall to get her frustrations out, calling him almost every name in the book. The highlight of our experience together was when we went to a Men At Work concert. When the band played, we rocked out: snapping our fingers, swinging our hips, singing the lyrics to "Down Under." One day, I went to the library and checked out a book to help me go through Becky's obstinate teenage period of her life. It was a book for stepparents called *The Successful Stepparent* by Helen Thomson. The book gave me insight into stepchildren and their loyalties, and how innocent and nonobjective they can be when dealing with a stepmom. It must have been very painful for the children to go through a divorce. First, they suffered with Joe during the marriage with Eileen, and then they suffered through the divorce itself. Then they saw me going through the suffering of two people I loved dearly, Mom and Doug.

I only hit Becky once, but she deserved it. She played on my sanity sometimes, and I hated it. But when the going gets tough, the only way to go to the top is up. She moved from our house into a new apartment. That hate was compensated by love when she moved out and said that she was going into the army. She played the flute in the army band. She married and became a member of the army band along with her husband. They were placed in the infantry division and sent to the Persian Gulf, participating in Desert Shield and Desert Storm. President George H. W. Bush had called off the troops, so their lives were spared. I cried despondently when she was over there. I thought she was going to die. I sent her a music box playing the tune "Fur Elise" to cheer her sprits. Whatever it was between us became a sea of emotions of gratitude and appreciation, drenched with love and respect and honor that no stepparent in our situation could touch.

CHAPTER 15

HEALING THROUGH PAINTING

Doug's boyfriend, Doug, has AIDS. It's a sorrowful relationship between the two. They both have alcoholic parents and a member of their family who has been hospitalized for mental health reasons (me and Doug A.'s brother). But now my brother calls to tell me his lover has AIDS. I feel like pulling my hair out.

I leave an artificial rose and a graduation card for Becky. She is to graduate from high school. Her mom will be up for graduation, so I take the Greyhound to Eugene to meet my brother. While his friend is on a "healing" walk, Doug and I take in a Richard Pryor movie, not realizing how close death can be. I question whether, since his friend has AIDS, he will get it, too. Doug says that he has always been celibate.

When I return to Portland, I get a call from my brother. "I have AIDS."

What do I do? That just killed the spirit inside of me. A hundred questions are going through my mind. What's the next step? How long will he live? What can I do for him? I feel his pain. I don't know what to do with myself, and I feel pain for him and pain for our situation. Unbelieving, I tell him I will come and take care of him. He says, "Don't jump the gun."

I ask a doctor for help while my tears of confusion flood my heart. The doctor orders Xanax for me and says it will help me to forget. He seems insensitive toward the subject of AIDS and says he will do this instead of sending me to a psych ward. "But do I really need a psych ward?" "Isn't my reaction a normal reaction?"

He just shakes his head and says, "Not necessarily so."

My brother's disease fluctuates and every once in a while triggers a remission. I make him lots of gifts and send get-well cards, but I go overboard, and he sends a letter to me. It goes like this:

> *Dear Sherry, I have an opportunity to be out of town this weekend, and I would rather go than visit on Sunday. This brings up a request that I have—could you possibly back off a little bit for now? I really appreciate your concern, and that's enough for me. I hope you feel it isn't necessary to send so many cards. I would rather you save your money—it must be getting expensive. I'm in no position to return your cards, and it only seems to make me feel worse. So please! No more cards. Also, no more gifts. I don't have the room for them.*
>
> *Please understand that I still love you very much, but I do not have any energy for you right now. The best thing to do is to leave me alone for a while. And let me concentrate on healing myself and putting my life in order.*
>
> *Sorry we can't meet this weekend.*
>
> *I will let you know when we can get together again.*
>
> *Your brother*
> *Doug*

Doug is special to me and so supportive, but this letter hurts me, because I want to give my all to him. I love him, and I want his AIDS. "Please don't die," I cry.

I vividly remember one time when I broke up with Joe. I was in Eugene visiting Doug. We, Doug and I, went to a gay bar and danced to disco music. He would shimmy and shake his shoulders, and clumsily I would mimic him to learn his technique. He laughed. "Sherry, I had more fun dancing with you than anybody I have ever danced with!"

I had a feeling in my heart that he was going to die from AIDS. I thought so because of a premonition I had when he told me that he was gay. I always dreamed of him living in a gay green house and dying in it. He did end up living in a green house with a gay man. It was déjà vu all over again.

After my twentieth high-school reunion, Joe and I go to visit Doug, and he and I share cigarettes all night long, developing a bond that no one could pierce. We talk about the Christmas Eve incident that we clearly will never forget. Ralph had given Doug a flashlight to find me, and he beat him when he couldn't find me. But when I question him about the time Ralph ran upstairs, Doug wouldn't tell me what Ralph did to him. He says that he will never tell, "and you'll never find out, Sherry." And I don't think I did.

To conclude our evening, Doug makes me promise not to go back to the mental institution ever again, no matter what happens to him. I have been hospitalized five times and he figures it is enough. I agree and that is good enough.

I came back home from Eugene and made dolls out of clay that year. I dressed them up like the people I thought they resembled and gave them away with candy for gifts. I made one for Doug for his birthday and another for an RN friend of mine.

I remember when Doug's friend died. It is though it was happening today. I had a cyst behind my ear, and when I popped it, blood came shooting out at the mirror. Then I got into my car, headed down the street, and got into a wreck. I hit someone's fender as I bolted into another lane. When I arrived home, I purchased a second Greyhound bus ticket to travel to Eugene to take care of Doug's friend, not knowing that he had passed away. I had a feeling something was haywire. I met Doug in Eugene, and he let me know Doug A. had died. He asked me to stay for the wake.

I ironed my brother's clothes: a black silk bow tie, stiff white shirt, and black wool pants and suspenders. With his dusky-brown Afro and bright-blue eyes, he looked like a precious doll. I greeted everyone at the door when they came to pay their respects for his friend. There, on the fireplace, Doug had arranged all these delicate pictures and flowers for him and his friend.

The day of the wake I stopped smoking but started up again; all I could do is to heave my guts out all night long.

I come to see Jim Friesen, my counselor, for a session. Mom jumped out a tenth-story window in a retirement home and committed suicide the day before I see him. I take her picture with me. It is the one with her in her blue-and-white flowered muumuu, clutching a sunflower that she had grown so carefully in the Green District.

I drive to the restaurant in downtown Portland that she frequented and talk with the staff about her death. My knees are wobbly, and the earth is exploding, as if crumbling beneath me. I stand shaking in disbelief. Why did she have to jump? With tremors in my fingers, I hand them her picture to post on their bulletin board and leave. I can't remember their names or the restaurant I am at.

Everything is a blur; only their caring faces are brought to focus. Moisture pops out like sprinklers from the pores of my face. I race home, throw myself on my bed, and grab hold of a soft crocheted pillow that Mom had given me at one time as a present. Broken tears envelop her pillow. What I imagine to be rain, pouring down on me like glue, presses slippery strands of my red hair against my pale face. My clothes cling to my body as I lie sobbing in pain and sorrow. My mind succumbs to depression, and anxiety takes over. It is like a game they are playing with me. First depression and then anxiety takes turns with me, until my head becomes heavy and dizzy. I am wringing wet with sweat.

I can see her lifeless body on the cement, sprawled out by a garbage dumpster, where she had been discovered by a garbage collector that morning. She climbed on an apartment chair to get over the wall of the fire exit and plunged to her death. I want to scream, but a feeling inside holds me back. It is the feeling of helplessness you get when you lose a person you love and then realize that you can't have her back again. I enter the twilight zone. Visions of lilies in Salem's insane asylum dance through my head. David, my stepson, is there in the room next to me. He sees what sorry shape I am in. He doesn't say a word and leaves in a hurry. I know he is hurt.

I take it upon myself to feel guilty about her tragedy.

The day before she died, she rang me and said, "You don't have a job yet do you?" I was already working. She was drunk.

So I said, "Leave me alone!" and I hung up on her.

She called me back, and I let the phone ring for the time it took me to do some dishes and make a little lunch—about five minutes. Then she hung up. She was taking Xanax, like I did when I heard about Doug testing positive for HIV. I quit that pill cold turkey, but she couldn't.

I pretended that it was right for Doug to die and that I could stand anything. I visited Doug, and we hardly spoke. I couldn't cry. When I stopped the Xanax, all my emotions came out, and I couldn't stop crying. It masked my feeling, so I didn't have any feelings.

I think that is what happened to Mom when she was taken off Xanax. All her emotions came back to her, and she jumped. The doctor took her off her pill and it unmasked her feelings of grief and despair. She needed it bad.

Apparently, Mom mixed her pills with booze, and neighbors saw her hiding a bag underneath her coffee-stained beige coat while walking from the store.

In therapy, Jim tells me it isn't my fault that Mom has died. He says, "Remember your relaxation techniques when you can. Shut out the negativity. Things will get better. Try to get involved in your art. Paint a picture."

I remember when we were going to the AIDS meetings together, Mom and I were friends. There was friction between us, and she was being sarcastic, but I played a Roger Whittaker tape for her with the song "Memory." She was staring at the peach-gold full moon outside the passenger window, and the glow of it lit up her face and bounced off her round cheekbones. She sang, "All alone in the moonlight, I can smile at the old days, life was beautiful then." I could sense that she was thinking of her past and Doug and how long she'd be on earth, for she sat idly with no hope of tomorrow. As she cried, I gripped her hand in mine and cried with her. The poor dear soul. She told me that she wouldn't be here much longer, yet she had told me that many times before, and I didn't take her seriously. I wish I had.

We had a wake at our house. Doug came from Eugene. Everyone was happy to see him—my husband, my sister, her family, my Brazilian family, and Mom's friends. I appointed myself head orator. I drew everyone's attention by asking for a moment of silence. After I talked, I asked everyone to pitch in and say how our mom, Maria, had touched his or her lives.

I said, "I know that Mom had many sides to her. She had a good side, and she had a bad side, like all of us here. I'd like to think of her because of all the good things she did for me in her lifetime, like sewing clothes for me and Diana, her painting, and the work she did as a LPN."

Everyone began to blurt out facts and good things about her life and their relationships with her. Grieving has a weird way of making people open up. We say things that we normally wouldn't say to people. We all joined together crying. It made the wake very special.

My brother was quiet. He sat as if he was still processing what had just happened to Mom. He went to his car and bade farewell before we got him in our family photo. At least, Diana and I had a chance to kiss him good-bye on the forehead.

A year later we buried Mom's ashes in a valley facing Mount Hood in Oregon. In the summer, the grass would grow green; in the spring, the wildflowers would bloom; in the fall, leaves would turn red-orange; and in the winter, the heavy snow blanket would warmly caress and envelop her ashes, the center of her being. A white butterfly flew around as we sprinkled her ashes in the hole we dug. That truly was her place.

———

Now, when I remember my little curly-haired, blue-eyed brother, whom I use to hold in my arms and on my lap when he was young, I can't imagine why, if there is a God, this had to happen. It didn't seem possible that this sweet, mature, responsible human being was dying of AIDS.

Earlier, a neighbor said that she had made him chicken soup and placed it by his door. She heard him coughing a lot, but he wouldn't come outside. I guess with one last hope that he'd live, he had driven his car to the hospital and died. He had cut all ties with us. When the neighbor heard about his death on the radio, she told someone to call us.

When my brother was admitted to the hospital an MRI was taken of his brain. The results were given to the doctor by a lab technician who said that my brother's brain was almost gone. The doctor said that couldn't possibly be. "Doug had just graduated from UO and was on the dean's list for acting, and he drove himself to the hospital when he was dying." The lab technician assured the doctor that the head he examined was Doug's.

We opened his duffel bag. Inside were warm sweat clothes used in a sauna and chocolate candy bars. Doug passed away September 16, 1990. We sprinkled his ashes on one of the Sisters Mountains, so they would be with his friend Doug A.'s ashes. As a way of giving, Doug had been knitting tiny wool hats to donate to the premature babies at the hospital. Among the belongings he left behind was a box of the premature baby hats that he had knitted.

⁓

With a heavy heart I asked, "How could you do this, God, knowing how I felt about Doug and Mom? Why did they have to die?" Nothing seemed to connect for me. Nothing was right. I wanted the perfect solution to life now—on the spot. Wasn't there a way that I could have changed my mom? I didn't understand. How uncomfortable and miserable this was. Should I begin smoking cigarettes again? No, because this would be going backward.

So I did the next best thing. Through an agency, I was assigned to work with two elderly ladies with Alzheimer's, Fran and Eva. When I spotted the painting on the wall that their father had done, I expressed how I wished I could take painting lessons. I brought my oils to their house when I worked and let them doodle with them. What magnificent artwork they did! Eva recommended that I go to the Oregon Society of Artists in Portland to learn to paint.

"Take one more step," I said, sighing as I climbed up the steps to the Oregon Society of Artists. I didn't want to do this! They would just laugh at me. On the other hand, I had no alternative but to paint. "Another step to climb." My feet were full of lead, and my fingers began to tremble. "I will do this, and I will become successful at it. No one will know about my mom and brother. Here I am. I'm at the door. Please, God, help me."

Finally it was ten o'clock, and the door opened. "Hello! My name is Ree Barron, and I teach drawing and painting here. What is your name?"

"My name is Sherry Standing," I replied. "I only have two brushes, a few paints, and a canvas, but I would love to learn more about painting."

"Have a seat. You've come to the right place," Mr. Barron said.

"What a wonderful man," I thought.

The clock's hand moved to twelve, and I only did a few strokes on my canvas. He helped me organize my colors on my pallet: burnt sienna, alizarin crimson, cadmium red, cerulean blue, viridian green, cadmium yellow and titanium white. "What do you want to paint?"

I said, "A landscape."

He was a sensitive human being.

"I went to art class!" I screamed to Joe when I reached home. "It was exciting. My teacher is Ree Barron, a famous artist. He gave me a good lesson. Look what I did."

It was the beginning of a lake near trees and brush. It had brilliant colors.

This was my out, my key that unlocked my life's treasures and brought them out in the open. I blossomed. Doug's and my mom's deaths became distant realities each time that I painted.

Life was my pretty little puzzle. Each piece fit into place. As the paintbrush formed a picture on canvas, my mind was taking those discordant pieces of the puzzle and placing them in such a way that they formed a meaningful picture. Mom, and eventually Doug, became a sweet retrospection. They became a place in the back of my mind that I could visit when I wasn't expressing myself on canvas. It was an inconceivable trophy glittering in the sunlight. I was never so happy in my life.

Ree was over eighty years old when I knew him, and now he is gone. Ree died in his sleep. People all over paid their respects to him, and an artist named Berle Bledsoe painted a large watercolor portrait of Ree with a paintbrush in his hand, a class in the background. Something that Ree loved to do: paint.

Ree left a great impact on me. Never asked why I was the way I was, nothing about my mother or brother. I didn't come for talking about my troubles but to escape them for a while, and he made painting fun. He was always saying, "Let's get down to business."

Being rich in my connections to art during these difficult years, I saw an African American doctor for my condition of paranoid schizophrenia and depression. I met her at the Delaunay Clinic when I moved to Portland from Illinois. She tested me for manic-depression and treated me for both schizophrenia and depression. I had the utmost respect for this woman and adored her as a person. She was able to pull everything out of my past: my mom, my hospitalizations, and my smoking and drinking. The more we talked, the better I became. I took one l-tryptophan for sleep instead of Dalmane, a sleeping pill that I took for eight years, and when l-tryptophan was discontinued, I took Benadryl. She prescribed it for me to take before bedtime. Her work was more up-to-date on manic-depression than the help I received from Dr. Kirts.

I still saw Jim. I called him "Saint Jim," because he could receive and get rid of all the anguish and insecurities that I would impose on him. Within two and a half years, I lost Mom, Doug, and Dell, and it was almost too much for me to handle, but I was trying hard to live without a crutch at the same time, and I managed.

The doctor placed me on lithium. I took blood tests, and I was cleared for the medicine to be given to me. At first, I felt out of sorts with myself: heavy tongue, heavy breathing, heavy thoughts, fear that people were noticing me more, but I was determined to have a medicine work in my favor and against my mood swings. I shed the old life that clung to my being, and I began getting a taste of what it was like to have a new life again. The lithium worked for my manic-depressive interludes, and the depression and the mood swings subsided. The Stelazine, Artane, and Benadryl all seemed to do the trick for my paranoid schizophrenia and insomnia. And no restraints! I began to open up and talk to people again, and it wasn't so bad. I was beginning to like myself, and I made friends.

I remember working with an RN friend, Lee, at Mount St. Joseph, when Doug took sick. I called her Mindy for short because her last name was too long to pronounce. She was always caring about people's ills. She was a robust supervisor. A couple of patients died in our arms; one was foaming at the mouth. Before the patient died, Mindy grabbed her, held her head, and called me to come. We both held on to the dear elderly lady, who didn't have but an ounce of life in her. Then her head dropped. Mindy closed her eyes and told me she had a seizure. It was so sad, but Mindy was strong to catch her and help her die in comfort. Later, I cared for and comforted nine other patients by myself as they took their journey from my arms to heaven.

Joe and I got married, and Mindy and her husband put on a celebration. But after the honeymoon was over, Mindy's cigarette habit resulted in cancer. As Mindy became more dependent on others to take care of her, I donated my time to help take care of her once a week. We had fun discussions on sex, love, religious books, and dying. She wasn't ready to die. She said, "There is too much I want to get done before I die. I want to see my kids get married and graduate from college." One of her daughters did graduate from Cornell University and became a psychologist.

Mindy would come back from the hospital with her face all swollen like a golf ball from chemotherapy, and it would "hurt so bad." Not only did her jaw ache with pain, but she had a case of shingles behind her ear, and she stated that the itching in her jaw devastated her.

The family named me a pallbearer for her funeral along with her godchild, Ruth. Ruth was growing flowers in her garden and making arrangements for happy and sad occasions. Sometimes, if you were just nice to her, she'd give you a bouquet from the garden. But now, it was Mindy's turn to receive the flowers and carry them to a heaven or a palace that we never heard of. She will live in my heart and mind forever.

It is so sad to think that as we live, our hopes and ambitions are someday laid to rest in a box or in an urn of ashes. I think of the many dreams and desires Mom and Doug could have fulfilled in their lifetimes. Mom wanted to get married again. She wanted to travel to Hawaii and then back to Brazil to unite with her family. She wanted to build a bigger, better garden. Doug wanted to become a film restorer, get married, live a better, less painful, and more stress-free life. It's sad. Was it really necessary for death to take over so suddenly? I guess I will never know the answer to that question, for they are both gone from me, and I must pick up where they left off.

I had quit working at Mount St. Joseph and began working for Interim Health Care, a home care agency, as an aide. I took care of a lady who had been married to a cofounder of Jantzen's Sportswear. There were many trappings of wealth that filled her small apartment. She had a grandfather clock, antique furniture, and Persian carpets. Being a no-nonsense believer in propriety and proper demeanor, she made her voice heard in the complex where I was taking care of her. Whenever she didn't like the way things were, she'd say, "I'm going to buy the place and fire them all." She told me not to cross my legs when seated—only the ankles.

When she had been in good health, she led an interesting life of travel and entertaining famous people in New York, Chicago, etc. At times she would tell me that Pavarotti would come by, and other musicians would play her piano to practice. As she would doze off, she would have the news going on TV. I had a hard time being myself around her, though her humor was cordial and genuine, and she wouldn't have minded if I let loose once in a while. Doug was diagnosed with AIDS when I worked there, and I never let her know what was going on. I was concerned that she would find out that I had a mental problem and I would get fired. I worked for her for three twelve-hour days a week, until I found myself running up against a post when she refused my help. So I quit trying and quit her case.

My next assignment was taking care of two sisters, Beverly and Donna, whom I started with four days after Mom died. I hid her death from them. I was grieving and thought it was imperative to hold my mom's suicide in, so they wouldn't be affected by it. I worked three and a half years at their home. Beverly had a pear-shaped body. She was basil headed with a capital *B*. She cooked everything with basil. I was taught to fix their meals with basil at lunch and dinnertime. Donna was daring. She had a Roman-shaped nose. She dared me to take her places, against my home health aide instructions. Both Donna and Beverly had worked at Ma Bell as PBX operators, so we had something in common. Donna wrote poems and was a handwriting analyst. That bothered me at first, because she was getting personal with me about my past. I don't think I ever told her and Beverly how Mom died, or about Doug, as a matter of fact. I thought that information was better kept to myself.

My last lengthy job at Interim was working for a lovely educated lady named Mrs. Alexander. She liked to smoke cigarettes and watch soap operas. My lungs began hurting me, so I had to resign.

There are benefits to caring for the elderly. You have access to huge chunks of history and culture in many areas. The drawback is dealing with very strong wills in bodies that no longer can measure up to the demands of a dynamic life. In frustration they often lash out at the underling, and you must be able to resist the temptation to personalize anything they say and do. This means that you can't remain with them for long. Also, because of their age and health concerns that bring you into their lives, they're near the end, and they pass on. I am surprised I was able to handle these negative things as well as I did. Perhaps I was stronger and tougher than I thought.

In the time I worked as a nurse's aide, I was in a study for schizophrenia and its treatment at Pacific Northwest Clinical Research Center. There was a wonderful, handsome man conducting the study. After he interviewed me, I was chosen to be the candidate for a newer medication called sertindole. My African American doctor had teamed up with Dr. Smith to do the study. I was so happy to be under their care and kept a diary every day of my change from Stelazine to sertindole and its effects.

I met Dr. Smith in 1993. He shook my hand and introduced himself. Dr. Smith not only was a great psychiatrist, he was an exceptionally exquisite actor. He was the most talented doctor I had ever come across. I witnessed him playing Mr. Kirby in *You Can't Take it with You,* Elisha Whitney in *Anything Goes,* Sir Toby Belch in *Twelfth Night, or What you Will,* and FDR, Lieutenant Ward, and Oliver Warbucks in the musical play, *Annie.* He made me laugh and cry. His portrayal of Oliver Warbucks was extraordinarily captivating and moving.

The minute he took my hand, I developed a big crush on that guy. But I was willing to be a test case and try something new anyway. So he asked questions about my past, and we went over a lot of things in my life. He asked me, "If you said something good about yourself, what would it be?"

I said, "It is spotting things when I'm out of control."

Then he asked, "What is your worst trait?"

I said, "Feeling sorry for myself."

He said, "All right."

I questioned him, "Am I a candidate for the study?"

He said yes, and I was elated.

His reality checks with me lasted years on end, and I still reap the rewards from his kindness. But first, I had to come for lab work and eventually get off the Stelazine. No piece of cake. It was work. Dr. Smith had three special people there at his office, Jan, Marsha, and Nancy Gail. They inspired me to paint and make dolls, always showing enthusiasm for my hobbies. They became good friends to me, taking an interest in my life. It was like being in a second family.

With their help, it was easier to cope with my symptoms of dry mouth, drooling, and dizziness. My body was not necessarily reacting to the new medication, but it was coming off Stelazine. I had been on Stelazine for about twenty-two years. But once my study drug kicked in, it was miraculous. My thinking was much clearer. There were no hallucinations. Dr. Smith was on the right track, and I was able to take a trip to Spain to see my nomad sister, Diana, who was traveling around Europe to teach. We were jiving to the same tune!

I had always wanted to go to Spain. Getting a chance to be overseas with Diana was a dream come true. The last time I did that, I was traveling to Brazil, and I was almost helpless on Stelazine.

I began working at an agency called Legacy Visiting Nurses, and I saved my money to see Diana. I had quit smoking one year before mom died and quit drinking after my separation from Joe. I was strong, and somehow, deep inside I knew it.

Sherry's Paintings

Native American Indian Girl

Northern California Coast from my hitchhiking journey

A Winter's Rose

In Memory of Renoir- Learning by Reproducing the Masters then moving on to my own style

Carrying the Little One home

Walking with Lily

Peppermint Lady at the Carnival

Mardi Gras

Julie A. Fast, Bipolar Disorder Management Specialist
She writes about it, speaks about it, and lives it!

My older sister, Diana (right), and I as the entertainers 1960

My brother Doug

My Mother Maria

CHAPTER 16

SPAIN AND SCHIZO-AFFECTIVE DISORDER

It was my first time traveling alone to another country. I didn't know quite how to react or what to say or do. When I arrived in Barcelona, there was no one waiting for the passengers at the airport. I went to a telephone to call my sister, and there was no answer. That could mean she was here or that she was lost. I cashed my traveler's checks at an exchange and raced down the stairs to the luggage department. My luggage was stuck in a corner, because I wasn't there to get it. I picked up my luggage and went through customs. They asked me where I was from, and I said, "The USA."

The attendant said, "Go right through!" I was scared, but I was not a quitter. No asking for cigarettes, whining for a beer, or screaming, stomping, or going crazy. Finally, I saw Diana. She was jumping up and down outside the airport door yelling, "Sherry, Sherry!" I met her outside, because that's where the passengers were picked up. Then we took the bus to her hostel.

During our stay in Barcelona, Diana and I frequented museums, temples, and parks. We went to see Antoni Gaudi's Temple de la Sagrada Familia. It was breathtaking. I was impressed with the lacy fixtures of gold, intricately intertwined, hanging from the temple's structure. At Park Güell's lower level, a funny yet disturbing thing was taking place. A pleasant-looking man was standing by the women's bathroom charging us twenty-five cents to use it. He counted out six sheets and handed the toilet paper to each of us.

I heard some Japanese girls laughing behind me and holding up their toilet paper. "Is this all we get? What if we need more?" I guess we would have had to go back and pay for more if we ran out.

Diana and I had an amazing time together. We slept in a hostel, a small room with a bathtub. In order to take a bath, we could only sit with our legs in the air. She took me to El Court Inglés, a big shopping center in Barcelona, to buy fresh fruit and clothes.

We talked of our heartthrobs, our heartbreaks, our accomplishments, and our plans for the future. Diana described her experiences as an elementary grade schoolteacher to me. Like me, she loved teaching children. She wrote a book called *Art Connections* with a fellow author, Kim Thompson. The book consisted of art history lessons, how to make paper, rubber stamps, and the like. In her earlier years of teaching, Diana went to a garage sale and bought a bathtub. You might think, "A bathtub? So what?" She placed a throw rug in it and painted a lion, a giraffe, and other jungle characters on the outside of the tub. When students wanted to read, they could go to the tub. It gave them an incentive to read, and they enjoyed reading in the tub.

Also, she had the idea from somewhere that if you sent up a hot-air balloon, it might travel overseas. She had her schoolchildren write peace sayings during the Persian Gulf War for children and adults involved in the war. She placed their sayings in the balloon and sent it off for another country. We discussed my stepdaughter Becky's involvement with Desert Storm and the well-being of Cathy and David. Diana shared stories about her son, Justin, too. He had excelled in school and track and acquired a bachelor's degree in psychology. Justin was the baby I almost dropped on his head.

After three days of fun we left Barcelona and journeyed to Empuries Y Figures. We saw Greek and Roman ruins next to the

Mediterranean Sea. On the way, Salvador Dali's museum was a treat. I was impressed with Dali's sculpture of eggs that was being exhibited at the entrance of the museum. I felt my mind being tilted and bent as I viewed Dali's surrealistic pieces and wondered if he had experienced the same tilting and bending while doing them.

My sister happened to come across this woman who lived in the town of Gerona. Diana was riding a train and met the woman, who she thought had fallen, so she helped her up. She gave Diana her name and address and asked her to come and visit. Her name was Frau Zeheimer, and she stayed with Cecilia, who owned a ranch in Figuries.

Cecilia was a petite woman, and headstrong. Her ex-husband was a prominent artist in Spain. She owned a lush vegetable garden with persimmon and apple trees that were planted beside each other in the outlying area of the garden. Fig trees decorated the landscape behind a picketed gate, and blooming flowers beautified the design of the property in its rich soil. She plucked a prize tomato from her garden and offered it to us in her calloused hand. Untouched by the gusts of wind that tossed the aging ends of her soft brunette hair into spirals, she went about her business, weeding and watering. There were cats and dogs, and such a wild musk smell in her house that it was hard to sleep, but I slept anyway. Just before bedtime, I came downstairs to where Cecilia had a pot of water boiling in an open fireplace. We spoke in Spanish and some English about life, art, and children. After sharing a cup of hot chocolate (rich chocolate made in Spain), I went back upstairs and fell asleep. Insomnia, which I had in the past, was no longer an issue with me. The Benadryl was working well. When I woke up, Diana and I went to Frau's part of the ranch at 9:00 a.m. sharp for coffee.

Frau, a tall, white-haired, slender woman, was clumsily smoking a cigarette with her stiff upper lip hanging onto a white weed. She peered over her shoulder at us while she drew her cookie sheets out of the oven, dropping ashes on the burned hot pads she wore as gloves on her hands. She had just baked a hundred Christmas cookies for a charity and handed us some to sample.

After our visit, we bade Frau and Cecilia farewell and left for our next destination—Cadaqués, the city by the sea. Diana was taking care of a friend's house in Cadaqués while the tenant was on vacation. We walked the tenant's dog, Carlos, every day. This was next to paradise. Diana had met Suzanna, Susie, and Aroona in a cantina there, all bold and creative women of Cadaqué's upper social class. One day Diana had Susie over for dinner. Susie wore octagon-shaped glasses and appeared to be wealthy, but gracious. Her towering physique just missed the top of the entryway of the tenant's house by five inches. The way she carried herself and her vocabulary showed signs of sophistication, but the expressions on her face caused me to wonder if she was going to ridicule me, compliment me, or do both at the same time. One could tell she traveled in the elite circles by the way she talked about her professional life and the way she dressed. I gorged myself with dessert and ran to the bedroom, passing out with my clothes on. I was just like a drunk.

Diana woke me up and said, "Are you all right?"

"Yep, I'm OK," I said and went back to sleep.

I thought I had too much sugar, but the next day we went to Suzanna's restaurant. She displayed all these desserts on a table. There was no limit to the chocolate mousse, caramel cheesecake, and chocolate fudge cake being served. I think we tasted them all.

Close to the restaurant was the jade-green Mediterranean swaying gently and calmly over the marbled rocks that sketched the contours of the city. A beauty salon was located on the cobbled streets north of the city. I showed a picture of Melanie Griffith with her hair done on top of her head to the beauty operator there. I pointed to the picture, and the beautician started shaking her head. Then she motioned to her daughter, who proceeded to straighten my hair. My sister, who had dropped me off, came back to the studio. She looked all over and couldn't find me. She was looking for someone with her hair on top of her head in curls. When she came to her senses, she spotted me. We were in stitches, we laughed so hard.

We walked up a cliff to a lighthouse. Overlooking the city, I could see a stretch of cadmium-red rooftops. As I closed my eyes,

I visualized a slim and wiry bullfighter with a black ponytail, a hat pointed at the top corners, and an enormous red cape that was painted with red paint. As he swooped his arm across the city with his painted cape, it would land and spatter red on the rooftops. Inspired by the gift that I imagined the bullfighter had given me, I edged myself back down the cliff next to my sister, grabbing brush and branches as we slid on the rocks. The following night, we went to Susie's house for dinner, but after our meal, I told Diana I had to go home to take my pills. We headed for home, and I said to Diana, with my arm on her shoulder, "I can wait for the pills if you want to go to a souvenir shop."

She blew up and said, "Why did you lie to me about your pill? I was enjoying myself."

I told her, "Just forget it. I'll just leave."

She asked, "Where are you going?"

I said, "I don't know." Then we half made up.

The next day, I wrote a letter to her, and she wrote back. Then we apologized to each other and bonded. In Barcelona, the sun shone ever so brightly on the waters, silhouetting the boats in the harbor and the people in the city. You see, after I had written my sister a note on the bus back from Cadaqués to Barcelona, we cried and forgave each other, and things were all right. I love her so much and always will.

It was a trip I will always remember. I learned that you can talk your troubles out instead of holding them in. It is so important to be honest. You release the guilt that is inside. What will someone do to you if you do tell the truth? There is nothing to lose. I gained a new confidence in myself and others by speaking it.

───

When I arrived home in Portland, I had the pictures of my oil paintings made into holiday calendars at a printing shop near my area. I mailed Jim one with a letter attached. I received a heartwarming response from him, thanking me for the calendar and welcoming me back. He said that he would treasure the calendar as a reminder of our conversations over the years and how far I'd come with my healing journey. It made me feel good.

More doors opened up for me after Jim's response. I was still working for Legacy. My Alzheimer's patient died within a month, but I received a letter from my company, which I was very proud of. It went like this:

LEGACY VISITING NURSES ASSOCIATION;

Sherry Joiner attended my mother, Mrs. Rosemary Lee, from March 1995 until January 1996. During this time, Mrs. Lee, who had Alzheimer's disease, suffered a marked deterioration of both mental faculties and physical strength. The care she received from Sherry was highly skilled and tenderly compassionate. Sherry's treatment of Mrs. Lee was invariably respectful and friendly; so much so the sound of Sherry's voice never failed to evoke a smile from her patient. We feel extremely fortunate to have had Sherry with our mother for so long; her goodness contributed much: both to our mother and to us. We are immensely grateful to her and commend her highly.

Daughter of my patient, Rosemary

I was photographed in the metro section of the *Oregonian* newspaper that year, with another Alzheimer's client from Legacy, as her husband looked on.

The sertindole study ended, and I was taken off the medication in 1998. It was no longer effective. Dr. Ward Smith, the psychiatrist who was the head of the study and who made TV and radio commercials to help people with depression, anxiety, and mental illnesses, suggested a new medicine. It worked even better than the sertindole. The drug's name was Zyprexa. It sounded something like a Greek goddess. I thought Dr. Smith was transforming into somewhat of a mythical god, too, prescribing medicine that actually worked in my brain and could keep my mind sound and strong. Because he cared about keeping me well and happy, he discussed my problems and choices in life with me and was there for reality checks and crises.

There were no side effects to the Zyprexa, yet the medicine only lasted three years in my system. Then my schizophrenia took off to the downside. But I was normal and together when I took it and hardly needed a sleeping pill.

The certified nursing assistant program at Legacy folded, and I went back to work at the Mount St. Joseph extended care facility as an aide on the Alzheimer's unit. My disease began to spiral, and I was diagnosed with schizo-affective disorder.

CHAPTER 17

ADJUSTING MY MEDS

A close friend of mine named Shirley was shot in the back and paralyzed from the waist down. We had an argument about sharing responsibilities at Mount St. Joseph, and the next day Shirley went to her friend's apartment. Her friend's boyfriend was jealous, because she went out on him, so he charged into the apartment to shoot her. When the gun went off, the bullet missed her and hit Shirley. I was crushed, yet I had the strength and resilience to go on. I went to see her in the hospital, and after seeing her, even though I was feeling her pain and devastation, I was able to keep it together.

There were other nightmarish challenges ahead. Another coworker at Mount St. Joseph came down with AIDS. I passed a kidney stone, but again, I did not go crazy. I was attending a stressful activity directing class in the meantime and stuck with it, even though I was seeing and hearing things. I hiked up the street after work, and a guy stopped his car, pulled down his pants, and exposed himself to me. I just looked at him quietly and studied him. He opened his car door. I moved quickly to the back of his car to get his license plate number. He smiled and drove off. I hurried home and called the cops, and they came. I described the man to them and gave them his license plate number. I said, "I've seen a man's genitals before. But what if some little girl saw that? He would take her mind forever."

The policeman comforted me saying, "We'll find his car and talk to him."

I was seeing a new counselor, Dr. Loyal Marsh, since Jim needed to change hours, and I couldn't comply with the time change. When I told Dr. Marsh about the exposer, he said, "We get these perverts all the time. Portland is full of them. They joke about how beautiful their victims think their body is. Unfortunately, that's the pathetic kind of reality we have to live with every day, I'm afraid."

Everything happened to me so fast—in a period of one month. Though I kept my sanity, these occurrences began to take a toll on me. They almost did me in, but I was strong. Dr. Smith came to my rescue and became my permanent psychiatrist. I worked and talked out each episode in therapy with him and Dr. Marsh. They prevented me from going into the hospital.

In therapy, Dr. Smith held up his hand and counted the stresses on his five fingers, illustrating what I had gone through in one month.

"That's a lot, Sherry," he said. "Sometimes people experience that in a whole lifetime, but you experienced those episodes in a month! Some people do hear voices and see things jumping out at them. With hard work, talking it out in therapy, and taking your medication, you will live through it." Dr. Smith saved my life by saving my brain and not sending me to the hospital.

We talked about each problem separately, how I could best deal with the stresses, and how I could single out my stresses. To keep on top of it, I was encouraged to get involved, talk to my sister and friends, write down things that bothered me, call the crisis line if I needed to, make dolls, paint, swim, and walk. I continued to visit my friend in the hospital. As time went on, because of my complete trust in Dr. Smith, I was back to normal.

I was gaining weight on the Zyprexa, so we tried a new medication called Geodon. When I first took the pill it was OK, but when I was changing over from Zyprexa to Geodon, I had hallucinations.

I wasn't getting enough sleep at night from changing to the Geodon and the stress of work, so Dr. Smith ordered a sleeping pill called Remeron. I was in a hurry to get more sleep and took too much of it. I wasn't sleeping right, because I had to fight the corporate managers of my new job at Monterey Court, an Alzheimer's residential facility. They had cut my working hours without warning or higher pay. Unfortunately, I was working graveyard.

It happened one night when I helped out a patient, an obese man with a gray crew cut who was having a heart attack. I was mentally and physically drained from helping him out and carrying the stress of my hours being cut. When I got home, I took too much of the Remeron. I'm sure the Geodon would have helped me in different circumstances.

I received a letter from my girlfriend, Wilma, in Illinois. She was arranging furniture, flowers, and figurines. I also received the *Artist's Magazine* in the mail from my sister. The combination of the two would help me stabilize my intense emotions and withstand the chemical crisis that I was about to undergo the minute I walked into Dr. Smith's office.

Dealing with pleasure and mental pain at the same time wasn't easy to do. In fact, it was impossible. So before I went to see Dr. Smith, I followed certain steps in order to draw strength from my weaknesses. I started to make up things in my mind, such as equating Wilma's arrangement of furniture, flowers, and figurines to the menagerie in *The Glass Menagerie* by Tennessee Williams. I read that play and gave a speech on it many years ago in high-school

English class. Mrs. Ashworth had assigned the speech to me. I was getting a sense of security relating to it.

Ever since I had been faced with bad visions in my life, I held onto the uncontrollable factors that molded and shaped my inner being. I escaped into a world of miniature sculptures and miniature glass figurines, almost as Laura did in the play with her menagerie of animals. I associated being weakened by my condition of polio with Laura's condition of pleurisy. To get rid of stress and constant turmoil with myself and others, I let my imagination run wild. It was the tiny menagerie that led me to this escape when I was experiencing tough and stressful times. The menagerie of a blue unicorn, a baby elephant, a wooden duck, a fighting rooster, and a jade Heisey tiger, seemed to be the reality that said, "Take control."

When I received Wilma's letter about her arrangement, it caused me to think of my own creations that I had made in sculpture class before I was hospitalized in Kishwaukee. I compared the image of my doll with its firm texture to the hardness and durability of the glass unicorn in the menagerie. It was the harshness of the breaking of the doll's foot that made me clearly see how sick and fragile I was. It hurt my feelings when the doll's foot broke off. I put her in her crib and prayed for her. After realizing that the doll didn't possess the qualities of life that human beings had, I had to come up with the same truth that Laura did in *The Glass Menagerie*; when its horn broke, she discovered the unicorn was "only a horse." Discarding my hurt feelings for my creation, I finally perceived that my doll was "only a doll" with a broken foot.

Closing my eyes, I replaced the image of the glass menagerie with the image of the blue-glazed clay figurines I made in class. They were the bowling pins on a card table that I gave to Doug, pointing with their thumbs. Their properties were smooth and hard, like Wilma's smooth glass swans and solid glass horse sitting on her dining-room table. They were pointing in one direction: to the center. The message: stay in touch with the center of your being. I didn't realize it at the time, but if I had tuned into it more closely, maybe my problems would have been solved.

There were other aspects to Wilma's arrangement from which I drew a deeper meaning to the understanding of myself. I remember being hypnotized on a big comfy chair in her living room as a means of quitting smoking. Her furniture was always warm and comfortable. I counted from toe to head and then back down again, and I disappeared into myself and found a world of self-actualization and reality. I thought about Laura and the menagerie. I began creating thoughts of passion: passion for my life, passion for my health, passion for my creativity, passion for my mind. It was there that I could find answers to my own questions—questions about why I was the way I was and how I could tackle this disease. I started to draw strength through self-talk and self-discipline. I was going to succeed in life, no matter what it took. As my journey continued, I wrote down steps for me to move forward. I repeated to myself, "I'm going to live a happy life regardless of what happens." I asked myself, "How can I stay in touch with reality? How can I become better at life?" Then, I began to make amends.

Wilma's colorful flowers came into play. I wanted to give one to my mom, my brother, my sister, and anyone else I had harmed. Flowers to me are a symbol of the blossoming of life. Each time I opened my heart to people, my insides would bloom. The flowers became akin to my brother's gift to his friend who died of AIDS. They were the roses Mindy took with her on her walk to heaven, and they were the jonquils that Amanda used to decorate before the arrivals of her gentlemen callers in *The Glass Menagerie*.

I focused on the furniture, the figurines, and the flowers that Wilma wrote about once more, not each one as a separate unit but as a whole. They provided the delicate blueprint and framework of my life: delicate like the blue unicorn or the wings of the wooden duck. They brought my troubled thoughts to a head inside of me. Fighting against myself, I met my challenge and was able to leave the unreal world behind and make great strides to change it.

But now Joe, who had married me, and whom I had been living with all this time, argued with me. We both knew that my imbalance was out of control, because of the bizarre things I was doing at home. For instance, one day I passed out due to exhaustion from working. While I was sleeping on my bed, a gray cat that was pregnant sneaked into the house. As I awoke I heard something moving. I thought it was a mouse, and I called for my husband to come to my room to investigate. He checked under my bed. Lo and behold, there were five newborn kittens mewing beneath my bed. She'd had a litter of kittens! Joe placed them carefully in a box and moved them to a different spot of the house. I don't know how she could have had kittens there. The space was small and confined. Nothing like that had ever happened to me. I figured she must have been protecting me in her motherly way.

Three days later, I made a doll of myself with a kit that I bought at a store. It turned into a voodoo doll with dark eyes and pincushion stomach. I had gotten carried away. I was pretty deranged at the time, and I was thinking of my past suicide attempts. I clumsily sewed a button where the doll's heart would be. I cried. I was hurting my mind. I asked my new counselor, Loyal Marsh, what was going on with me. He said to stay away from my history memory book (pertaining to what I was writing) and think of something new. So I did for several weeks. The psychosis eased off.

After receiving the *Artist's Magazine* from Diana, I told Joe I would go see Dr. Smith and get help. It was a long journey in my car, but I was ready to face reality. No more mental explosions. All I could focus on was the tiny menagerie—Wilma's arrangement—and the software I was reading about in the magazine. Dr. Smith drove over to see me at his office, and I let loose. He called Joe, and we all talked. I suggested that I go back to work for two more weeks and then quit. He said yes.

He talked to Joe as I read the *Artist's Magazine,* chomping on a stick of spearmint gum. I turned what was ugly and distorted in me into a nice pleasant trip of lesser psychotic dimensions. Reality became a friend that day. I had so much in life to give and to fight for. Dr. Smith stopped the Geodon, prescribed two 10 mg Zyprexa, and sleep.

At a follow-up appointment it was obvious that these measures had worked. I quit my job at the Alzheimer's place, and I started to do things that were important to me and for my psychosis. I painted pictures, sought out positive people to be around, and read good books. I wrote diaries and sewed hands on infant, toddler, and preschool books. I found strength, love, and understanding helping children. There was glimpse of happiness for me with Geodon, and at the time I took it, I was starting to think clearly. But the transition from Zyprexa to Geodon caused me to have auditory and visual hallucinations, so as a result, I settled for Zyprexa. I began working through my problems with Dr. Smith, a doctor who cared about helping adults and children with paranoia, depression, anxiety, and stress. He knew a world where there was a brighter life and a brighter future to be attained for everyone, and he put his best foot forward to help anyone in need that he possibly could.

CHAPTER 18

ORIGIN OF SHERRY'S MASTER PLAN

I started to write e-mails to Dr. Smith about my work and life. Sifting through these e-mails, I found information about my disease and how I took care of it. The letters showed that I had taken good care of my schizo-affective disorder, from which I had suffered for more than thirty-eight years.

Even though my mental makeup was one of manic-depression and schizophrenic interludes, my thoughts were sound, and my mind was at a state of readiness. This was possible because the Zyprexa that I took in the past as an experimental drug for bipolar disorder was working, and all the other medicines had quit working in my system. The Zyprexa that was prescribed by Dr. Smith showed the best results. I received approval from my family and friends for being on it.

The information pointed out that after five years of continually taking Zyprexa along with the lithium, which was prescribed for depression, I gained weight and maintained unhealthy sleep patterns. I was torn between fighting fat, being depressed with mood swings, and having normal psychological reactions to things. The side effects of this medicine caused me to suppress my thoughts in my daily routine.

    As I became a toddler teacher in a day-care center, the Zyprexa masked how I felt about life. It had done well by me for three years. It was a clean drug that enabled me to have clear thoughts. I liked the feelings I had gotten from the medication and how I was able to achieve them by becoming a teacher. But after a three-year period, I started to feel remorseful. I felt uneasy about taking it, because I gained weight, which fed my inferiority complex. The feeling became more intense, because I was fat. I lost my self-respect and respect for others, and I wasn't true to my belief system, which said, "When you respect others, you respect yourself in return." I hoped to extend myself to society, but how could I? I was so mixed up and depressed.

    I began working steadily at the day care. I thought it would help. I loved teaching the infants, toddlers, and older children in the complex, but I lacked the ability to move around freely. I injured my back by turning the wrong way at the diaper table while diapering a baby at work. After being sent to an urgent care facility, I was seen by a spinal surgeon. A month later, I had an operation for a slipped lumbar disk. Because of that, I was unable to peel away my excess weight. I became addicted to chocolates, pastries, sugary drinks, and Three Musketeers bars, which made me look like all the fattening things that I ate. I had no self-control. The thought of leaving a trail of humungous globules of fat behind when I died weighed on my mind. It was pretty pathetic. I wanted to take the Zyprexa and stay mentally well, but it was so contradictory to my lifestyle that it just about drove me nuts.

    Death and sadness plagued my conscience at the time. There was my mom's suicide, my brother dying of AIDS, and the deaths of my very close friends that I was still working through. There were my suicide attempts, my hospitalizations, and my trip to San Francisco when I was strangled. All these experiences were too difficult to forget, even with in-depth counseling.

    It's like having a horrible nightmare, looking up out of my casket, smothering in thought. As I lie suffocating in my sleeping terror, someone places an hourglass dated 2017 on my forehead. I unconsciously drift off. "Will I be the one who is bumped off next?" I ask. I try to reach out at the faces of terror, trying to touch them as they fade in the distance, chanting "You screwed up! You screwed up!" I begin to scream, "Help me! Help me!" My mind is smoldering with defeat. I feel penetrated by a powerful jolt of darkness sweeping over my mind, as it did when I was a small child with polio, and Mom was divorcing my dad. It stings me time and time again like the sting of the long needle in the hospital ward when I was being institutionalized.

Mom didn't really ask to be where she was. All she wanted was to come to the United States, marry, and have children. Every time she had a relationship with a man, he supplied her with booze and led her down a one-way street. Was it all right to blame her for ending up a helpless alcoholic and wanting to end her life?

She used to tell me, "When you die, you go into your closet and look for your pink prom dress, Sherry. It's the one that is more beautiful than all the other ones you have, and then you walk out of the closet like a changed redhead, more beautiful than before. It is as simple as that." I wonder if she walked into that closet. Guess I will never know.

I recall my brother Doug and how he loved life, giving all his kindness and talent to the world. He didn't deserve his fate either. He must have been naturally gay at birth. He was born into a family of women. Not knowing his father, he entertained himself by dressing up in our fancy dresses. Now there is better medicine to prolong the lives of some of the HIV and AIDS patients; however, healing didn't come soon enough for poor Doug. Driving himself to the hospital, hoping he would live, he slowly passed away. He left a White sewing machine for me to sew with, which helped me to create my baby and preschool books. I loved him for that. As he left, the sweet earth grasped his precious hands and enveloped his ashes.

My fear of death was lessened when I visited with my angel, Alanna, who was at my high-school reunion. She had been my inspiration, my friend, and a true guide to my serenity, always reminding me that there were better days ahead. She had become a physical therapist and was strong in her convictions about life. Alanna contracted cancer in five of her organs, and the thought of leaving herself and leaving this earth was weighing on her mind, but she was only concerned about everyone having a good time.

A frail peace-loving redhead, she sat with her hand in mine, both feet planted in her oxford shoes. She told me to remember her favorite sayings: "In the shade, Slade," "Ditto, Kiddo" and "That's the facts, Max," and to use them in case anyone gave me any flack. She gleamed my way and smiled. A shadow kissed my heart, and the strong bond that we formed silently ascended into the air. I know we will be friends forever. In late August 2007, the month of our class reunion and her birthday, she passed away. It was the prettiest time of year.

With these tragedies, the losses of my friends and family, and my traumatic experiences, I still stayed on top of my elusive delusional world. I would work through the depression and paranoia that plunged into my heart and touched my soul in the years ahead. What was past could never be relived again, and what was real would take its place in the most fragile essence of reality. I had resigned myself to entertain a world of truth, and through my struggles, I would prevail.

It was true—to stay on top, I tried to push suffering and sorrow aside, but I also went one step further. I began to keep a journal in my head to organize my thoughts. I began to write down a plan meticulously. I put emphasis on "meticulously," because it was something that I had to push myself to do when writing down details on paper. Be meticulous. I was not an accurate person at times. With my faults, I stumbled and put the right things in the wrong places, where they didn't belong. It was like French braiding my hair, making sure I didn't get a single strand of hair out of place. Still, I skipped braids now and then, just because I thought the outcome would be better. I was only to find out later that the braid was too loose.

As I reviewed my diary, I figured out a code and typed it on the computer and sent it to Dr. Smith. With his help, Sherry's Master Plan was founded. Every time I sent him a message, I typed it in under that heading.

The plan was implemented when I was a toddler teacher reading *Feeling Good* by David Burns, MD. Loyal Marsh recommended it to me to read for my depression. After reading the book, I adopted the symbols M for master and P for pleasure, and I used a scale numbered from 0 to 10 (10 being the highest pleasure level or activity). I used them in my journal, and they were quite effective. It seemed to work.

The procedures I used to prepare for the days ahead to combat the daily crises that I might encounter as a toddler teacher are exemplified in this sample.

Sherry's Master Plan, November 2003

November 4, 2003

8:00 a.m. to 9:00 a.m. Woke up, took a shower, and drank Diet Coke. Took meds, ate breakfast. M 10 P 10
9:00 a.m. to 10:00 a.m. Drove to appointment. M 10
10:00 a.m. to 11:00 a.m. Session with Dr. Smith. M 10 P 10
12:00 noon. Ate lunch and took vitamins.
12:00 p.m. to 1:00 p.m. Got mail, drove to Safeway, purchased meds. M 10 P 10
1:00 p.m. to 2:00 p.m. Got ready for work. M 10
2:00 p.m. to 3:00 p.m. Drove to work. M 10
3:00 p.m. to 4:00 p.m. Diapered toddlers, gave them snack. M 8 P 6

4:00 p.m. to 5:00 p.m. Put on "Brown Bear" skit with the kids and read to them. P 10
5:00 p.m. to 6:00 p.m. Vacuumed, mopped, sprayed toys, and did dishes. M 10
6:00 p.m. to 7:00 p.m. Drove home. M 10
7:00 p.m. to 8:00 p.m. Made dinner and took meds. M 10
9:00 p.m. to 10:00 p.m. Watched TV, started a painting of a pregnant woman, and took vitamins. P 10
Good night, I went to sleep.

November 5, 2003

9:00 a.m. to 10:00 a.m. Woke up, ate breakfast. Took meds and drank a Diet Coke. M 10 P 10
10:00 a.m. to 11:00 a.m. Got dressed. M 10
Noon to 1:00 p.m. Took vitamins and ate lunch. M 10
1:00 p.m. to 2:00 p.m. Visited with friend from the Oregon Society of Artists who lives in retirement home. P 10 Called surgeon's office about physical therapy for my back. M 8. Still in the air.
2:00 p.m. to 3:00 p.m. Picked up check and drove to work. M 10
3:00 p.m. to 4:00 p.m. Changed toddlers' diapers and gave them snack. Did "Polar Bear" skit with them. Michael liked snakes. P 10
4:00 p.m. to 5:00 p.m. Picked up toys, washed the bathroom, sprayed the toys, vacuumed, and did the dishes after poop check. M 10 P 7
5:00 p.m. to 6:00 p.m. Mopped. M 10
6:00 p.m. to 7:00 p.m. Drove home, went grocery shopping. M 10 P 10
7:00 p.m. to 8:00 p.m. Ate dinner. Took meds. M 10
8:00 p.m. to 9:00 p.m. Took bath and watched TV. P 10

9:00 p.m. to 10:00 p.m. Took vitamins. Intermittently drifted to my dining room to see if I could touch up something that I painted before I went to sleep. Good night, Sher.

Dr. Smith said, "Great job. I have printed this one out and am putting it in your chart for reference when you return. Keep up the good work."

November 6, 2003

9:00 a.m. to 10:00 a.m. Woke up, showered, and drank Diet Coke. M 10
10:00 a.m. to 11:00 a.m. Ate breakfast and took meds. M 10 P 10
11:00 a.m. to noon. Called Providence for PT appointment. I can use my insurance, and my doctor will fax over a slip to Providence for my appointments. M 10 P 10
Noon to 1:00 p.m. Talked to my sister over the phone, ate lunch, and took vitamins. P 10
1:00 p.m. to 2:00 p.m. Went to Fred Meyers to buy shampoo. P 10
2:00 p.m. to 3:00 p.m. Got ready for work and drove to work. M 10 P 20
3:00 p.m. to 4:00 p.m. Changed children's diapers. Did "This Old Man" skit with my bag of tricks. Read to children. Got into a conflict with coteacher who wanted to take the books out of the room. Weird stuff. M 10 P 8
4:00 p.m. to 5:00 p.m. Cleaned bathroom and mopped. M 10

5:00 p.m. to 6:00 p.m. Took Yolanda home. M 10
6:00 p.m. to 7:00 p.m. Took a bath and ate dinner. M 10 P 10
8:00 p.m. to 9:00 p.m. Painted as I worked on pregnant lady picture.
9:00 p.m. to 10:00 p.m. Read *Women of the Silk* by Gail Tsukiyama.
11:00 p.m. Went to sleep.

November 7, 2003

7:00 a.m. to 8:00 a.m. Woke up, took a shower, ate breakfast. Took meds and drank Diet Coke. M 10
8:00 a.m. to 9:00 a.m. Drove to the dentist for a crown to be put on my tooth. M 10
9:00 a.m. to 11:30 a.m. Ate lunch and took vitamins. M 10 P 10
12:30 p.m. Went shopping for Latina hair conditioner for my Brazilian hair and looked for the book, *Making Peace with your Parents*. No luck on the book or cassette yet. P 5
2:00 p.m. to 3:00 p.m. Got ready for work. M 10
3:00 p.m. to 4:00 p.m. Changed diapers, passed out snacks, sang songs with the kids. M 10
4:00 p.m. to 5:00 p.m. Brought art books for children to learn colors. There was a nude picture in one of the books, and one little boy wanted to see it. I turned the page quickly so that he didn't see the woman exposed. I wasn't sure what his parents would think, and it is just as well that I shouldn't be the one he learns from at this age. M 10
5:00 p.m. to 6:00 p.m. Sprayed toys, vacuumed, and mopped. M 10
6:00 p.m. to 7:00 p.m. Was dissatisfied about co-teacher and her sarcastic remarks to the children and me, so I talked to another teacher about it. M 10
7:00 p.m. to 8:00 p.m. Drove home, ate dinner, and took meds. M 10

8:00 p.m. Took a long hot bath, worked on my painting, and continued reading the *Women of the Silk*. P 10
Finally getting rid of the curse of the full moon. It is neat!

⌒

Dr. Smith said, "It seems you are doing quite well, with only a few marks below ten. I'll bet just keeping track gives you a sense of mastery and accomplishment. Keeping a journal has been shown to be very useful. Good job."

As I perceived my activities being carried out under this plan, I saw that each step, each thought and task I completed successfully, I mastered with pleasure. In addition, my achievements were helping me become motivated. I had more self-confidence, attained more independence, and fostered more discipline. I was becoming proud of myself, and with the support of Dr. Smith, Loyal Marsh, my husband, Joe, and my sister, Diana, I was finally getting myself together.

In the final weeks and days of November, I accomplished

1. giving "Brown Bear," "Polar Bear," and "Three Little Pigs" skits to the toddlers with toys and stuffed animals I found in secondhand stores (after I washed the toys thoroughly);
2. sewing a rabbit doll dress;
3. giving a ride home to a girl from work three times a week;
4. changing more diapers;
5. practicing my Portuguese and Spanish lessons;
6. going to a post-polio syndrome class when it was snowed in;
7. finishing the portrait of my pregnant co-teacher in the infant room;

8. working on a scrapbook for Diana, who traveled all around Europe on a teacher's service grant;
9. going to therapy in the pool;
10. continuing to work.

My mastering and pleasure scores were still high, but there were times when the scenario didn't ring true. In December and January, I was teetering on a tightrope of depression and paranoia. My scores rose, but the way I documented my tasks seemed inconsistent. I entertained thoughts of suicide before I went to sleep. I was still fat, and my husband said that I couldn't fit into my clothes anymore. Then there was the day when I came home crying, because I thought that I had lifted a child wrong. I was feeling guilty, and I obsessed about it when there was nothing to obsess or feel guilty about. I hadn't done anything wrong. My mind started to take a toll. I was on a circus ride of emotions. It made me feel inadequate and uncertain.

CHAPTER 19

SEIZURE

"Mr. Geodon," my new pill (as I called him), was my other self: apart from me but on the outskirts of my mind. He took on human characteristics. As I medicated myself with "him," I would blame him for my bad days and hallucinations, as well as give him credit for my good moods and intervals of success.

I had taken a turn for the worse and was defeated by the side effects of my disease. I contacted Dr. Smith in desperation. He recommended that I return to taking the Geodon. I had taken it in 2001 and had a rough time with it, but I felt I needed a drug that would get me out of this trapped state of mind. I knew that changing from one medication to the other caused me to have hallucinations, yet I wanted to take the chance. Zyprexa had lost its luster.

Five factors came into play in my transformation:

1. I changed over from Zyprexa to Geodon.
2. During the time that I started taking Geodon again, I began walking a lot. One day, I walked up the street to the park, but I failed to notice that someone was following me. A young man driving a blue pickup truck became my stalker. I drove my car to the park to feel more secure. When I was at the other end of the enclosure, I saw him get out of his truck and walk around to my car. He wrote down my license plate number. When I got home, I called the police. An officer came to my door, and I discussed the incident with him. He said that he would keep an eye on him. I relayed to the officer that it was around school property, and I feared for the schoolchildren as I feared for myself.
3. My supervisor at the day-care center was mourning for her mom, who was dying. I was sympathizing with her. I don't rightly know how this came about, but I had bought a bottle of grapefruit juice and was walking around the park on a rainy day praying for her. I couldn't remember if I was supposed to drink the grapefruit juice or not. I was taking Lipitor at the time for high cholesterol. In addition, I was eating a lot of gumdrops, candy, and chocolate kisses, and I was overweight.
4. The anniversary of Mom's death was two weeks away, and I unconsciously hid it from everyone at work. I think I did that because it was close to my birthday.
5. I was giving a girl at work free rides home. I barely knew her and went far out of my way, disclosing things about myself that I might be paranoid about.

The night Dr. Smith prescribed the Geodon, I took 100 mg, the way he prescribed it, but I couldn't sleep. My mind was a vacant lot: full of empty air, abandoned by thought, and lacking in hope. If I blinked, I would wake up. If I had a hair out of place, I stayed up. My heart pounded and echoed through my chest cavity. Each breath, like steam escaping from a boiling kettle, kept me awake. The short hand on the clock spun off its wire, and at two o'clock, I fell asleep. At three o'clock, I woke up shaking. My bed was vibrating. I felt myself levitating up from my bed. Was it just my imagination, or was I nuts? In my mind, I became the star of the movie *The Exorcist*. I went into convulsions and wet all over myself. I had been gagging on my own phlegm. Could this be happening to me? I walked into the kitchen. My husband was sleeping in the next room. I pulled radishes out of the vegetable drawer in the refrigerator. Next, I found some onions and carrots and a turnip in the bowl on top of the kitchen counter and devoured them quickly. I searched the medicine cabinet, found a thermometer, and took my temperature. It was high. I called my family doctor frantically. The answering service said that she wouldn't be in the office until the next day.

I tried to fake it. I knew I had to go to work that day. Meditation helped. I put on a CD of the ocean and drifted off but still with some shallow awareness. My days ran together, so I don't know if I went in to work that day or the next. In either case, I went to work very groggy, and I tried to help myself by teaching at a different angle, with a different style, telling no one what I had gone through.

The Latina whom I had taken home from work was trying to get my job in the toddler room. I called her a bitch when she tried to make believe I wasn't doing my job. She had been forceful and intense, telling me to pick something up. It hadn't fallen to the ground yet. I thought she was playing games with me. I am paying to this day for saying "bitch" in the toddler room. I went to Christine and told her what I said.

Our supervisor, Christine, had dark-brown eyes that cased you up and down on matters of importance. She told you how wrong you were if she didn't agree with you. She could cause you to react like a childish schoolgirl even if you were right. She had an important meeting with Yolanda (the Latina) and me.

I spoke up and said, "Christine, my car had a dent in it, and my husband was all out of sorts about it. I thought Yolanda might have put a dent in my car when she opened my passenger door up. I guess it could have been anyone or anything that did it, and I am sorry."

I must have had some paranoid thinking. I also said, "I was giving Yolanda free rides, and all I wanted was a Diet Coke, but I didn't get one." I broke down, and tears creased my face with black mascara, causing me to look like a black witch moth. I think that finding out that the supervisor's mom was dying touched me deeply. I was moved by it. It affected Yolanda, too, because she couldn't be objective with me. She knew that Christine's mom was going to die, and that is why she struck out at me in the toddler room. Christine was her good friend. Yolanda was also dealing with a grandmother who left her. We both had overreacted. It was February. I told Christine that my mom had died this time of year and that my family had buried her ashes in the valley of Mount Hood. "Strikingly enough, a white butterfly flew around her grave. She always loved butterflies," I said.

Christine took me aside and asked me, "What is wrong with you?"

I explained, "I had a seizure. It had an adverse effect on me."

I had sympathized with her about her mom's illness in part because it was so close to my mom's death anniversary. But I didn't mind the empathy I felt for her. "It happens to all girlfriends when they are losing a loved one, doesn't it?" I asked. We just hugged. Yolanda and I apologized, and Christine asked us never to come into work with a serious illness or problem again. Later, Yolanda bought me two Diet Cokes and told me that I was her best friend at work. She was sweet.

The next couple of nights, I tried the Geodon again. Same adverse effect from day to night. I was afraid of my convulsions. My battle to stay sane in an insane world was almost too debilitating for words. The circulating electrons of my brain were flaring out like a tornado, and each cell conquered the very essence of my being.

I made it to see my family doctor, Dr. Ruth Wilcox, the next day. I told her about my convulsions and about the radishes, turnip, onions, carrots, and thermometer. It took an hour to get blood work and be diagnosed. She was very warm and attentive to what was going on. I told her about my Christmas Eve experience with Ralph, Mom, and Doug.

She asked, "Sherry, how long have I known you?" She didn't realize what I had gone through. She gave me a warm hug and assured me that everything would be all right. Joe waited patiently outside in the waiting area. The diagnosis was a seizure. I'm going to live!

During the time I was seeing Dr. Ruth (the nickname that was given to her by her patients), I was also e-mailing Dr. Smith. I had written detailed descriptions in my e-mails of what was happening. Even though I seemed to be sinking in quicksand, he was there at my beck and call. I told Dr. Smith what Dr. Ruth said about the seizure, and he saw me immediately. I said that I wanted to continue with the Geodon regardless. I just needed a way to sleep. He prescribed 90 mg of Geodon. It was a bit too much, so with trial and error he prescribed Geodon four times a day, 20 mg at a time, instead of once a day. He also prescribed 75 mg of Benadryl for sleep, because I was leery about going back to the Geodon-Remeron combination I had taken in 2001. Later the Geodon was decreased, first by 10 mg and then by 20 mg, so that my system could adjust. I took it three times a day at 20 mg.

I remember posing for a picture when I had lost some weight, my red hair short, standing next to a painting that I did of the moon. I had painted a clown's face on one half of the moon, and on the other half I painted an oblong greenish, murky-colored E, with brilliant triangles of gold green and blue. Deep red, blue, and purple roses bordered the painting. I attached the picture to a sheet of typing paper and made a want ad: Help Wanted, Geodon Man in the Moon. I gave it to Dr. Smith. He got a kick out of it.

Geodon, "the man in the moon," came to life in my consciousness. I would see images clearer, hear and understand what was going on better. My thinking and reasoning power was more effective after taking it. As my new pill stimulated my awareness and replenished the cells of my brain, I began to make better decisions. I eliminated the sugar in my diet and gave up chocolate. I ate right, slept well, and woke up looking forward to the next day. As I yielded to the psychological changes that were brought about because of my seizure and the change from Zyprexa to Geodon, my mind became stronger and my body healthier. I broadened my sensitivity toward the needs of others and myself, became attuned to the purpose of my disease, and found ways to consult it.

CHAPTER 20

PRESCHOOL TEACHER

"Beware and take caution of dark images." That is what my new counselor, Todd Ransford, warned me when we discussed the Star Wars film *Revenge of the Sith.*

It was not in my best interest to connect with the darkness and gloom, as I had done in the past. Christine's mom had passed away, and I had leftover confusion from seeing the movie. When I took my grandson to see *Revenge of the Sith,* I suffered weird side effects from it. Todd said that I get things turned around in my mind when I see dark, ill-fated movies. "The bad images triggered some bad thoughts and brought out disagreeable experiences that were hidden in your mind." He was right. I had to shake this acute sense that preoccupied me with death once again.

After talking with Todd, I felt assured that if I kept my thoughts on the children and my projects and used self-hypnosis, the bad images would eventually leave me.

Todd listened and agreed with me on most of my principles. He was a compassionate and intelligent counselor. Even though I felt deprived of a flawless childhood, he instilled a vision in me of breaking free from the past, and he helped me to take the crucial steps to make it happen.

When I first came to see him at the request of Dr. Smith, I didn't know what to expect. I went over my past and cried about the pain my family and I went through: the alcoholic mother; the abusive stepfather; the brother with AIDS; my polio; my hospitalizations; stabbing myself with a screwdriver; lying on the freeway waiting for a truck to run over me; my boyfriends, Joe (now my husband) and Gene, his brother; my hitchhiking and dancing days; San Francisco; and anything else I could think of. I just let loose.

He did counseling with me in sections: opening up one session, hypnosis in another. When I entered his office he asked me how I was feeling, and I let him know that my past still bothered me. He asked questions about me to draw a response from me, so that I could work out my problems myself. Before our hypnosis session, he said, "Have you ever tried hypnosis?"

I said yes.

"Would you like to have another session of it?"

I said yes.

He said, "You may sit or lie down. Keep your eyes open or closed, whichever you feel comfortable with." There was a couch, so I lay down. He said, "Imagine yourself as a little girl. This is one of the happiest moments of your life. You are smiling, having fun. You may see yourself in a picture. Perhaps looking in a mirror, smiling, showing off a new dress that you just received or posing in a pink bonnet when you were two. It is your birthday. Your aunt and friends are around you, and you are having fun. You are proud. Then as you count to ten, take deep breaths, and relax. As your tragedies enter your mind, place them in chronological order: your struggle with polio, the brutal abuse from men and at home, Salem, your hospitalizations. Pay attention to your breathing. When you reach ten, remember that happy girl again. Remember her face. You will remember the people around you and the ones who have helped you out in life. Give thanks to them." Then he told me to pretend I was by the ocean and could feel the ocean air on my face. "Breathe in, relax," he said.

I didn't have a care in the world. As he counted to one, he praised me for my good qualities while I practiced deep breathing. I felt lifted and could let go of all the suffering. In the next session, we did role playing and getting in touch with the now. I would give him an example of someone who rubbed me the wrong way one day, and he would pretend he was that person and would give me feedback. Our other sessions involved me slowly opening up to him about my years in teaching and getting rid of the demons, which I'm still working on.

I found a purpose in relating to him. I told him about my opposition to the Iraq war and a dream I had of the World Trade Center going down on September 11, the same time that it happened. I learned to strengthen my mind as I practiced yoga breathing and read a few excerpts from the book of Buddha.

The birds were singing, and the moon was rising. Rain made miniature pools of rainbows on my doorstep. I welcomed it. The rain was a healthy and cleansing gift of nature. I was just embarking on a new celebration and awakening with good sleep and a healthy attitude toward teaching. As I worked my cellulite off as a toddler teacher, I thought about changing my job title. I saw a preschool opening in the office at the day-care center, and I messaged my sister about it. She said, "Go for it!"

I filled out the preschool teacher application indicating that I was ready and willing to teach. I had attended eight teaching seminars and felt qualified. The following week, I practiced memorization and recited history dates, lyrics to songs, and the sequences of words in a sentence. I stood on my head a lot and let the blood rush to my apex, so that I could concentrate better. When it was time to hit the sack, I placed over my forehead an open *Mailbox 2003–2004 Preschool Yearbook* on the subject that I was to teach the next day, and I slept with it. This helped me think of key words and key phrases by putting them in my consciousness. Within a few days I collected materials for fishing poles, a shell clock, and collage for the theme of the week, the ocean. I was ready to face young America once again, and Christine accepted me with open arms.

There were thirty children and a young head teacher named Anne, who taught with me in the preschool. I tried to look professional. I wore black slacks and a neatly ironed shirt. I stayed smooth, steady, and connected. Anne and another teacher would gossip about the new teachers, and I think the news got out in the preschool room that I had called someone a bitch in the toddler room. At first the children didn't respect me. They would chant, "Sherry is a baby, Sherry is a baby."

I'd look at them and say, "Sure. What is it you want, baby?" That quieted them down. Then we made a joke about it. You had to have a little bit of toughness and a sense of humor when it came to teaching under those circumstances. The next week, another boy had a cog in his noggin, an idea in his head. He rebelled over having to wash his hands. He organized the kids calling, "Come on, guys!" They threw all their chairs on the floor. It was like the domino effect. I called Christine, and she got it under control.

I won their respect as challenges came along the way, and I was able to confront the power struggles that were presented to me. I used tools and techniques such as catching the children off guard and making them feel more wanted. I went to seminars and teacher meetings to learn verbalization in activities. There was a cream called "boo-boo cream" that I used.

Boo-boo cream was a hand lotion made of milk. I had the parents read the label and sign a consent form for us to use it with the students. Then I had it OK'd by Christine. When a child fell and skinned his elbow or knee or felt that he needed some boo-boo cream for making a boo-boo better, I would bring out the bottle of cream, which had three sides to it. Each side was labeled: silly cream, grumpy cream, or boo-boo cream. I would rub their choice of cream on their hands to let them know that their boo-boo would go away.

If I was using the boo-boo cream, for instance, I would let the child know how special, beautiful, and courageous she or he was.

"Things will get better. Your owie will get better and go away," I'd say.

With silly cream, I would rub their elbow and laugh with them. I'd tell them they could make someone laugh today, and they would have an incredibly funny day. Grumpy cream was for the child feeling grumpy. I would ask the child if he was having a bad day and why. I would talk with him. I would say, "It is going to be a great day. Think positive thoughts. You truly are a special person." It worked.

There was a variety of songs and finger plays that I would break into when the children started running around in circles and losing control. By using an interpretation of the song "Frere Jacques" that claimed the right to have feelings, I was I was able to help myself and the children get more in touch with our emotions. We would make expressions on our faces of whatever mood we were in and sing the song.

I acquired teaching ideas from preschool books: a lesson plan to help the children with their five senses and a Valentine's Day activity to help me with my mom's passing turned out to be the most helpful. All my lesson plans helped me to become stronger mentally as I interacted with the kids. I centered on educating the children by helping them make their own "five senses" book. I illustrated the five senses on the cover of the book, and the children drew and colored pictures of their sense organs on the pages. To help them with word associations and touching and feeling, I made a felt board with materials of different textures. They ranged from hard to soft, and rough to smooth. The children could pass by it during the day and feel the textures, telling me and the other children and their parents their opinions about what they felt.

For the sense of taste, I asked the children if they would like to make a cookie of a special texture. They all jumped for joy, and we made oatmeal cookies with oatmeal, water, sugar, baking soda, vanilla and eggs. Well, almost sugar. Our oatmeal cookie saga proved to be a fiasco instead of a pleasurable event. We made the oatmeal cookies with salt instead of sugar because I mistook the salt container for sugar and measured out three-quarters of a cup of salt. I didn't know that the salt was in the container with a red lid, and the sugar was in a container with a blue lid. The lids had been changed the previous month. I used the red-lidded container. Our cookies baked, to our delight, and we got ready to eat them. Then the supervisor tasted one and said, "Oh no!" She informed me what happened.

I looked at the children and said, "Class, you know how I told you no one is perfect? Everyone makes mistakes. Well, Miss Sherry makes mistakes, too. She's not perfect. It was a big boo-boo. I put salt in the cookies by mistake. I thought it was sugar. I am so sorry. I hope that you can forgive me. Maybe we will make cookies again real soon."

"How did you put salt in the cookies, Miss Sherry?" asked Roberta, one of my favorite A students. She had chestnut brown hair and dark eyes.

I explained, "There were containers holding the salt and sugar with different colors of lids, and I used the salt container, because I didn't know the lids had been changed." One by one, the children came up to me to give me a hug. They forgave me. I learned my lesson, and I think everybody learned a lesson that day. I was very careful from then on to make sure I got the sugar instead of salt.

Kirsten, who was sweet, two and a half, with blue eyes and platinum-blonde hair, motioned to me. "Look! Come here."

She sat me down, pointed to my eyes, and said, "Eyes." Then she pointed to my nose and said, "Nose," then to my ears and said, "Ears." Next she pointed to my mouth and said, "Mouth," and then to my chin. "Chin." She smiled and said, "See!" This was all I needed to complete my day. What a helpful child. She somehow knew my day wasn't going right, and she was so sweet to let me know. It took a little teacher to know a teacher. I finished my day feeling high-spirited.

By the end of the week I was feeling much better and had weathered the storm. We played Listening Lotto, where we heard a sound on a CD and matched it to the illustrated sound on our lotto card. I created a testing table on display with chocolate bars, finger food, grapes, and broccoli on it. The children were blindfolded and tasted the food as they put it on their plates. They all guessed what the food was by feeling, smelling, and tasting. In the process, they experienced what it was like to be blind.

The next morning, the kids were spinning like tops. I had them spin at arm's length apart to relieve their aggressions. Judy was playing her part as the preschool pill, but she got over it. Fridays were always trying. I gave calendar and circle time and had the children suggest and vote on a name for their group. They came up with "The Mommy-Loving Tickling Group." We got the giggles inside. Then I asked the class what their favorite exercise was, and they said, "Somersaults and cartwheels." They all got wound up, so I had them lie on the floor, close their eyes, and envision a mountain or a quiet peaceful place. I invited them to pretend they were next to a mountain, and they could smell the green grass all around. "Smell the flowers—the daffodils, carnations, dandelions, and roses—growing there," I said.

Then I asked them to imagine they were by a stream. The water was cool, and you could drink it. The stream became a waterfall, and you could stick your head in the water and feel its coolness and freshness. I said, "As you shake the water out of your hair onto your shoulders, it is cold and wet. After being in the hot sun all day long, the coolness is relaxing. When you are ready to awaken you will become a smiling blooming rose, and you are welcome to sit on the bench."

I went through a lot of changes. In the month of February, I started composing lessons for the children and myself that promoted healing and began to strengthen my mental condition. Working with the children was like working with magic.

On Valentine's Day, we made valentine holders and played a game of hearts. I cut out a big pink heart from valentine paper. The children colored a certain number of miniature hearts on the big heart. Various hearts with different numbers of hearts on them were passed around. In a circle I would hold up the ace of hearts, the child who was given the ace of hearts would clap once. The child with the two of hearts would jump twice, the child with the three of hearts would tap his head three times, the child with the four of hearts would touch his ear four times, and the child with the five of hearts would sit down. The rules changed a bit each time the game was played. It depended on what the children's suggestions were for playing the game.

Then I brought out a red velvet rose that I had bought from the floral department at a local grocery store. They did a painting from the rose. Their colors were vibrant. They were blooming everywhere. I was able to help them develop their artistic skills by painting with nature. I gained satisfaction from watching the children grow, and I was growing, too. The grieving for my mom became easier. The activity helped me develop a new perspective on life.

My life was getting better, though I didn't want to believe it. It seemed too good to be true. I tried to get rid of self-doubt, but it looked me in the face and challenged me to think otherwise. Still, I was making progress. I was given an Employee of the Month for Compassion award in the preschool room. But just before I got the award, an incident happened that I will never forget. I was on my break in my car, and as I looked out the corner of my eye, I saw two cars collide head on into the curb next to me. The people in the one car were not injured, but I saw a man frantically give CPR to a person in the other car. He was exhausted. There were people with their cell phones, and one had called the paramedics. I came up to the rescuer and said, "I will take over."

I felt the injured man's chest. He was heavyset and couldn't move out from underneath the steering wheel. He was conscious, so I asked him to take deep breaths as I counted to ten with him, and we breathed together until the paramedics arrived. As I slowly walked back to the preschool room, stumbling over a toe or two, I looked like a drunk trying to find himself. I told Anne what had happened, and she sent a message to Christine. Christine entered the preschool room from the toddler room and asked me if I was all right. I replied, "Yes, but I'm a little shaky."

Shortly after, an Employee of the Month for Compassion award was hung beside my preschool teacher photo on the bulletin board in the room. I was proud and beside myself. I ran to the infant room to share the news with the teachers. Now, I thought to myself, I'll have to work harder than ever to live up to my title. I couldn't settle for a nice gesture. It went to my head.

I took a CPR course at the day care as a requirement for teaching. I remember the instructor saying that I probably wouldn't be able to save anyone. He didn't realize what an impact that statement had on me. All I could think about was that helping that man was not enough. I knew my material by heart from my nurse's aide days, and I was the only one who knew the procedure, but his comments hurt me. I felt inadequate. He ended up thanking me for my participation when the class was over. Still, his critical statement—that I couldn't save anyone—made me feel small and like a failure, not good enough. I questioned and doubted myself. The supervisor did write on my award that I was compassionate and brought my homework with me. I know she was bragging. But did I need to do more homework to keep my title? Why did I weave this web of uncertainty when someone had been just nice to me? Why did I let others break down my self-esteem?

Not long after the accident, the sunny weather cast me a spell. I was walking up the street from my house, and in my mind I would visualize what I saw on the outside. Trees became pink cotton-candy and white popcorn happiness. The blue jays flew by, and the squirrels danced up the telephone poles. This was life to me. The mere colors of spring captured in their entirety. I started believing in myself again and thought about how I could recreate spring's beauty with my ingenuity. Arriving at the preschool, I walked boldly into the kitchen, chin in the air, head thrown back, and headed toward the microwave. I popped the two bags of popcorn that I had brought from home. There was a space on the wall big enough for a large paper tree, so I gave the children handfuls of popcorn, and we glued it to the tree that I assembled on the wall. I was crossing my fingers in hopes of making apple blossoms with the popcorn on the tree, but I wasn't holding my breath. Some of the younger children were grabbing the popcorn and sticking it in their mouths before they got to the tree. Regardless, I kept the leftover popcorn that wasn't glued to the wall and used it for our snack, and we marveled at our production.

The next week, I came into the classroom with a daisy held behind my back. "Children," I said. "Do you want to hear something I wrote?"

"What's it about?" They jumped up and down.

"It's about spring!" I said.

"Yeah! Yeah!" they yelled. They saw I was holding something behind my back.

"This is the one Miss Sherry made up herself. It goes like this..."

"Spring"

Spring is here. But golly gee whiz,
I wonder where my flower is.
I planted the seed not very long ago,
But now my backyard is dry.
Is it going to snow?
Ah! But here it comes up, up, up,
Flowing its petals in a tiny cup,
Its colors so bright, so gay, so free.
Is this the flower I planted for me?

As I recited my poem, I brought the daisy from behind my back. The children took turns holding the flower and practicing the poem. Most of the children made up their own poems. I was amazed. It was incredible to feel that I was helping someone experience the springtime as I did. I wrote the poem when I was in junior high school in 1963. My memory hadn't failed me.

So much of my childhood was being lived through my students: the innocence of being young; the pleasant wonderment of being alive and having a new friend; the thirst for knowledge; asking questions. What is that for? Where does it come from? Why do you do that? What time is it? How does it work? Where does it go?

I don't know how I lost all that in my lifetime. It seemed like my only gain for years had been to survive on drugs that made my head spin and made me make U-turns. I wish that I had had more time to be with my brother and sister; to run free in the hills in the Green District; to build more sweet memories with them; to roller-skate endless times and miles on the rumbling floors of the Salt Lake City, Roseburg, and Portland rinks and laugh till we burst our seams; to blow dandelions with them as the flowers matured in the spring. What would life be without shakiness, poor concentration, insomnia, depression, and paranoia? I would be a free spirit, but I guess if the symptoms of their serious illness ceased to exist, anyone would be a free spirit. Some are more fortunate than others.

Yet life always has two sides to it, and I started showing signs of optimism. My mind was developing as I taught preschool, and with every door that closed, another door opened. Instead of being the "energizer bunny," I became the energized teacher. I went hunting for age-appropriate books at the Woodstock, Holgate, and Midland Libraries in Multnomah County to accommodate the themes of the week and help the children read. I met two librarians, Joan and Cathy, who directed me to new resource materials on the subject of "kid-friendly" books.

In circle time, I taught the children how to read, do a calendar, follow preschool rules, and sing songs, and I taught about the themes of the week. I would read a book in relationship to the theme and ask questions.

I used some of these ideas for reading:

1. To familiarize the children with reading a book, I made a poster with "when," "why," "who," and "what about" written on the poster and pointed to those words as we read the story. It helped the children with reading comprehension and to converse more freely among themselves about the concept of the book.
2. I passed a basketball to the children as a tool to help them learn letters to read. They would catch the ball and tell me the letter of the alphabet that they were standing in front of. We had a gigantic letter A–Z panel, with pictures illustrating the letters, along the back of the bench. (A gift from my sister, Diana.) This enhanced the children's ability to recognize letters and to form words, especially the younger preschoolers, who were beginning to learn phonics.
3. I helped them view the first four letters of their names by writing down each name in capital letters on a strip of paper. I pulled the strip of paper with their name on it through a paper window that had a slit on the each side of it. The children sounded and mouthed the letters of their names. As the letters appeared, the children would name themselves as they learned to read and spell their names.
4. Sometimes I would pass the beginning letter of the child's name on a card to the child with that name and instruct him to get ready to wash his hands for snack at snack time. Other times I would bring out flash cards to help the child associate the object or name on the card with a letter, by sight or sounding the vowels or consonants of the words.
5. I would have a little walk around during the week and point to objects in the room. I'd have the children pronounce the words and tell me what they saw. I explained to them what letter it began with as I pointed to the object. The older preschoolers would write stories about their experience and what they learned in our writing area.

6. Likewise in picking up, I would have, for instance, the numeral 4 and the word "four" printed on a card with an illustration of four hearts drawn on the face of it. I placed it in a basket. As I came over to one child, I handed the card to him or her and asked him or her to pick up four items in the play area while waiting to wash for snack. I did the same with five other numbers that corresponded to numbers on the cards.
7. I used the blackboard to demonstrate how to write a letter or a number.
8. I sprayed shaving cream on the art tables, and we would practice making letters in shaving cream with our fingers.
9. I made activity books for them to go over with the teacher's help and to color in to accommodate the themes of the week: polar bears, the seasons, sports, dinosaurs, disabilities, incredible me, and foods from other countries.

Teaching changed the direction of my psychosis. I was able to live up to my expectations, and I loved every minute of it.

CHAPTER 21

DINKY

Miss Anne and I ultimately got along well. You could say we chose to have a relationship in which we agreed to disagree. She was thirty years younger than me, mature, and talented. To me it didn't make a difference what age you were—you had it or you didn't, and she definitely had it as a teacher. She had an overwhelming abundance of love for the children, and the children loved her. She was a little mother to them. Her acts of caring and compassion were over the top.

The state came in one day while we were teaching and reprimanded Anne for some reason. No one explained to me what was going on or why, and it was disturbing. I was given a warning for not paying closer attention. This was my first warning. I could have three before they let me go. I hadn't seen anything, since I was concentrating on napping the kids on the other side of the room. I felt sorry for Anne. She went around like a lost puppy for days. Her ego was squished. I told her that we needed better communication. As time went on, our teaching practices got better, but there were times when they would collide. Regardless of the circumstances, we were a team, and we would invariably work things out.

Once or twice she interrupted me. When I was reading a fire safety book to the children, for instance, I got to the part where it said, "What do you do in case of a fire?" I said, "If the neighbor's house is on fire, you get to the phone and dial 911."

Anne stepped in and said, "That's not what you do first."

"I know," I continued. "If your house is on fire, you get out of the way of the fire and get out of the house. If your clothes catch fire, you stop, drop, and roll."

It was a benefit to us to get our meaning across, and I was more than happy to have her intervene if she wanted to, especially on topics of safety. Sometimes things went smoothly for us, and sometimes they didn't. Life is that way. We did the best job we could. Anne was a good teacher, and I found it worth my while to work with someone of her caliber.

I remember teaching the children how to cook at school. They learned how to make gingerbread houses at Christmastime, and popcorn balls, cakes, brownies, and cookies on other holidays. In the springtime, it was animal critters made out of vegetables. For all other occasions we made sugar-free foods like puddings and Jell-O, or smoothies and applesauce and other healthy foods. Nothing fancy, but I wanted to give them a taste of something new to experience in the classroom.

As I lay back on the bed that my husband, Joe, built of wood for me, I reminisced about the fun I had teaching that spring and summer. There were promising times with peaceful weather, and the kids made the greatness happen. Dr. Smith had to raise my Geodon level a couple of times, because I was seeing demons, due to my Catholic upbringing and beliefs in two powers. I don't know why the dark side of religion had such an impact on me, a schizophrenic, but it did. The voices would come to remind me of the beatings Doug and I got at Christmastime. I'd hear the sharp cold screams of my brother being beaten and most likely molested, by Ralph. Doug had showed me, when I was in Eugene, the position

Ralph put him in while he was on top of him. The voices whispered, "Don't go there, don't go there, you fool!" Ralph was the man I was afraid of. He was the devil who haunted me all of my life and in all of my dreams. I couldn't quite come to the reality of having a normal life with him as a stepdad. I believed that my illusion was real—that there was a devil, and Ralph was it—but there was something else that triggered my illusions. The eye and hand contact I made with the inmates in Salem; their disturbed habits, strange configurations, and distorted faces. They caused me to imagine things and see things that didn't exist, and because of it I had feelings that my dreams were real. I'd have flashbacks of Salem and lacked the strength to combat them. I tried to break the spell that imprisoned my mind, as the bogeyman of the spiritual worked on me to possess my soul.

With my dosage of Geodon being raised to 70 mg, my sleep became more regular. But due to stress, the Geodon needed to come up to a level of 80 mg. With the extra dose, I started to have bad dreams again, and I didn't feel quite right. I felt heavy and drugged, and I was still having visions of a demon. It was hard to kick. But I tried to ride it out. Swimming two days a week and walking to the end of the street kept me busy. Checking in with my counselor renewed my strength. I continued my work at the preschool. I listened to the doctor faithfully and returned to the lower dose when asked to do so. In the past, 60 mg was my consistent dose, but I did quite well with 80 mg. As time went on, I adjusted to 80 mg, and it became my comfort zone. The bogeyman had left my soul, and life became less stressful.

Thank the good man upstairs that my visions were few and far between. Gratefully, I had a little faithful companion who wouldn't let me fail. He gave me a boost for life and an incentive to teach preschool. He was my little cocker spaniel, Dinky. Dinky had come to us from Panama with his little sweetheart friend, Sweetie. My stepdaughter Becky had given him to us while she was stationed in the army in Panama. He had been with Joe and me since he was a pup. But my sweet little darling Dinky was dying. He lived to the age of seventeen and became blind and deaf in his old doggie years. He became incontinent. How I loved that little man. He had given me so much joy. He was someone to tell my most intimate dreams and secrets to.

In the autumn, I walked up the street from my house naming the fall leaves. The crisp yellow leaves became grandma's apples as my eyes would puddle up. Ruby-purplish leaves became plump ruby cherries. I walked on, and there were golden coffee-stained leaves that symbolized the stripping away of life and the delicacy of a new beginning.

Dinky was a magical pup in every sense of the word. He was a special and unique puppy dog. When I had to put Sweetie to sleep because she had complications with her legs and spine, he put his paw over my right eye to stop me from crying. His sweet-smelling strawberry-blond fur absorbed my tears of anguish as I grieved for my mother and brother. He helped me paint a picture by moving his paw in a circular motion on my canvas to make the painting look like cotton-candy skies. We ran and jumped and danced together with the seagulls in the park.

I had some esoteric knowledge of what pain was, especially the pain when a pet or loved one died, particularly a dog. It was awful. I was angry with God. One of the exercises I learned from Todd, and in a pain management class I took to deal with pain, was to close my eyes, visualize the color of my anger, and give it a size and shape. It was a new technique that I had never used before, and it helped me gain a new perspective on my emotions. I closed my eyes, and I colored anger green, as in envy, because I saw anger when I was envious. It had sharp edges like a triangle. When I was a young girl, the sharp tones of a triangle hurt my ears, and I saw anger as hurtful. Next, I colored love as red, like a heart on Valentine's Day, and my heart inside projected a reddish glow from it.

As this practice took up residence in my mind, I began to extend positive feelings to myself and other people. When I'd stop at a stoplight in my car, and someone pulled ahead of me when it was my turn to go, I would think of a phrase to change my thoughts of aggravation to good ones. For instance, I started thinking this:

There are people who are losing their loved ones in this world who have needs to be met. May they find help.

There are people without limbs and broken limbs and diseases who needed to be comforted. May they find peace.

There are disadvantaged people with handicaps or disabilities who have needs to be attended to. May their sadness cease.

I extended my love to them and the car in front of me. I proceeded after the green light with a whole new outlook.

As my beautiful red heart overtook me, I began to feel better and less impatient with myself. I put my importance on the here and now and how to spend it. Are my present moments being spent in a healthy way? What is the best road to take in getting well? It really did matter what frame of mind I was in in relationship to my pain. If I felt lousy, my pain level would skyrocket.

I wasn't angry with God anymore. After all, he gave me Dinky to make me happy. I'm not sore with him. God is my friend, my creator. I am on purpose, and everything I do is meant to be. I think we are all celestial beings. We are an inspiration to this world, like dogs, cats, horses, and birds. We are all made of different brains to think, but we will always try to get along and remember not to hurt others or ourselves. It is our nature. I think when you get off course, you are locked up in the "loony bin," as my husband calls it. And it is usually a downhill slide from there. Dinky kept me out of the loony bin for the seventeen years that he was my pet. He was a forever-faithful friend. I had known him by his love and undeniable genuineness and contagious sense of humor. I know that Dinky will be waiting for me in the closet someday. His kisses will last forever. Dink passed away in an animal hospital, September 11, 2004.

CHAPTER 22

BRAZIL

I just received a letter from my cousin Mickey, Aunt Deanna's son. He said that he and his wife, Susan, were going to Brazil to visit our family. Uncle Dao, Mom's brother who passed away, had made a CD in Brazil with his harmonica playing from the soundtrack of the movie *Dr. Zhivago*, and "Somewhere My Love" was one of my favorites. It reminded me of him, and as a result, I wanted to see how his wife, Terizhiniha, and his daughter, Fatima, were doing in Natal. I also wanted to visit Cousin Myrna, her family, and Aunt Joanihihia in Joao Pessoa. I didn't know if I would get the chance to go back there again.

I decided to fly to Brazil by myself and meet Mick and Sue there. When I applied for a newer passport, because my document from Spain had expired, the Brazilian embassy contacted my cousin Myrna's house to see if that was where I was going, since her house was my last destination on my trip. The Brazilian embassy gave me the OK.

Before I left, there were a couple of things I had to take care of. I needed to break the news to Dr. Smith. I walked into his office at

Summit Research. He was no longer at Pacific Northwest Clinical Research. He had become founder and director of this huge medical mental health facility in Portland.

"So you are going to Brazil, eh?" Dr. Smith asked, with his swirling white hair caressing his face, feet resting on his desktop, and kind blue eyes with a twinkle that could read you like a book. He was concentrating on something he wrote as the tablet lay comfortably on his lap. He twisted a pencil between his shining white teeth. "Let me help you figure out the times you need to be taking your meds on your trip."

Sao Paulo was six time zones away, so he calculated the best time of day for me to take my morning, noon, and evening meds starting in Portland, changing in Florida, then again to Brazil time, including the changes in my thirteen-hour flight. He wrote me out a schedule and bade me farewell. I went to Walgreens and bought a watch with multiple time zones on it and a pill category container.

I couldn't believe I was actually going to my mom's homeland. And I was going by myself. It had been twenty-six years since my last trip there. I remember how depressed and perplexed I was with Mom when I went in 1978. She was hitting the bottle most of the time. I couldn't think straight or breathe right.

Life has a funny way of overturning depression and mending it with waves of happiness through daily experience and growth. I was living my present moments and having a great time thinking and planning for my destination. Nothing could stop me.

Two nights before I left, I packed and repacked my suitcase and my fanny pack. I counted my pills a hundred and ten times. I shook them to see if they were still in their bottles. I was thinking I'd be stopped at customs, because I was sure the airlines wouldn't let me on with my medication. The next day put me to the test.

"I'm afraid to go, Joe," I said.

"Oh, you'll be all right," he replied.

"What if they open my case at customs and see my medication?"

"Dr. Smith wrote you a slip for your pills. You'll be all right. Do you still have it in your fanny pack?"

"Yes, I do. Will I see you later?"

"Have fun in Brazil."

We kissed and embraced.

As I walked up to the metal detector from the concourse of the Portland International Airport, I put my backpack on the belt. My heart sank. Would I ever see Joe and the kids again? I tried to block out the anxiety by singing a song called "White Flag," by Dido. My ship resembled the aircraft and the white flag was the ghost of the past that was eating away inside of me.

I imagined a blank canvas before me. As I painted an ocean scene, I visualized me with Fatima and Myrna on the white sandy beach near the turquoise water: Myrna smiling with the big porcelain bowl in her hand, her turquoise-green eyes and olive skin accentuating the waves; Fatima dancing around with her hands circling in the wind in the blue-and-yellow flowered dress that I had brought her. I imagined my time with Aunt Joanihihia, Mom's sister, carrying on a conversation in Portuguese with me at the convent, and the nuns singing, "The hills are alive." Maybe everything would be the same. Who knows? Does anyone age in Brazil? I wondered.

I caught the plane to Sao Paulo. As I sat down, I witnessed the moonlight passing silently behind the clouds. It was the most serene moment. Goose bumps disappeared beneath my skin. Catching on to how to use the pill schedule that Dr. Smith gave me silenced the propellers churning away in my mind as we changed from Florida time to Brazil time. When it was time to take my medication, I was excited and couldn't wait to begin my new mission.

Before I reached Natal, I was routed to Belem from Sao Paulo. At the Belem airport, I brought my medication and vitamins pills with me to the bathroom. I was in there for about ten minutes. There was a little bottle of red dye stuff on the top of the toilet tank. When I came out of the bathroom, an airport official approached me, speaking Portuguese. She asked me to go into the bathroom with her. I was getting edgy. She asked if the bottle was mine. I told her, "Nao meu," meaning not mine. She dismissed me. Apparently, it was a bottle of poison, I think. Someone must have pulled a prank. I was having paranoid thinking that a man I was sitting with on the plane planted it there just to spite me, because I wouldn't talk to him. He did look suspicious.

At my final destination, all that panic and anxiety about getting delayed at customs and being arrested for my medication went out the door, like so many of my obsessive ideas that were forced to go and begged never to return again.

I met Fatima, Sue, and Mickey in Natal. Fatima tried on the dress I brought her and swayed and danced in the warm Brazilian breeze. A certain song encircled my head. I started to sing the song "Vincent" by Don McLean. It was a song about the Dutch artist Vincent van Gogh. He died a year after he painted his famous *Starry Night* painting. The song reminded me of my mother as a nurse, when she painted with oils—how she tried to maintain her sanity, and how she tried to break free from depression. We saw the documentary *Vincent: The Life and Death of Vincent Van Gogh* by Paul Cox, a month before she passed. I remember how she had talked me into seeing the movie. "Look, Sherry, wasn't he a beautiful painter? And so sensitive," she would say. Singing her song in the country that she loved changed my view toward her completely. It moved me.

Mickey, Sue, and I traveled to Joao Pessoa and stayed a few days at Myrna's. As we swam in the turquoise body of the Atlantic Ocean, Mickey picked a starfish up with his toes and handed it to me. Near the Ilha de Areia Vermelha, I snorkeled with sunglasses (imitation goggles). I saw fish that I had never seen before. I didn't know they existed. The tropical fish were so extraordinarily brilliant in color that they seemed to absorb a direct ray of light and reflect patterns from kaleidoscopes that bounced off my arms and legs. I was in paradise. Forgiveness, sorrow, and pain had swept from my face, and once again I felt a reason for healing and living again. By traveling to this exotic place, my strength and confidence were renewed.

Before we left Joao Pessoa, we visited my aunt Joanihihia, Mom's sister. She was a nun, and she was dying of Alzheimer's in the convent hospital. When the nuns became ill, they were cared for at the hospital adjacent the convent. She had been very close to my mom. Myrna was caring and attentive to Joanihihia's needs. She'd stroke her hands and kiss her forehead. My aunt softly closed her eyes. I reached for her fingers. She clutched my right hand in hers. Myrna said, "Sobrinha (niece) Sherry is here."

I repeated, "Irma Maria, Irma Deanna, Irma, Leo, Irma Clara, Irma Beatris, and Irma Paula amor voces," meaning all her sisters loved her. "Eu saudades voces tanto." I miss you always.

I carried a note in my head that one of Mom's other sisters had given to me when I went to college at OSU. It was from Aunt Beatris. From memorizing the prayer on my aunt's card throughout the years, I repeated the words to Aunt Joanihihia. It was the Peace Prayer by Saint Francis of Assisi.

Lord make me an instrument of thy peace,
where there is hatred, let me sow love;
where there is injury, pardon...

After, "and it is in dying that we are born to eternal life," I added,

"Where there is need, let there be no need,
Where there is no trust, let there be trust,
And where there is war, let there be peace."

She didn't want to let my hand go, I could tell. It was hard to say good-bye to Auntie. I wished I had kept her letters from Brazil when I was growing up. I am grateful to have saved a few cards, but at the time, I didn't understand much Portuguese. I was fortunate to have her grace, and because of it, I was able to grow and forgive through my experience with her in Joao Pessoa.

CHAPTER 23

HOME FROM BRAZIL

It was an inviting atmosphere the day I walked through the entrance of the preschool room. I brought back music makers, large wooden crayons made out of palm trees, Brazilian street vendor dolls called baiana women, individual colored clay sacks containing cornstarch that you could make faces out of, Portuguese coloring books, and the sunshine. The children ran up to me and embraced me around the legs.

Anne and I prettied up the preschool room with stockings and ornaments. The children put their hands in paint and made handprints on their reindeer's head for antlers. At show-and-tell time, I showed the doll that my nephew, Justin, and his wife, Heidi, had given me one Christmas.

The doll had a porcelain face with tiny wrinkles in the creases of her mouth and around her blue eyes. Dangling on a golden string, she spun with a branch of Christmas holly draped across her snow-white hair. Butterfly wings were attached to her back, and a burgundy velvet jumpsuit hugged her plump figure. Tiny burgundy posts fitted her lobes, and golden slippers and lustrous ribbons brought accent to her attire. In her hand was a magic wand, the tool that all fairy godmothers are so noted for. I passed her around for each child to hold and ask questions. The children were excited. They asked me, "What does a fairy godmother do?" I told them that she would grant their wishes like the one in the *Cinderella* book. I heard oohs and aahs as they held tight to her magic wand and closed their eyes.

I gazed out the window of the preschool room. The branches on the enchanted winter trees were turned inside out and upside down. The pale green leaves were lifeless sheaths of lace hanging on to their last veins of hope. Depression wrapped a thick cloth like a shroud about my head. Three questions spun around in my head as I tried to convince myself that I was taking responsibility for my class and myself. The questions were not new to me. Todd and Diana had asked me to ask myself these many times:

1. Why do I feel this way?
2. What can I do about it?
3. How can I change it?

As I drove home from the preschool that night, the road was slick and wet with puddles that turned into Dr. Seuss's Cat in the Hat's skinny arms caressing the wheels of my car. I proceeded as the Cat's long tail caressed my bumper and anchored me. I felt a hard rock hit the hood of my car. It knocked and bounced off the hood, till it cracked open the door to my mind. I said, "Take it easy. Take it easy." I shivered at the fact that the impact could have shattered my skull to pieces. I reached my house and unlocked the front door. I wedged inside and sat down. I sat back in my chair and realized that my imagination must have gotten the best of me. I was forced to deal with puzzles in my head, and logic.

It was time to face myself and come to terms with life once again, so I called my sister. I thought she might have some inkling of where I had been and where I was coming from. She told me to get one of my poster boards that I used for teaching and with a marking pen relive Christmastime with Ralph, Maria, and Doug.

"Draw in detail everything that happened Christmas Eve: when you left OSU as a college student to come home for the holidays; getting drunk with Mom and Ralph; Ralph hitting you for being molested by Sandy and for having a German girlfriend; Mom hitting Ralph over the head with a fireplace poker; and Ralph running upstairs to take it out on Doug. Then draw a detailed picture of how you want your Christmas to be on the poster board."

I drew my pictures true to life and then not so true to life. Now I wasn't so unhappy. I liked the untrue nature of the pictures that were on my poster board. I could pretend and remember Mom, Ralph, Doug, and me opening presents and having a grand time. I traveled back to OSU in my mind as a happy person. I found out I could change the scenario of Christmastime and the events and believe only what I wanted to believe about it. I sailed through that Christmas without any scars.

As the month of February crept up on me, grieving was still preeminent. This was the month of my mom's suicide. I was questioning everything around me that was thwarting my way: Had I sent that invisible dagger that pierced her heart and caused her to jump? I should have listened to her when she said, "I'm going to die, and there is nothing that you can do about it, Sherry." Did she jump because I went to Oregon State Hospital and suffered a mental illness? Was it the life of promiscuity I lived so long ago? Should I not have hung up on her because she was drunk the day she jumped?

Since Mom died, these questions had sunk into my consciousness with no way to escape. I was trying to process these things and protect my mind from going off the deep end, but I dealt with these issues in a haphazard way. I couldn't connect the dots. I was going through the same feelings I had for her before she jumped, when she jumped, and now after she jumped. Suicide is so cold and heartless. You never ever seem to reach a closure with your feelings. I had to put a lid on it. I made an urgent appointment to see Dr. Smith, and he suggested that I write to my mother in a way of healing and see what happened. I wrote:

Dear Mother,

So many times you have helped me develop my own ideas and tried in your own way to say, "I am sorry, Sherry, for all I have done to you." But so many times I have wanted to say, "It is all right, but it was your fault."

Actually, it wasn't your fault for the way life had dealt with you, the problems you faced with men, or the drinking problem you had. I have run into many men in my lifetime with a drinking problem, and I have met my own fate with booze. It was not your fault about Salem. You saved my life, because I was very sick from Ralph and the men who were in my life.

So you were a drunk. Beneath that was a woman with a philosophy as beautiful and peaceful and harmonious as the deep blue sea. I would not have been able to give without the love that you gave me in the beginning.

Maria is your name. God and your parents gave you that name, because you were a virgin. They thought you were the Virgin Mary.

Hats off to you, my dear mother, for being so pure and for taking all the stuff that men did to you. Still, you tried to raise us.

Doug was your son. He did not feel appropriately raised by you. I'll let him talk to you up there and give you his own forgiveness.

Knowing Doug, he will.

Diana and I will come to terms in our own way. We were bitter when you left, but things are better now.

I turned fifty-six today. Some people, family, celebrated my birthday, and I celebrated it with the kids, getting mad at them for one reason or another. I am so sorry I raised my temper.

I talked with Dr. Smith and Joe about a student who celebrated his birthday the same day as mine. We gave each other a big hug for our special day. I feel sorry for him because he suffers from ADHD. But he and I are fortunate.

I am so lucky and happy with my life! I am in love with Joe. And Dr. Smith, my doctor, is the best doctor.

This is my birthday, dear mother. I miss you. It is a day of forgiving and for giving, receiving, and sharing.

I love you, I dream of you, and most important, I forgive you.

Let the sun shine down on you in heaven,

Sherry

CHAPTER 24

GRANDEUR ILLUSIONS

There was an invisible tiger hurling itself inside of me. I knew it. I was consumed by its hot breath as it made its way to the dark images that festered outside my head. I could visualize its sharp fangs grasping my forehead and chin, growling lifeless breaths in my face. I didn't give into it. After all, I had children to care for, and they loved me and depended on me.

Easter holiday was nearing and *The Passion of the Christ*, coproduced by Mel Gibson, was playing in the theaters. I had feelings that I was Jesus Christ, and I was having bad images. Because I had been strapped to my bed on Good Friday in 1976, I felt a strong connection to that movie. I thought Jesus could have been strapped to the cross like I was strapped to my hospital bed, and I was feeling his pain while I was twisting my wrists, yelling, trying to get out of the heavy leather straps. I had distorted religion and allowed it to influence my thinking and have power over me. Not letting the experience cool down a bit, I let the distortion run its course. I figured out that it was my upbringing by a mother who was Catholic and drank, and my belief in two powers, God and Satan, that caused me to have grandeur illusions and to think insane thoughts. Ever since I was little, coming home from church, I became fearful of a dreadful creature—like a black hairy monster—overpowering me. Mom always told me the devil was coming to fetch me if I did wrong. In my head, I created illusions of grandeur, as if I were Jesus or some supreme being, so that I could ward off the demon. But no one ever told me I wasn't Jesus Christ, and I had to work it out in my head. As I became afflicted with mental illness, the task became harder. I would shake my hands and sweat and feel all-powerful. I thought that I could miraculously change people and circumstances.

I am not Christ, but I need to be reminded of that time and time again. My head gets so swollen with conceit and confusion that it plays tricks on me, especially when taking a new medication or when my medication dose is off. I need to turn off my Christ image by self-talk and discuss my symptoms with my counselor, Todd, and my psychiatrist, Dr. Smith. After living in the unreal world for a portion of my life, a reality check and an endorsement are appropriate in helping me overcome my fear and maintain my sanity. They assure me that my visions and elevated thoughts are just my imagination, and to erase them from my memory will take work.

I had only been on the Geodon for a year, and even though my thought processes were clearer sometimes, there were steps I needed to take to get well. So I wrote in my journals and continued painting in art class and at home. I painted my students' portraits. I had a gallery showing, and one of my students showed up with his parents to see his portrait. He was doing somersaults, tumbling all over the tiled floor when he discovered his picture. His sad brown eyes were like a lost puppy's, and the moisture would form in front of his pupil, as if he was crying for no reason. His features were sharp: high cheekbones and rough lips. He was a challenge to paint, but that made it all the more fun to paint him.

On Saturday, I went to art class. A particular art teacher named Dorothy was teaching. She was subtle in her remarks and her eyes, like the color of the Atlantic Ocean, had a musical feel to them as they reflected back onto me. Oddly enough, she once lived at the beach and was painting an ocean scene. It was hard to distinguish her still-life paintings from a photograph; they were so real. I got involved in all kinds of formulas as I trained myself in learning the artistic techniques of the professor. I was afraid that if my head got much bigger as I painted, I would evolve into a female creature. The features of one side of the face would be male, and the other side of the face would be female, and they would call me "Sherry da Vinci."

"Ah, come on, Sherry, you can't be that good," I said to myself. But I was not disillusioned by the potential I had as an artist, and I dared to try anything once. I was persistent, and I couldn't give it up.

Rose, the next subject, had deep brown eyes that led you around in a circle in the picture. Each time I learned a new skin tone and showed how I identified with the professor's techniques, Dorothy would comment on my painting and give me a bigger head than the one that I came in with. "Brilliant," she'd say, as I painted the skin tones on Rose's face. "Fabulous! You got the shading just right." She marveled as I brought the picture to life.

Rose became a precious gift to my mind and to my eyes. My shadow colors were a little dab of burnt sienna, burnt umber, and a tinge of cadmium red light for rouge. My night was something out of *South Pacific*. My head, my self-consciousness, and karma were still never quite the same.

I remember traveling to see my sister Easter weekend on the Greyhound bus. I learned to acquire more self-esteem and grace just by being with Diana. My life would open up and blossom with each step, made firmer by her encouragement. I found out there was something positive to be said about Easter. I had been so immersed in the activities with the kids and the Easter celebration that I forgot all about being Jesus Christ.

Diana, her new husband, Bob, and I took in a play about the paranormal at the Cabaret Theater in Ashland, a local theater downtown to which actors came from all over. Afterward she took me to the store and bought me new shoes: blue-leather spider-web sandals with straps and rubber soles. The brand name was Keen. There was no hidden meaning to it. I didn't connect the episode of when I painted the Keane paintings with red paint—before I went to Salem—to the sandals. "It is what it is," as my husband would say over and over again to me to get me to face reality. I gave myself a big endorsement for not dwelling on and obsessing over the resemblance.

When I came back to Portland, Dr. Smith adjusted my medication because I was having some problems. I went back to 80 mg of Geodon and continued on a sleeping pill called Remeron. Dr. Smith had prescribed the Remeron for me from the time that I went to Brazil up till now. The Benadryl was no longer effective. I got too shaky, and I needed something stronger. My husband knew what I went through with the Geodon-Remeron combination before, and he was reluctant for me to take it, but this was different. We agreed that I would do better taking the Remeron this time.

Miss Anne and I attended an Applebaum Teacher's Training Institute seminar in the late spring. It was located at Village Inn, on the north side of the freeway from our school.

We sat down in a large auditorium where the seminar commenced. We wrote our names down on a blank piece of paper, along with the day-care center we were from, then passed them to the front of the auditorium. As 150 sat quietly, we listened to the speaker, who was tall, slender, with sandy-red hair: a stark resemblance to Ichabod Crane. I started to get nervous. It wasn't the nervousness where you get tense and ready to bite your fingernails. It was a butterfly-in-the-stomach nervousness like something was going to happen. Like when I was at an Obama town hall meeting at the Kid's Unlimited Gymnasium in Medford, Oregon, and asked the candidate in front of two thousand people, "With all the criticism you get from the press and your opponents, what tools and techniques do you use to maintain your composure?" His reply was honest and to the point. He said that he had love and respect for his country and for himself. He respected the role of the military and their sacrifice in keeping our nation strong. He was going to spend important time on the issues and he expected being attacked by other politicians. It didn't bother him. He also remarked that he avoided the tabloids, and he said that his daughters said that he had a sense of humor.

    I guess it was that kind of nervousness that shook me up and made me remember what the candidate had said that day. But at the Applebaum seminar I was more intense, not prepared. The material the speaker was presenting—about the angry defiant kids, how to handle kids who talk back, children who didn't listen, information about the mistakes parents make, and what parents need to do during divorce and separation—triggered my stomach to do backflips.

    There was a drawing before the break, and they drew my name from a hat. I won the T-shirt with the world stamped on it. People around me applauded. I felt proud; I couldn't believe it. My eyes started to puddle up. How long had it been since I had won something? I walked up to the center of the stage, and the moderator handed me my prize.

    The meeting started up again after the break. The speaker was talking about children in the classroom and their modes of communication. He pointed several questions to the audience: Why do you think that we need communication? How do you prefer to correspond: by writing letters, telephone, e-mail, or music? How did it change your life?

    I raised my hand. "I prefer to correspond and communicate by letters. I got a letter and it changed my life."

Speaker: "Identify yourself and tell us why."

"My name is Sherry Joiner." I repeated my name because he didn't remember me, I guess. "In 1972 I received a letter in the mail, because I was fighting for equal pay on my job. The attorney general in Salem, Oregon, sent me a check from my employer for my case and said that from now on, there would be equal pay for equal work in the work force. I was one of the first women in the United States to receive a reimbursement for fighting for her equal pay rights on a job."

As I talked, my heart drained. I felt a giant fist reaching down my throat, pushing farther, blocking my esophagus, stopping the air that was passing through my mouth as I frantically tried to breathe. My hand shook like I was pressing my knuckles against a wall, and the pressure on my knuckles caused my fingers to crack, erode, and crumble. The pressure got the best of me. I lost my voice part of the way through my response, and my knees began to bounce like a basketball player dribbling for a pass on a basketball court. Finally, I regained more stability and was able to finish what I was trying to convey to the audience.

I could hear oohs and aahs in the crowd. "She was the first woman to fight for us."

At that moment, I sat basking in glory and felt proud, thinking that if anyone touched me, they would turn to gold. It was the first time I opened up to a crowd about this issue. It got better each time I talked about it. All of my fighting had come to a halt at last.

When Anne and I came back from the seminar, a teacher named Lois was working in the toddler room. Lois, a middle-aged, blue-eyed, buxom blonde, was a new addition to the day care.

"How was the seminar?" she asked.

We told her it was fine, and Anne bragged about the way I brought up my equal pay case. Lois and I struck up a conversation, and I invited her and her husband over for dinner at my pad. We were doing an early childhood assessment study together and bonded well. But my first impressions of people in this business were deceiving at times, and sometimes the teachers were out for themselves. I found out the energy I invested in trusting her as a friend would turn on me. I disclosed facts about my stay in the mental institution and my dancing to her. She said that she was a child-abuse worker, and her mother had difficult depressive states like me. Feeling she would understand my situation, I extended my compassion. I hoped there was a chance that I could help Lois get in touch with her mom by relaying information about my schizo-affective disorder. But my logic was slipping and needed a fine-tuning.

Mother's Day came with a bit of peace in the storms of life. I had discovered that everyone around the world was having some sort of a crisis. Even though I thought that I had been hit the hardest, I hadn't. People all around me were trying to manage and make their way through life, facing bad financial circumstances, illness, abandonment, war, or grieving. We all had our crosses to bear; some were more burdened than others. But my cross was no longer heavy. I was missing Mom, but the grieving had gotten better. My armor was finally built up to defend me against attacks on my emotions.

The children and I made Mother's Day hug boxes. It was an endearing time, a time of compassion and admiration for our moms. Through interaction, we learned patience and forgiveness as we guided our favorite illustrated hug into our boxes. We placed chocolate kisses and confetti inside the boxes and tied them with golden ribbons. I helped them write "I love you," and we sent them merrily on their way.

Later that day, I came to the toddler room with my preschool kids and thought I heard Christine say, "What's her problem?" Did she mean me? Did I hear her right? Or was I being just a little bit paranoid?

CHAPTER 25

THE HIERARCHY

I became a head teacher. The establishment gave me full responsibility for the preschool room, since I had been there the longest. My title wasn't posted on a board or anything, but they assumed that I was fit for the job. I had lingering thoughts about going back to college, but I figured that the day care was where I belonged and where I was needed. I was still searching my soul and trying my best not to act on impulse. Christine left, and Lois became supervisor. Anne went to another branch of the day care to teach preschool.

There could have been a little clarification about what Christine said in the toddler room about the girl's problem, but it didn't happen. Instead, I carried it with me and conducted a Christmas concert at preschool with both age groups, the two-and-a-half- to three-and-a-half-year-olds and three-and-a-half-year-olds to five-year-olds. It was phenomenal how many times I had the children rehearse "We Wish You a Merry Christmas," Jingle Bells," and "Santa Claus Is Coming to Town." It became a ritual. The children performed the concert right on cue. I remember when little Mary, one of the singers, with her short, bouncy brown hair, stood up from her chair next to the platform where we were performing and went bouncing off unexpectedly in the opposite direction. She headed for a seat in the audience. It was when they were singing, "Dashing through the snow." It was so cute. It fit in perfectly with the musical. It reaffirmed my feeling that it was fun to be a teacher. After the concert, I could hear giggles and then more giggles as the children laughed about themselves and with Mary. It was something to behold.

Communication started to become hazy and broke down. A teacher named Faye became my coteacher. Faye was big-boned, bold, and beautiful—a sweet and strong African American woman. I'd say she was in her twenties or early thirties. She was the most talented person whom I worked with. She sang, played the piano, played baseball, and made beaded bracelets and necklaces with the children. When I called the abuse line about a parent's abuse of a child, Faye told me that she had such respect for me. That was so like Faye—kind and sweet. But the storms of life were lurking around the corner. She took it back, because I was talking to a child who was venting about her parents at nap time. The room was supposed to be quiet.

In January I directed a play for our school called *Where The Wild Things Are,* by Maurice Sendak. I made programs with my computer and passed them around to the parents, the staff, and the students. I offered Faye the part of scenic director. She accepted and helped the children paint a forest and jungle scenes, attaching their pictures to the inside of the windows.

I wasn't looking for trouble, but I stood a knock away from its door. Faye had befriended Yolanda's daughter Juanita, who was a substitute preschool teacher. Juanita was a teenager with beautiful black flowing hair. She was conceited. She walked as if everyone was beneath her, with her chin up in the air, a pinched-up nose, and her head held high. I kept my distance when it came time to work with her. Only once did I say, "Juanita, you need to respect me like you respect Faye." She had turned me in for messy counter tops.

It became a power struggle between Faye and me, and I was written up for cluttered counters and a messy preschool room. I thought everyone could have pitched in and picked up. It was important to keep my materials on the teacher's counter, so they were within reach. But I was given a second warning. It got to the point where, in frustration, I listed five things to Faye that we needed to work on in the preschool room. One of them was, "Please do not criticize me in front of the kids."

Lois didn't like this mode of communication and became suspicious of me. She yelled at me and said, "There's the door." Then she asked me back. I struggled with my inner being, sending e-mails to Dr. Smith. I was trying to get my act and life in order in hopes of becoming more conscientious and caring. In Sherry's Master Plan, which had been symbols and charts, I wrote a description of what was going on to Dr. Smith.

Dear Dr. Smith:

Today I will be the most conscientious and positive person that I can be. I will address each issue with love, no matter how hard or how long it takes. I will remember that I am not perfect, and I too have fallen, only to be lifted up by people who cared and loved me. Some loved me enough to die for me. My teaching will be of responsibility, guidance, patience, understanding, and grace. I will try harder to make the path straight and smooth for the children to endure. I will remember the lessons of my past. Children have problems, too, and they are just trying to work through them. It takes time. And I will practice forgiveness toward Lois and Faye. I will work cooperatively and congruently with Faye as a team today and bend where I need to bend. It will be a great day. I will take pictures of our masterpiece, the bunny cake, and go to the library. I will pack for the coast after work. My lesson plan is completed. Sherry

Dr. Smith's reply:

"You continue to inspire. Attitude is so much of life. Congratulations for figuring that out. Keep up the good work."

⌒

The next week, I injured my knee putting up mats. I hadn't reported my injury right away to SAFE, because Lois's dad had come down with a serious illness the day I was injured. I thought she needed me. But something was amiss.

Helen, who was a new employee, took my place while I was on leave. She continued the ritual of singing my bonding songs with the children. When I came back for a short visit, unbelievingly I watched her sing and playact "Three Little Monkeys Swinging in a Tree" and "ABCs," because that is what I used to do with the kids.

Lois asked me, "Isn't Helen going to make a good teacher?"

I nodded my head, not knowing what Lois was thinking.

The following week, I was released to full duty from workmen's comp. I had the children line up to go outside to play on the playground. Little Samuel was still in the bathroom. Juanita was supposed to be the coteacher with me. She counted the children before we went out to the playground. I counted nineteen (I always counted the children). There were supposed to be twenty. I asked where Samuel was. She told me he was in the infant room, so I took her word for it. I thought he had gone to be with the teachers there when he had finished pottying. I proceeded to tell the children to give me the high five: ears open, eyes open, mouth closed, hands to yourselves, and pay attention to teacher, as I held up my fingers pressing each one down to the palm of my hand. We went to the playground.

Suddenly, Helen came running out to the playground, air sounding tight in her chest. "Lois is mad at you, because you left Samuel in the bathroom."

I knew something was wrong. Lois was not talking to me herself, and I hadn't done anything wrong.

The police came, but they didn't need to question me about the incident. Lois waited two days to talk to me. I painted with the kids that morning. As I went into the bathroom, I looked into the mirror and noticed red paint splattered on the front of my shirt. In a flicker of a second, the red paint reminded me of the red paint I had splashed over the Keane pictures of children. I hurriedly scrubbed it off. I went out to the playground with the children.

Shelly, another toddler teacher, came out to the playground and said, "You are wanted in the office." She didn't look happy. Bottom lip lowered in disgust.

As I entered the office door of the preschool, the owner of the day care, Bertha, was standing there with Lois. "You'd better sit down," they said.

"You are fired for leaving Samuel in the bathroom," Bertha remarked in a nonchalant tone of voice.

I couldn't believe this was real. I was getting fired. I sat staring at her sweaty tennis shoes. They reeked of rotten eggs, like the ones I smelled in Mom's boarding house where she worked when I was little. My imagination was getting the best of me, yet I remained calm. I glanced at the polished floor beneath her foot, thinking how she could maintain a day-care center that well when she wasn't able to keep help like me and couldn't keep us up to ratio sometimes. I couldn't stomach the situation. It was a setup. I had just gotten my release to full duty from workmen's comp, and I had been there for four years. Maybe it was because Bertha's daughter, Yvette, the director, yelled at me for not producing my insurance number on time when she asked for enrollment one day. I thought no one was supposed to know that number.

Bertha told me it was my third warning and to pack my things and go. Was it taking my break first in order to take my pills on time? Was it taking time off to have a counseling and psychiatric session once a month? Could it be not reporting my injury on time because Lois's dad became seriously ill?

I said to Bertha, "Even if Juanita told me that Samuel was in the infant room?"

Bertha looked down below her chin and replied, "You should have walked back there to look for yourself. Juanita isn't teacher qualified."

I went to the wall in the preschool room and grabbed hold of the huge dinosaur mural that hung in the quiet area. It was a gift from my stepdaughter Becky. I wasn't going to let them have it. I tore down the mural. I began to take down the kindness tree that I made with the kids. Bertha stopped me. "Not that tree."

I said, "It's mine. I made it with the kids." I spared it. Lois stepped into the room.

"I didn't know Juanita wasn't teacher qualified, Lois," I said, keeping my tears back.

Lois, with a silly grin on her face, commented, "You knew it all along."

Then I shifted gears. I blurted out, "I couldn't tell. She was always hanging around in your office."

I reached over to the ABC panel on the wall that my sister bought me for the school. I used to play catch basketball with the youngsters standing in front of the letters of the alphabet. I ripped the panel off the wall. Then I got my things and put them into a box. Two weeks before they let me go, they'd asked me to remove the portraits I painted of the children. They had been in the storeroom at the day care for a long time, and it didn't seem fair that I was asked to remove them. That should have told me something then.

Next, I asked Lois for my multicultural painting that I did of the preschool. She handed it to me and laughed to Joan. The children in the painting were standing on their heads, jumping rope, playing jacks, riding bikes, and playing ring-around-a-rosy outside the preschool. There were coffee stains on it. Maybe one of the teachers did it to get back at me. Who knows? Ironically, I later entered the painting in a volunteer show, and it hangs in Doernbecher Children's Hospital today. But time was running out for me. I was getting paranoid. Entertaining bad and dark thoughts was not my nature. My meds were due in fifteen minutes.

The last thing I remember doing was walking to the playground and throwing my arms around the children. I told them that I was leaving, and I cried. The children and I flooded the playground with tears. They hugged me. The boy who had been abused looked up at me, and tears streamed down his cheeks. An African American infant teacher, Priscilla, came out of the infant room, and we hugged each other and sobbed. Faye stood tall on the concrete next to the slides and opened her arms. She said, "You are a good teacher, Teacher Sherry." I did love that woman, despite our differences.

It was the longest drive home. Why did this have to happen? Where did I go wrong? Being a teacher was a dream of mine that became tangible. The day care gave me the opportunity to teach children by showing them my love. But why now and why this?

The Cat in the Hat's long skinny arms grabbed the wheel of my Volkswagen. I had loved children all of my life. I wanted to help every one of them I possibly could, with their skills and the everyday problems that they faced in a world of disease, war, dysfunction, violence, hunger, and abandonment. Then why did this happen to me?

The Cat gnawed at my tires. Was it disclosing the fact that I was bipolar to Lois? My car slowed down. Was it standing up for myself in seminars, expressing my knowledge, and confessing my beliefs to the world? My car took a right. Was it attending the same church my hierarchy went to? Was it because I ceased to go there because of the pope's views on homosexuality and pardoning priests for molesting parishioners? Or was it the pure meanness and vindictiveness of a friend named Lois, who betrayed me? My car stopped. I was saturated with tears. My only way out was to think of all the good times I had at school and my life's experiences. I could hear my brother's voice from heaven. "Don't do anything crazy. Life has done enough to you." The

Cat in the Hat was leaving now. The only way to fight this was time. I made it to the driveway. Joe was there to meet me and hugged me.

"I got fired," I said.

"I'm sorry, Bunky." He grabbed me and held me tight.

CHAPTER 26

WRITING LETTERS TO MYSELF

When I returned home, I called Dr. Smith and told him that I was let go. It was the saddest day of my life. By the tone of his voice, he was unhappy, too. I had forgotten my library books and pictures I had taken of the class. I called Lois, but she didn't answer my calls. So I left her a message at the center on the answering machine implying that it would be embarrassing and awkward if I had to come and pick up my teaching materials. Still no answer. I had been sewing a hands-on preschool book and finished it to show the kids. It consisted of their photos on the front page. The other pages were full of activities sewed in the book, like buttoning flowers, and matching planets, matching shapes, tying shoes. I brought it to the playground as a form of healing and closure.

Two five-year-old girls cupped their heads in their hands and sobbed. Their tears soaked the necklines of their dresses. They couldn't look me in the face. They pleaded, "Miss Sherry, don't go." Lois handed me my books and pictures. Somehow the animosity that I felt toward her had vanished, and I felt a healing fill me. As I closed the gate to the playground, Roberta called out, "Miss Sherry, come back to see us real soon!"

I replied, "I will," knowing that I could never step foot on the premises again.

I went to see Todd, and we talked at great length about my leaving and how I could be a productive human being again. He perceived my work situation as one where I was the winner. I had prospered by reaching out to the children, teaching them how to read, helping them with their identities, and working through their problems. By making bulletin boards with them, helping them to socialize, introducing arts and crafts, and strengthening their knowledge with scientific experiments and social studies, physical education, and math, I excelled. He said that because I reached out to them, I had enriched not one, but many lives.

Todd explained to me that being let go was not a reflection on me. It was a reflection on the day-care center I was working at. They were the ones who had failed and would suffer, because I was a good teacher.

"They will remember you. It may take time to heal, but you have made a mark on their lives."

I was relieved, so I went to Southeast Works, a nonstop employment center, and I was assigned an advocate named Gwen. She helped me with my resume, and then she helped me find a job and later to get disability insurance. While I was looking for work, I received unemployment, because I was fired for an unjust cause. I looked into college possibilities in the interim. I read two great books by Wayne W. Dyer: *The Power of Intention: Learning to Co-Create Your World Your Way* and *Inspiration: Your Ultimate Calling*. They helped me with my psychosis, to discover ways to alleviate the stress that I had undergone at the day care, and to overcome my world of inferiority.

I learned to acquire unconditional forgiveness and to give unconditionally. I started writing a journal about what I wanted for the world and myself. I wrote the names of the persons for whom I was grateful on my calendar each day. I adopted philosophies and made up sayings to fit my lifestyle: Sometimes winning in life is just being there.

Participating helped me to accept defeat.

These are some of my favorite sayings:

1. The key to life is having a higher power, admitting your faults, and forgiving your friends.
2. When you have a positive outlook, every door will open up to you.
3. Be satisfied with your circle of friends, because no one can replace the chain that links you together.
4. Be thankful for your mentors, doctors, nurses, and relatives, for they are a real treasure in the changing fortunes of time.
5. When we forgive, we release the binds we have attached to ourselves and other people.
6. Live your true identity, and you will live a life of luxury.
7. If something is too hard to deal with, don't deal with it.

I started writing in my journal in my quiet bedroom, where I sought peace and solitude. Something told me to glance over my shoulder at my dark-green Brazilian wrap with its light green stars. It's a Brazilian flag with its blue hemisphere enclosed in a yellow diamond with the banner, ODEM E PROGRESSO, and twenty-two sweeping yellow stars. It was dangling off the broken curtain rod. It danced in the breeze of the open window. I thought about my beautiful family back in Brazil and my friends. About the kids and experiences of the past. I began to write two healing letters to myself.

My letter to myself:

Dear Sherry,

You are going to have a one big nourishing self-talk with yourself.

The kids where you worked loved you.

You painted their portraits and came to work early every day to teach them compassion, love, and respect. You even attended multitudes of seminars to help their minds and bodies become strong.

And you say you aren't good enough? You are the best you can be. You are good enough the way you are.

Whenever you are down, remember what an inspiration you have been to the kids and what more you still can be.

Many of our choices in life can be wrong, but they are our choices, and there was a reason for every one of them. So when you make a choice in life to talk—with a friend, a coworker, or a boss—use your words the way you have told the children to do so many times. Learn from your mistakes. The decision to change your mind is yours, and the distortion of the realities that you weave in your mind will work its way through into a beautiful smiling blooming rose someday.

My letter to myself to say good-bye to the day care:

Dear Self:

I want so much to make amends with the girls at the day care. So much resentment has eaten me up inside. Not a day goes by that I don't feel the urge to compensate or apologize for the miscommunication or hurtful feelings. Faye, I only want you to know this: I miss you even though we haven't seen eye to eye. I'm sorry if you thought I was being so controlling around you. You probably thought you were only trying to help at times. I am sorry if you felt that I didn't give you enough credit. They say time heals all wounds. I might say it healed mine. You were a friend, a fine worker, and the kids loved you. I hope you are feeling better about your life, and I hope that you succeed in whatever you do.

Juanita, I want you to know that sometimes in life we meet people who think they are better than we are. I have often thought that I was better than you, because you snitched on me about my counters and irrelevant things. I hope you will always be my equal, so that when we march into heaven, we will be side by side, shaking hands. You are young and growing. It takes time. Being a teenager is hard. When I was a teenager, I was very obstinate, too, but later things changed. Things will change for you. I'm sorry I hurt your mom's feelings. I forgive you.

And Lois, you were my good friend. I'm sorry our relationship didn't grow into something great. Be at peace with yourself.

Kids, I love and miss you. I do very much!

You made my day. Thank you for the stories you wrote, your fabulous artwork, and your imagination. Thank you for putting up mats and helping with bulletin boards, using your manners, waiting in line, listening, and being as sweet and helpful to each other as you have been. You were my life's purpose. You had such a sense of humor. Please take care and listen to your parents. Think good thoughts. You are forever in my heart and in my mind. Live the best of life and be happy.

Love,
Miss Sherry

CHAPTER 27

THE BIPOLAR CHILD

I passed birch, holly, and spruce fern trees gaily decorating the street: The birch with its long, frail, bare limbs sweeping the ground, the holly wearing a prickly skirt of green leaves and bright red berries, and the spruce fern standing statuesque with its viridian-green and powder-blue branches. A drop of water touched my eyelid. It landed in a puddle of water in the reflection of a photographer's inverted image. It was unlike the starry night or the sunny day we had a day or two ago that gave birth to a new meaning of freedom in the wintertime. Instead, ice crystals had formed and left a blanket of snow on the playground on Christmas 2006.

I was having trouble with a student at a new school. He and his brothers were notorious for kicking, biting, and spitting at other kids. The boys were a trio. This student in particular had a mental disability, so I decided to go to the library and educate myself. He was a bipolar grade-school student. The more I read, the more I got involved, and the more demented I felt. He was depressed because of an accident: the death of a loved one in the family. As a result, his stress caused him to act out. He was striking out at his classmates because of his condition and his brothers' influence on him. I came back to school and tried to relate to him. I finally got through, but Dr. Smith had to prescribe me a higher dose of Geodon for me in the process. The dosage went down in a couple of days.

I left a Post-it, with five stars drawn on it, by the table where Tim sat. I explained that if he hit or kicked a fellow student or refused to listen to instructions, he would lose a star. I would ask him to tell me why he hit, and then I would ask him to apologize if it was his fault. I told him that it was not OK to hurt other people's bodies or feelings, and I would talk with him in the quiet area of the room. If he was good and kept all his stars till the end of the week, I would buy him a prize. He could also get a prize at the end of the week for picking up things in the room. It worked pretty well. I bought him rad stickers of his choice and pencils that were up-to-date with the times.

Things were piling up on me: getting involved with Tim's condition, failure to control the grade-school class, Mom's death anniversary, being let go from the day care, and dreams of demons. It was a combination of everything. I saw Dr. Smith two weeks in a row, one day each week. Mentally, I was in sorry shape. He put me on a higher dose of Geodon again and prescribed Seroquel, two 25 mg pills, for sleep. It worked liked a charm, and my sleep was never better. I was finally sleeping soundly, and my Geodon was back to 80 mg. I was happy. I no longer took the Remeron and was thrilled to get off of it. Remeron did serve its purpose, but nothing worked better than the Seroquel. It was a godsend. It was cleaner and more effective. I could fall asleep an hour after I took it. With the Remeron, it took three hours to drift off to slumber.

One of the exercises I did to help myself was putting on a DVD called *Relaxation and Breathing for Meditation with Rodney Yee*. I learned to take long breaths. I controlled my breath by putting my legs in the air, up against the front door, and breathing the air in from my "lower rib, to the upper rib, and then to the collarbone." I used the mantra "water belly, river breath, sky mind" as I imagined a waterfall flowing over my body. I was finally attaining a peace of mind, and my psyche was more tranquil. The stress was gone. I also listened to Louise Hay's self-affirmation tapes, which assisted me when I wasn't doing the yoga breathing. I read helpful children's books like *Hands Are Not for Hitting* and *Words Are Not for Hurting,* by Martine Agassi, PhD, which aided me in conveying to the children the message of being good to yourself. These books also taught me the lesson of being good to myself and valuing my body and other people's feelings.

On Christmas morning, I woke up to find a package under the tree from my sister, Diana. She called me the night before to see if I had gotten anything, but to my surprise, my husband put the packages under the tree without me knowing. To my amazement, I found a doll with a long pointed nose and golden spectacles. She wore a red-and-white dress and a flowered cap that covered the top of her long gray-yarn hair. But her most amazing feature was her mouth, which was big enough to swallow all the creatures in the song "The Old Lady Who Swallowed a Fly." She came equipped with a package of animal stuffies and the book *There Was an Old Lady Who Swallowed a Fly* by Simms Taback. Ever since I was little, Diana always knew how to cheer me; her heart reached the many corners of my mind.

Having a better understanding of my mental disability over the past years has made me a better, well-rounded person today. I have learned responsibility and tolerance for my disease. Instead of avoiding a problem, trying to take my life, or hitchhiking to faraway places, I cope by talking my problems out with a counselor and a doctor. Having control over my life by taking medication, I am able to set goals for myself like forgiving, sharing, and helping others. I am reaping the rewards of life by giving a meditation-relaxation exercise with my lectures at a psych ward for the National Alliance on Mental Illness (NAMI) Multnomah in Portland, Oregon.

As I begin the exercise, I have the patients sit down and place their feet on the floor and their hands in their laps. I say, "There is a box next to your feet and a string next to the box." I have them put all their cares, woes, and troubles into the box, tie up the box with the string, and send it up to a fluffy white cloud till they no longer see the box, and even the end of the string is gone. Then I say, "Come back to your feet." I count from one to ten, toe to head, and ten to one, head to toe, saying self-affirmations. We breathe together after each count. After the meditation, the patients give me feedback. They say they are more relaxed, and some say their jitteriness is gone. It is really gratifying. It is also a privilege to speak at the University of Portland, Concordia University, Emmanuel and Providence hospitals, and Summit Research for In Our Own Voice, a program of NAMI, where I put emphasis on my dark days, acceptance, treatment, coping skills and successes, and hopes and dreams. I get a positive response from people who are helped by my presentations.

Every morning when I get up, I think of my challenges and the great things I get to do. I get to help people. I get to work. I make it to my appointments. I e-mail and write my family and friends. I can continue my relationships with people. By seeing Dr. Smith, who prescribed the right combination of medication for my schizoaffective disorder and a recent doctor, Dr. Somusetty, who has continued prescribing the same medication for my condition, I have soared to the liberation of my sanity.

I would have freaked out when Mom committed suicide, my brother died of AIDS, or when I lost my job, but I took care of my guilt, depression, and stress when crises arose. Referring to Sherry's Master Plan helped me to spot when I was going out of control and discover how much I could accomplish in a day. Writing letters of healing to my mom and me, reading uplifting books, walking, painting, and meditating made my journey to sanity complete. Knowing what I do now—about learning to grow and handling with what life has dealt me—has made me strong and adaptable.

I came to my fortieth high-school reunion with a brightly colored purple-and-gold butterfly cane with a metallic sheen, which my sister had bought me in Ashland. The cheerleaders wanted me to do a yell with them. At first I hesitated, but then I decided to go ahead. I stood and shook my booty. I saw my best friend, Linda, there. It could have been a better connection, but I settled for what it was. Alice, Natie, and Nancy, my close high-school friends, made their appearance, and Maria, Judy, Sue, and Patty, the cheerleaders, delivered warm and congenial hugs. Miles and experiences had kept us apart. They were unaware of what happened to me in the Green District. Life was unbearable then. Connie Funkle wasn't there, but at the thirtieth reunion, after all those years, she made it a point to come up to me and tell me she was sorry for what she put me through in junior high and high school.

On February 18, 2011, I had a photo op with President Obama at Intel, Hillsboro, Oregon. A group of ladies and me, from Ladies in Blue, a political group associated with Organizing for America, were phone banking, and we were asked to meet with the president when he came to Intel.

Sherry and President Barack Obama
Photography by Pete Souza

AUTHOR'S NOTE:

In life, I've learned that you need to have a belief in a mental health system. Support groups like doctors, counselors, family members, peers, and mental health organizations, where you can participate and discuss your ideas about your mental health and get sound advice back, are important components of the system. Knowledge obtained from literature, mental health organizations, and doctors help to promote self-esteem and self-discipline. They activate the nucleus of the system. The nucleus is called communication.

I find at the heart of communication, I am able to work through my problems, deal with my problems, forgive, and say, "I'm sorry for my mistakes." One of the important aspects of my communication is learning from my mistakes and not blaming myself or feeling guilty for something that is beyond my control. Loving myself the way I am and having respect for myself in everything I do is essential in nurturing my system.

With communication I get all my questions answered in therapy and describe in detail what my problem is. If my health-care provider doesn't get the message, I write him an e-mail or letter, and sometimes I'll end on an optimistic note. I might say, "Guess

I'll go for a walk or paint today," as I work out my problem in an e-mail.

When I'm in a crisis, calling the crisis line and having a safety plan are both essential in keeping my commitment to my mental health. It is important to discuss my problems with a doctor, a counselor, or a family member to get a reality check and feedback during this critical time. I find writing down my problems when a crisis occurs helps me to evaluate what is going on with me and helps me to get more control over myself. Most important in my interaction with people is that I couldn't do it sanely without medication. I take my medication every day without missing a dose, no matter what people tell me or think I should do, especially if they aren't my doctor. I've come to accept my disease and take responsibility for my life.

Since I was sixteen, I received several diagnoses: paranoid schizophrenia, bipolar disorder, and schizo-affective disorder. I wish I had sought help from a doctor and talked to a counselor and received medication for my psychosis when I first needed it, but I didn't. I don't think I would have suffered this mental anguish and struggled so hard in my life to find myself if I had sought help in the beginning. However, I can only live to make my present moments better. Each present moment takes up a lot of energy, so I won't waste it on the past. As I journey through recovery, I will put my regrets and hate aside and replace them with healing words, love, and good thoughts. I am glad to be here and to have a second chance to live.

I hope this book will help you through some steps to give you strength and control to get you in touch with your stress and imbalance. You don't need to suffer. Get a good counselor and psychiatrist. Trust him and do what he says to do. A pill is not hard to take, if it is the right one.

Life is a gift.

Sherry Standing Joiner

ABOUT THE AUTHOR

A native Oregonian, Sherry M. Joiner has lived with schizoaffective disorder for decades, an experience she drew upon strongly for her memoir, *Sherry Goes Sane*. She has spoken in psychiatric wards, hospitals, and universities for the National Alliance on Mental Illness, and also as a speaker for In Our Own Voice. Her article, "Bringing Peace and Happiness to the Psych Ward," appeared in the 2013 Spring Edition of the *NAMI Voice* newsletter, published nationally.

Passionate about helping those with special needs, Sherry has worked as a preschool teacher for children with ADHD, autism, and bipolar disorder. She also worked as a certified nurse's aide for twenty years, assisting patients with cancer, dementia, and Alzheimer's disease. Her certificates include Recognizing and Reporting Child Abuse, Violence and Prevention, Impact of ADHD, and Social Development and The Special Needs Child.